Readings in Ancient History

Edited by
Claude Eilers

Dept. of Classics
McMaster University

Copyright © 2012 by Claude Eilers
All rights reserved. This book or any portion thereof may not be reproduced or used in any manner whatsoever without the express written permission of the publisher.

Printed in Canada.

First Printing, 2012
Reprinted with corrections, 2013, 2014

Dept. of Classics
McMaster University
L8S 4M2

Contents

1. GREECE IN THE HEROIC AND DARK AGES

Reading 1a: The Greek Bronze Age and Homer's Iliad 1
  Adapted from Samuel Butler, Homer. The Iliad of Homer (Longmans, Green and Co.: London, 1898).

Reading 1b: Hesiod, Works and Days 21
  Adapted from Hugh G. Evelyn-White, **Hesiod. Works and Days** (William Heinemann Ltd.: London, 1914).

2. TYRANNY, OLIGARCHY, DEMOCRACY

Reading 2a. Herodotus: The Tyranny of Cypselus 30
  Adapted from A. D. Godley, **Herodotus, with an English translation** (Cambridge. Harvard University Press, 1920).

Reading 2b. Herodotus: The Pisistratids 35
  Adapted from A. D. Godley, **Herodotus, with an English translation** (Cambridge. Harvard University Press, 1920).

Reading 2c. Aristotle: The Pisistratids 38
  Adapted from H. Rackham (1868-1944), **The Athenian Constitution** (London: William Heinemann Ltd., 1952).

Reading 2d. Herodotus: The Persian Debate 42
  Adapted from A. D. Godley, **Herodotus, with an English translation** (Cambridge. Harvard University Press, 1920).

Reading 2e. The Old Oligarch 45
  Adapted from H. G. Dakyns, **The Works of Xenophon** (Macmillan and Co., 1897).

3. ATHENS AND SPARTA

Reading 3a. Thucydides: The Spartan Debate 48
  Adapted from Benjamin Jowett, **Thucydides translated into English** (Oxford. Clarendon Press. 1881).

Reading 3b. Thucydides: Pericles' Funeral Oration 58
  Adapted from Benjamin Jowett, **Thucydides translated into English** (Oxford: Clarendon Press, 1881).

4. THE PELOPONNESIAN WAR

Reading 4a. The Revolt at Mytiline 64
<small>Adapted from Benjamin Jowett, *Thucydides translated into English* (Oxford: Clarendon Press, 1881).</small>

Reading 4b. The Melian Dialogue 73
<small>Adapted from Benjamin Jowett, *Thucydides translated into English* (Oxford: Clarendon Press, 1881).</small>

5. THE HELLENISTIC WORLD

Reading 5a. Hellenism and Indigenous Cultures 79
<small>Adapted from Frank Cole Babbitt (trans.), Plutarch, Moralia, vol. 4 (Cambridge, Mass., Harvard University Press, 1936).</small>

Reading 5b. A Description of Alexandria 81
<small>Adapted from W. Falconer, *The Geography of Strabo, Literally translated*, vol. 3 (London. George Bell & Sons. 1960).</small>

Reading 5c. The Achaean League 85
<small>Adapted from W.R. Paton (trans.), Polybius, The Histories, vol. 6, Books 28-39 (Cambridge, Mass., Harvard University Press, 1927)</small>

Reading 5d Lucian, The Cynic 89
<small>Adapted from H.W. Fowler and F.G. Fowler, *The Works of Lucian of Samosata* (Oxford: The Clarendon Press, 1905)</small>

6. ROMAN EXPANSION

Reading 6a. Polybius: the Roman Constitution 95
<small>Adapted from Evelyn S. Shuckburgh, **Polybius, Histories** (London: Macmillan. 1889).</small>

Reading 6b. Livy: The Case of Spurius Ligustinus 101
<small>Adapted from Rev. Canon Roberts, *Livy. History of Rome, an English Translation* (New York. E. P. Dutton and Co. 1912).</small>

7. THE GRACCHI

Reading 7a. Plutarch: Tiberius Graccus 104
<small>Adapted from Bernadotte Perrin, *Plutarch. Plutarch's Lives with an English Translation*. (London. William Heinemann Ltd. 1926.)</small>

Reading 7b. Plutarch: Gaius Graccus 112
<small>Adapted from Bernadotte Perrin (1847-1920), *Plutarch's Lives with an English Translation*. (London: William Heinemann Ltd., 1926)</small>

8. THE AUGUSTAN REORGANIZATION

Reading 8a. Vergil, Aeneid *121*

Adapted from John Conington, *The Works of Vergil translated into English Prose* (Philadelphia: David McKay, 1893).

Reading 8b. The Achievements of the Divine Augustus *131*

Adapted from Frederick William Shipley (1871-1945), *The Res Gestae of Augustus* (London, Heinemann, 1924).

Reading 8c. Tacitus on Augustus' Reign *137*

Adapted from A.J. Church and W.J. Brodribb, *Annals of Tacitus* (London: Macmillan and Co., 1876)

9. THE JULIO-CLAUDIANS

Reading 9a. Tacitus: The Trial of Piso *143*

Adapted from A.J. Church and W.J. Brodribb, *Annals of Tacitus* (London: Macmillan and Co., 1876)

10. ROMAN RELIGION

Reading 10a. Livy on the Reforms of Numa *158*

Adapted from Rev. Canon Roberts, *Livy. Books I and II With An English Translation*. (Cambridge, MA. Harvard University Press. London. William Heinemann Ltd. 1919.)

Reading 10b. Cicero: Address to the Pontifices *161*

Adapted from C. D. Yonge, *The Orations of Marcus Tullius Cicero* (London: George Bell & Sons, 1891).

Reading 10c. Plutarch on the Vestal Virgins *163*

Adapted from Bernadotte Perrin, *Plutarch. Plutarch's Lives with an English Translation* (London: William Heinemann, 1914).

Reading 10d. Pliny on Early Christians *165*

Translation by C. Eilers.

Reading 10e. Apuleius on the Cult of Isis *168*

Adapted from Stephen Gaselee, *The Golden Ass, being the Metamorphoses of Lucius Apuleius* (London: William Heinemann, 1915).

Chapter 1:
Greece in the Heroic and Dark Ages

READING 1A: THE GREEK BRONZE AGE AND HOMER'S *ILIAD*

The Iliad is the earliest surviving work of European literature, and one of the greatest. Its date, and that of its sister poem, the Odyssey, is debatable, but most scholars place the composition of these epics in the second half of the eighth century B.C. We call this period the Greek Renaissance, a period of rapid growth and social and cultural change, marking the end of the Dark Age and the first stage of the formation of citizen-states in Greece. While the poem as we have it was composed at this time, this was the culmination of a long process of evolution. The poem was passed down orally from generation to generation by bards who, in each generation, changed and added to what had been passed down to them, re-composing the poem as they sang it. Our Iliad represents the final (except for small changes) version of the poem, which became authoritative and was ultimately set down and fixed in writing. The poem is set not at this time of final composition, but in an earlier age, during a legendary war between the Greeks and the Trojans. The Greeks dated the Trojan War to around 1200 B.C., and while it is uncertain that there ever was such a war, the surface features of the world described in the poem—places, buildings, arms and armour—do belong to this time period of the late Bronze Age, some five hundred years before the poem's composition. This age is remembered in the poem as a time of larger-than-life heroes, a time when gods still came down from Olympus and walked among men.

The Iliad tells the story of only a few weeks during the last year of a ten year war (the Iliad and Odyssey were originally part of a cycle of epic poems covering the entire Trojan War). It tells the story of the wrath of Achilles, the greatest warrior of the Greeks. It is his anger and its consequences that comprise the content of the poem. While the death of Achilles and the fall of Troy are not part of this narrative, they are the inevitable results of the sequence of events initiated by the quarrel between Agamemnon, the leader of the Achaeans (the word, together with Danaans and Argives, for the Greeks in Homer), and Achilles. This quarrel soon led to the active involvement and interference of the gods, since Achilles was half-divine, which in turn led to the suffering and death of several characters because of divine will. The Homeric gods are anthropomorphic in nature, containing all human traits, good and bad. They mingle with mortals, helping their favourites and opposing those they dislike.

The Homeric poems were assumed to be fantasy until the late nineteenth century, when Heinrich Schliemann dug at the sites commemorated in the Homeric poems, first at the place the poems describe as the site of Troy, in Asia Minor (now Turkey), and then at the place the poems describe as the site of Mycenae (in southern Greece). In both places he found ancient cities, unearthing a lost late Bronze Age Aegean civilization. Furthermore, he found at these sites artifacts corresponding to objects (bronze weaponry, boar's tusk helmets, etc.) described in the poems. Thus it appeared that the world described in Homer was historical (albeit turned into legend as a time of heroes), describing a period that we now call—after Schliemann's second city, the city of Agamemnon in the poems—the Mycenaean period. Yet it turns out not to be that simple. As we have learned more about the Mycenaean period (especially through the Linear B tablets), it has become clear that although many surface features of the poems—artifacts and places—belong to the late Bronze Age, the social world—social and economic conditions, social and political organization—does not reflect the Bronze Age but a later period during the poems' long development, either (the point is disputed) the mid to late Dark Age (tenth or ninth centuries) or the Greek Renaissance.

While you read this passage, consider the following questions:
- What are some of the problems faced by historians who want to use Homer as a source of information about historical conditions?
- What are the social conditions (political structure, social status, values, economy) of the world the poem depicts?

Homer *Iliad* 1: The Quarrel

Sing, O goddess, about the anger of Achilles son of Peleus, that brought countless ills upon the Achaeans. Many a brave soul did it send hurrying down to Hades, and many a hero did it yield a prey to dogs and vultures, for so was the will of Zeus fulfilled from the day on which the son of Atreus, king of men, and great Achilles, first quarrelled with one another.

And which of the gods was it that set them on to quarrel? It was the son of Zeus and Leto; for he was angry with the king and sent a pestilence upon the host to plague the people, [10] because the son of Atreus had dishonored Chryses his priest. Now Chryses had come to the ships of the Achaeans to free his daughter, and had brought with him a great ransom: moreover he bore in his hand the scepter of

Apollo wreathed with a suppliant's wreath and he besought the Achaeans, but most of all the two sons of Atreus, who were their chiefs.

"Sons of Atreus, and all other Achaeans, may the gods who dwell in Olympus grant you to sack the city of Priam, and to reach your homes in safety; but free my daughter, and accept a ransom for her, in reverence to Apollo, son of Zeus."

On this the rest of the Achaeans with one voice were for respecting the priest and taking the ransom that he offered; but not so Agamemnon, who spoke fiercely to him and sent him roughly away.

[25] "Old man, let me not find you tarrying about our ships, nor yet coming hereafter. Your scepter of the god and your wreath shall profit you nothing. I will not free her. She shall grow old in my house at Argos far from her own home, busying herself with her loom and visiting my couch; so go, and do not provoke me or it shall be the worse for you."

The old man feared him and obeyed. Not a word he spoke, but went by the shore of the sounding sea and prayed apart to King Apollo whom lovely Leto had borne.

[35] "Hear me, O god of the silver bow, you who protect Chryse and holy Cilla and rule Tenedos with your might, hear me O god of Sminthe. If I have ever decked your temple with garlands, or burned for you thigh-bones in fat of bulls or goats, grant my prayer, and let your arrows avenge these my tears upon the Danaans."

Thus did he pray, and Apollo heard his prayer. He came down furious from the summits of Olympus, with his bow and his quiver upon his shoulder, [45] and the arrows rattled on his back with the rage that trembled within him. He sat himself down away from the ships with a face as dark as night, and his silver bow rang death as he shot his arrow in the midst of them.

First he smote their mules and their hounds, but presently he aimed his shafts at the people themselves, and all day long the pyres of the dead were burning. For nine whole days he shot his arrows among the people, but upon the tenth day Achilles called them in assembly, inspired to do this by Hera, [55] who saw the Achaeans dying and had compassion upon them. Then, when they were got together, Achilles rose and spoke among them.

"Son of Atreus, I feel that we should now turn roving home if we would escape destruction, for we are being cut down by war and pestilence at once. Let us ask some priest or seer, or some reader of dreams (for dreams, too, are of Zeus) who can tell us why Phoebus Apollo is so angry, and say whether it is for some vow that we have broken, or the sacrifice of a hecatomb that we have not performed, and whether he will accept the savor of lambs and goats without blemish, so as to take away the plague from us."

With these words he sat down, and Calchas son of Thestor, wisest of augurs, who knew things past, present, and future, rose to speak. [70] He it was who had guided the Achaeans with their fleet to Ilion, through the prophesyings with which Phoebus Apollo had inspired him. With all sincerity and goodwill he addressed them thus: …

"The god is angry neither about vow nor hecatomb, but for his priest's sake, whom Agamemnon has dishonored, in that he would not free his daughter nor take a ransom for her; [95] therefore has he sent these evils upon us, and will yet send others. He will not deliver the Danaans from this pestilence till Agamemnon has restored the girl without fee or ransom to her father, and has sent a holy hecatomb to Chryse. Thus we may perhaps appease Apollo."

When he had thus spoken he sat down, and among them arose the king, son of Atreus, wide-ruling Agamemnon, deeply anger. His black heart was filled with fury, and his eyes were blazing like fire. To Calchas first of all he spoke, with a look that threatened violence:

[105] "Prophet of evil, never yet have you spoken to me a pleasant thing; evil is always dear to your heart to prophesy, but a word of good you have never yet spoken, nor brought to pass. And now among the Danaans you claim in prophecy that for this reason the god who strikes from afar brings woes upon them, that I would not accept the glorious ransom for the girl, the daughter of Chryses, since I much prefer to keep her in my home. For certainly I prefer her to Clytemnestra, my wedded wife, since she is not inferior to her, either in form or in stature, or in mind, or in any handiwork. Yet even so will I give her back, if that is better; I would rather the people be safe than perish. But provide me with a prize of honour immediately, lest I alone of the Argives be without one, since that would not be proper. For you all see this, that my prize goes elsewhere."

[120] In answer to him spoke swift-footed brilliant Achilles:

"Most glorious son of Atreus, greediest of all: how shall the great-hearted Achaeans give you a prize? We have no hoard of wealth in common store. Whatever we took by pillage from the cities has been distributed, [125] and it is not right to gather these things back from the army. No. Give back the girl to the god, and we Achaeans will pay you back three and fourfold, if ever Zeus allows us to sack the well-walled city of Troy."

In answer to him spoke lord Agamemnon:

[130] "Although you are mighty, godlike Achilles, you should not seek to deceive me like this with your wit; for you will not get by me nor persuade me. Are you willing for me to sit here idly in want, while you order me to give her back, while you yourself may keep your prize? No, the great-hearted Achaeans must give me a prize that I find appropriate, and worth just as much. If they do not, I will come and take your prize, or that of Ajax, or I will seize and carry away that of Odysseus. Whomever I come to will be angry. But these things we will consider later. [140] Let us now drag a black ship to the shining sea, and quickly gather suitable rowers into it, and place on board a hecatomb to sacrifice, and embark on it the fair-cheeked daughter of Chryses herself. Let one prudent man be its commander, either Ajax, or Idomeneus, or brilliant Odysseus, or you, son of Peleus, of all men most extreme, so that on our behalf you may appease the god who strikes from afar by offering sacrifice."

Glaring from beneath his brows swift-footed Achilles spoke to him:

"My word! How clothed in shamelessness you are! You always are thinking of gain! How can any man of the Achaeans obey your words with a ready heart, [150] whether to go on a journey or to fight against men with force? It was not on account of our Trojan enemies that I came here to fight, since they have done no wrong to me.

They have never driven off my cattle or my horses, nor ever in deep-soiled Phthia did they lay waste the harvest, for many things lie between us—shadowy mountains and sounding sea. But we followed you, shameless one, so that you might rejoice, seeking to win recompense from the Trojans for Menelaus and for yourself, dog-face. This you disregard, and take no heed of. [160] And now you threaten that you will yourself take my prize away from me, for which I toiled so much, which the sons of the Achaeans gave to me. Never have I received a prize as good as yours after the Achaeans have sacked a well-inhabited citadel of the Trojans. But my hands always undertake the brunt of furious battle. If ever an apportionment comes, however, your prize is always greater, while I take to my ships a small but dear reward, even though I have worn myself out in the fighting. Now I will go back to Phthia, since it is far better to return home with my beaked ships. I do not intend to pile up riches and wealth for you while I am being dishonoured."

[172] Then the king of men, Agamemnon, answered him:

"Flee then, if your heart urges you. I will not beg you to remain for my sake. With me are others who will honour me, and above all Zeus, the lord of counsel. Of all the kings whom Zeus nurtures, you are the most hateful to me. For strife is always dear to you, and wars and battles. If you are very strong, it was a god, I think, who gave you this gift. Go home with your ships and your companions and lord it over the Myrmidons there. I do not care for you, [180] nor will I heed your wrath. But this is my threat to you: because Phoebus Apollo takes from me the daughter of Chryses, I will send her back with my ship and my companions, but I will myself come to your tent and take the fair-cheeked Briseis, your prize. In this way you will understand how much mightier I am than you, and so others will shrink from declaring themselves my equal and likening themselves to me to my face."

So he spoke. Anger came upon the son of Peleus, and within his shaggy breast his heart was divided, whether he should draw his sharp sword from beside his thigh and slay the son of Atreus, or stay his anger and curb his spirit. …

Now again the son of Peleus addressed the son of Atreus with violent words, not at all ceasing from his anger:

[223] "You wine-soaked dog-face, with the heart of a fawn! You never have had enough courage to arm for battle along with your people, or to go forth to an ambush with the chiefs of the Achaeans. Doing that seems to you just like death. Indeed, you think it better to deprive of his prize whoever speaks against you in the wide camp of the Achaeans. You people-devouring king! You rule over nobodies. This is your final piece of insolence. But I will speak against you, and will swear a mighty oath to this. I swear by this staff, that shall never more put forth leaves or shoots since first it left its stump among the mountains, [235] nor shall it again grow green, for the bronze has stripped it on all sides of leaves and bark, and now the sons of the Achaeans carry it in their hands when they act as judges, those who guard the ordinances that come from Zeus. And this shall be for you a mighty oath. Surely some day the sons of the Achaeans one and all, will long for Achilles. And on that day you will not be able to help them at all, for all your grief, when many shall fall dying before man-slaying Hector. But you will eat

your heart out and curse yourself because you dishonoured the best of the Achaeans."

[244] So spoke the son of Peleus, and down to the earth he dashed the staff studded with golden nails, and himself sat down, while over against him the son of Atreus continued to vent his wrath.

Then among them arose Nestor, sweet of speech, the clear-voiced orator of the Pylians, from whose tongue flowed speech sweeter than honey. Two generations of mortal men had passed away in the course of his lifetime, who had been born and reared with him in sacred Pylos, and he was now king among the third. He with good intent addressed the gathering and spoke among them:

> [253] "Comrades, great grief has come upon the land of Achaea. Truly would Priam and the sons of Priam rejoice, and the rest of the Trojans would be most glad at heart, were they to hear all this of you two quarrelling, you who are chief among the Danaans in counsel and chief in war. Listen to me, for you are both younger than I. In earlier times I moved among men more warlike than you, and never did they despise me. ... [272] So also should you obey, since to obey is better. Agamemon, mighty though you are, do not take away the girl, but let her be, as the sons of the Achaeans first gave her to noble Achilles as a prize. Son of Peleus, do not be minded to strive with a king, might against might! For it is no common honour that is the portion of a sceptre-holding king, to whom Zeus gives glory. If you are a stronger fighter, and a goddess mother bore you, nevertheless he is the mightier, since he is king over more. Son of Atreus, check your rage. Indeed, I beg you to let go your anger against Achilles, who is for all the Achaeans a mighty bulwark in evil war."

In answer to him spoke lord Agamemnon:

> [285] "All these things, old man, to be sure, you have spoken as is right. But this man wishes to be above all others; over all he wishes to rule and over all to be king, and to all to give orders; in this, I think, there is someone who will not obey. If the gods who exist for ever made him a spearman, do they therefore license him to keep uttering insults?"

Brilliant Achilles broke in upon him and replied:

> [292] "Surely I will be called cowardly and of no account, if I should yield to you in every matter that you say. On others lay these commands, but do not give orders to me, for I do not think I shall obey you any longer. And another thing I will tell you, and take it to heart: with my hands I will not fight for the girl's sake either with you nor with any other, since you are taking away what you have given. But everything else that is mine by my swift black ship, [300] none of it will you take or carry away against my will. Come, just try, so that these too may know: immediately will your dark blood flow forth about my spear."

So when the two had made an end of contending with violent words, they rose, and broke up the gathering beside the ships of the Achaeans. The son of Peleus went his way to his huts and his balanced ships together with his friend Patroclus, and with his men. But the son of Atreus launched a swift ship on the sea, and chose for it twenty rowers, and drove on board 100 cattle as a hecatomb for the god, and brought the fair-cheeked daughter of Chryses and set her in the ship; and Odysseus of many wiles went on board to take command.

[312] So these embarked and sailed over the watery ways, while the son of Atreus bade the people purify themselves. And they purified themselves, and cast the defilement into the sea, and offered to Apollo perfect sacrifices of bulls and goats by the shore of the barren sea; and the savour thereof went up to heaven, eddying amid the smoke. Thus were they busied throughout the camp.

Agamemnon, however, did not cease from the strife with which he had first threatened Achilles. He called to Talthybius and Eurybates, who were his heralds and ready squires:

> [321] "Go to the hut of Achilles, Peleus' son, and take by the hand the fair-cheeked Briseis, and lead her hither; and if he give her not, I will myself go with a larger company and take her; that will be even the worse for him."

So saying he sent them forth, and laid upon them a stern command. Unwilling went the two along the shore of the barren sea, and came to the tents and the ships of the Myrmidons. They found Achilles sitting beside his tent and his black ship; and he was not glad at sight of them. The two, seized with dread and in awe of the king, stood, but spoke no word to him, nor made question. He understood in his heart, however, and spoke:

> [333] "Hail, heralds, messengers of Zeus and men, draw near. It is not you who are guilty in my sight, but Agamemnon, who sent you here to take the girl, Briseis. But come, Patroclus, sprung from Zeus, bring forth the girl, and give her to them to lead away. But let these two themselves be witnesses before the blessed gods and mortal men, and before him, that ruthless king, if hereafter there shall be need of me to ward off shameful ruin from the host. Truly he rages with baneful mind, and knows not at all to look both before and after, that his Achaeans might wage war in safety beside their ships."

[344] So he spoke, and Patroclus obeyed his dear comrade, and led from the hut the fair-cheeked Briseis, and gave her to them to lead away. So the two went back beside the ships of the Achaeans, and with them, all unwilling, went the woman. But Achilles burst into tears, and withdrew apart from his comrades, and sat down on the shore of the grey sea, looking forth over the wine-dark deep. Earnestly he prayed to his dear mother with hands outstretched:

> "Mother, surely Olympian Zeus, who thunders on high, ought to have given honour into my hands, since you bore me, though to so brief a span of life. But now he has honoured me not a bit. Truly the son of Atreus, wide-ruling Agamemnon has dishonoured me: for he has taken and keeps my prize through his own arrogant act."

[357] So he spoke, weeping, and his lady mother heard him, as she sat in the depths of the sea beside the old man, her father. And speedily she came forth from the grey sea like a mist, and sat down before him, as he wept, and she stroked him with her hand, and spoke to him, and called him by name:

> "My child, why do you weep? What sorrow has come upon your heart? Speak out; hide it not in your mind, that we both may know."

Then with heavy moaning spoke swift-footed Achilles to her:

> [364] "You know. Why then should I tell the tale to you who knows all? We went forth to Thebe, the sacred city of Eetion, and laid it waste, and brought here all the spoil.

This the sons of the Achaeans divided fairly among themselves, except for the son of Atreus, to whom they gave the fair-cheeked daughter of Chryses. However, Chryses, priest of Apollo, who strikes from afar, came to the swift ships of the bronze-clad Achaeans, to free his daughter, bearing ransom past counting. … [378] But Agamemnon, son of Atreus, sent him away harshly. So the old man went back again in anger; and Apollo heard his prayer, for he was very dear to him, and sent against the Argives an evil plague. Then the people began to die thick and fast, and the shafts of the god ranged everywhere throughout the wide camp of the Achaeans. But to us the prophet with sure knowledge declared the oracles of the god who strikes from afar. … [388] Now, the quick-glancing Achaeans are taking the maiden in a swift ship to Chryse, and are bearing gifts to the god; while the other woman the heralds have just now taken from my tent and led away, the daughter of Briseus, whom the sons of the Achaeans gave me. But, you, if you are able, guard your own son; go to Olympus and make prayer to Zeus, if ever you have gladdened his heart by word or deed. … [406] Sit by his side, and clasp his knees, in hope that he might perhaps wish to succour the Trojans, and for those others, the Achaeans, to pen them in among the sterns of their ships and around the sea as they are slain, so that they may all have profit of their king, and that the son of Atreus, wide-ruling Agamemnon may know his blindness in that he did no honour to the best of the Achaeans."

Then Thetis answered him as she wept:

[413] "Alas, my child, why did I rear you, cursed in my child-bearing? I wish that it had been your lot to remain by your ships without tears and without grief, since your span of life is brief and will not last for a long time; but now you are doomed to a speedy death and are laden with sorrow above all men. It was to an evil fate that I bore you in our halls. Yet in order to tell this your word to Zeus who delights in the thunderbolt I will myself go to snowy Olympus, in hope that he may be persuaded. But remain by your swift, sea-faring ships, and continue your wrath against the Achaeans, and refrain utterly from battle. … I will go to the house of Zeus with threshold of bronze, and will clasp his knees in prayer, and I think I shall win him."

[427] So saying, she went her way and left him where he was, angry at heart for the fair-girdled woman's sake, whom they had taken from him by force though he was unwilling

Meanwhile Odysseus came to Chryse bringing the holy hecatomb. When they had arrived within the deep harbour, they furled the sail, and stowed it in the black ship… and themselves went forth upon the shore of the sea. They brought forth the hecatomb for Apollo, who strikes from afar, and the daughter of Chryses also stepped forth from the sea-faring ship. Odysseus of many wiles then lead her to the altar, and place her in the arms of her dear father, saying to him:

[442] "Chryses, Agamemnon, king of men, sent me forth to bring to you your daughter, and to offer to Phoebus a holy hecatomb on the Danaans' behalf, that therewith we may propitiate the lord, who has now brought upon the Argives woeful lamentation."

So saying he placed her in his arms, and he joyfully took his dear child; but they made haste to set in array for the god the holy hecatomb around the well-built altar.... Then Chryses lifted up his hands, and prayed aloud for them:

[450] "Hear me, god of the silver bow, who stands over Chryse and holy Cilla, and rules mightily over Tenedos. As before you heard me when I prayed—to me you did honour, and mightily smote the host of the Achaeans—even so now fulfill me this my desire: ward off now from the Danaans the terrible pestilence."

So he prayed, and Phoebus Apollo heard him. Then, when they had prayed, and had sprinkled the barley grains, they first drew back the victims' heads, and cut their throats, and flayed them, and cut out the thighs and covered them [460] with a double layer of fat, and laid raw flesh thereon. And the old man burned them on stakes of wood, and made libation over them of gleaming wine; and beside him the young men held in their hands the five-pronged forks. But when the thigh-pieces were completely burned, and they had tasted the entrails, they cut up the rest and spitted it, and roasted it carefully, and drew all off the spits. Then, when they had ceased from their labour and had made ready the meal, they feasted, nor did their hearts lack anything of the equal feast....

[494] But Thetis did not forget the request of her son, but rose up from the wave of the sea, and at early morning went up to great heaven and Olympus. There she found the far-seeing son of Cronos sitting apart from the rest upon the topmost peak of many-ridged Olympus. So she sat down before him, and clasped his knees with her left hand, while with her right she touched him beneath the chin, and she spoke in prayer to king Zeus, son of Cronos:

[502] "Father Zeus, if ever amid the immortals I gave you aid by word or deed, grant me this prayer: do honour to my son, who is doomed to a speedy death beyond all other men; yet now Agamemnon, king of men, has dishonoured him, for he has taken and keeps his prize by his own arrogant act. But honour him, Olympian Zeus, lord of counsel; and give might to the Trojans, until the Achaeans do honour to my son, and magnify him with recompense."

So she spoke; but Zeus, the cloud-gatherer, spoke no word to her, but sat a long time in silence. ... Finally, greatly troubled, Zeus, the cloud-gatherer spoke to her:

[517] "Surely this will be sorry work, since you will set me on to engage in strife with Hera, when she shall anger me with taunting words. Even now she always upbraids me among the immortal gods, and declares that I give aid to the Trojans in battle. But for the present, depart again, lest Hera note something; and I will take thought for these things to bring all to pass. Come, I will bow my head to you, so that you may be certain...; no word of mine may be recalled, nor is false, nor unfulfilled, to which I bow my head."

[528] The son of Cronos spoke, and bowed his dark brow in assent, and the ambrosial locks waved from the king's immortal head; and he made great Olympus quake.

When the two had taken counsel together in this way, they parted; she leapt straightway into the deep sea from gleaming Olympus, and Zeus went to his own palace.

All the gods together rose from their seats before the face of their father; no one dared to await his coming, but they all rose up before him. ...[600] And for the whole day long till the setting of the sun they feasted, nor did their heart lack anything of the equal feast, nor of the beauteous lyre, that Apollo held, nor yet of the Muses, who sang, replying one to the other with sweet voices. But when the bright light of the sun was set, they went each to his own house to take their rest, where for each one a palace had been built with cunning skill by the famed Hephaestus, the limping god; and Zeus, the Olympian, lord of the lightning, went to his couch, where of old he took his rest, whenever sweet sleep came upon him. There went he up and slept, and beside him lay Hera of the golden throne.

Zeus sends a lying dream and Agamemnon tests the spirit of his men

[1] Now all the other gods and men, lords of chariots, slumbered the whole night through, but Zeus did not partake of sweet sleep, for he was pondering in his heart how he might honour Achilles and lay many low beside the ships of the Achaeans. And this plan seemed to his mind the best: to send to Agamemnon, son of Atreus, a destructive dream. So he spake, and addressed him with winged words:

[7] "Arise and go, you destructive Dream, to the swift ships of the Achaeans. Go to the hut of Agamemnon, son of Atreus, and tell him exactly what I tell you. Command him to arm the long-haired Achaeans with all speed, since now he will capture the broad-wayed city of the Trojans. For the immortals, that have homes upon Olympus, are no longer divided in counsel, since Hera won over all the gods' minds through her prayers, and over the Trojans hang woes."

So he spoke, and the Dream went on his way, just as he was commanded. Right away he came to the swift ships of the Achaeans, and came to Agamemnon, son of Atreus, and found him sleeping in his hut. So he took his stand above his head, in the likeness of the son of Neleus, even Nestor, whom above all the elders Agamemnon held in honour; likening himself to him, the Dream from heaven said:

[23] "Son of wise-hearted Atreus, the tamer of horses, listen to me, for I am a messenger from Zeus, who, far away though he be, cares for you and pities you. He begs you to arm the long-haired Achaeans with all speed, since now you will capture the broad-wayed city of the Trojans. For the immortals that have homes upon Olympus are no longer divided in counsel, since since Hera won over all the gods' minds through her prayers, and over the Trojans hang woes by the will of Zeus."

[35] So spoke the Dream and departed, and left him there, pondering in his heart on things that were not to be brought to pass. For in truth he concluded that he should take the city of Priam that very day, fool that he was! seeing he knew not what deeds Zeus was purposing, who was yet to bring woes and groanings on Trojans alike and Danaans throughout the course of stubborn fights. Then he awoke from sleep, and the divine voice was ringing in his ears. …

[50] Then Agamemnon bade the clear-voiced heralds summon to the place of gathering the long-haired Achaeans. And they made summons, and the men gathered full quickly. But the king first made the council of the great-souled elders to sit down beside the ship of Nestor, the king Pylos-born. And when he had

called them together, he contrived a cunning plan, and said:

[56] "Hearken, my friends, a Dream from heaven came to me in my sleep through the ambrosial night, and most like was it to goodly Nestor, in form and in stature and in build. It took its stand above my head, and spoke to me, saying … that I should arm the long-haired Achaeans with all speed, since now I would take the broad-wayed city of the Trojans. … So come now, if it is possible let us arm the sons of the Achaeans. First, however, I will test them in speech, as is right, and will tell them to flee with their ships; [75] but the rest of you go out among the host and prevent them from doing so."

With this he led the way from the assembly, and the other sceptered kings rose with him in obedience to the word of Agamemnon, and the people pressed forward to hear. … Nine heralds went crying about among them to quieten theselves and bid them listen to the kings, till at last they were got into their several places and ceased their clamor.

Then King Agamemnon rose, holding his scepter. This was the work of Hephaistos, who gave it to Zeus the son of Cronos. Zeus gave it to Hermes, slayer of Argos, guide and guardian. Lord Hermes gave it to Pelops, the mighty charioteer, andPelops to Atreus, shepherd of his people. Atreus, when he died, left it to Thyestes, rich in flocks, and Thyestes in his turn left it to be borne by Agamemnon, that he might be lord of all Argos and of the isles. Leaning, then, on his scepter, he addressed the Argives.

[110] "My friends heroes, servants of Ares, Zeus the son of Cronos has ensnared me through trickery. He gave me his solemn promise that I would sack the city of Priam before returning, but cruelly he has misled me, and is now bidding me return ingloriously to Argos with the loss of many men. Such is the will of Zeus, who has reduced many a proud city to dust, as he will yet lay others, for his power is above all. It will be a sorry tale hereafter that an Achaean host, at once so great and valiant, battled in vain against men fewer in number than themselves; but as yet the end is not in sight. … Nine years are gone; the timbers of our ships have rotted; their gear is sound no longer. Our wives and little ones at home look anxiously for our return, but the work that we came here to do has not been done. Now, therefore, let us all do as I say: let us sail back to our own land, for we shall not take Troy."

With these words he moved the hearts of the multitude, so many of them as knew not the cunning counsel of Agamemnon. They surged to and fro like the waves of the Icarian Sea, [145] when the east and south winds break from heaven's clouds to lash them; or as when the west wind sweeps over a field of grain and the ears bow beneath the blast, even so were they swayed as they flew with loud cries towards the ships, and the dust from under their feet rose heavenward. They cheered each other on to draw the ships into the sea; they cleared the channels in front of them; they began taking away the stays from underneath them, and the sky rang with their happy shouts, so eager were they to return home.

Then surely the Argives would have had a home coming after a fashion that was not fated. … [185] But Odysseus went straight up to Agamemnon and took from him his ancestral, imperishable staff. With this he went about among the ships of the Achaeans. Whenever he met a king or chieftain, he stood by him and restrained him with gentle words.

[190] "Sir, this flight is cowardly and unworthy. Stand your ground, and order your people also to keep their places. You do not yet know the full mind of Agamemnon; he was testing us, and before long will visit the Achaeans with his displeasure. [195] Were we not all at the council to hear what he then said; see to it lest he be angry and do us a mischief; for the honour of kings is great, and the hand of Zeus is with them."

But when he came across some man from the common people, who was making a noise, he struck him with his staff and rebuked him, saying,

[200] "What kind of foolishness has possessed you? Keep your peace, and listen to better men than yourself. You are a coward and no warrior; you are nobody either in fight or assembly. We cannot all be kings; it is not well that there should be many masters; [205] one man must be supreme, one king to whom the son of scheming Cronos has given the scepter and divine laws to rule over you all."

In this way did he stride with authority through the host, and the people hurried back to the assembly from their tents and ships with a sound as the thunder of surf when it comes crashing down upon the shore, and all the sea is in an uproar. [210] The rest now took their seats and kept to their own places, but Thersites still went on wagging his unbridled tongue, a man of of measureless and seditious speech, who railed endlessly against all who were in authority, and cared not what he said, [215] provided that he might make the Achaeans laugh. He was the ugliest man of all those that came before Troy: bandy-legged, lame of one foot, with his two shoulders rounded and hunched over his chest. His head ran up to a point, but there was little hair on the top of it. [220] Achilles and Odysseus hated him worst of all, for it was with them that he was most likely to argue. Now, however, with a shrill squeaky voice he began heaping his abuse on Agamemnon. The Achaeans were angry and disgusted, yet still he kept on brawling and bawling at the son of Atreus.

[225] "Agamemnon what ails you now, and what more do you want? Your tents are filled with bronze and with fair women, for whenever we take a town we give you the pick of them. Do you want yet more gold, which some Trojan might give you as a ransom for his son, when I or some other Achaean has taken him prisoner? or is it some young girl to hide and sleep with? It is not well that you, the ruler of the Achaeans, should bring them into such misery. Weakling cowards, women rather than men, let us sail home, and leave this man here at Troy to stew in his own prizes of honor, and discover whether we were of any service to him or no. Achilles is a much better man than he is, and see how he has treated him: he has robbed him of his prize and is keeping it for himself. Achilles takes it meekly and shows no fight; if he did, son of Atreus, you would never again insult him."

Thus railed Thersites, but Odysseus at once went up to him and rebuked him sternly.

"Check your glib tongue, Thersites, and say not a word further. Do not presume to scold princes when you have none to back you. There is no viler creature come before Troy with the sons of Atreus than you. Drop this chatter about kings, and neither revile them nor keep harping about a homecoming. We do not yet know how things are going to be, nor whether the Achaeans are to return with good success or evil. How dare you shout at Agamemnon because the Danaans have awarded him so many prizes! I tell you, therefore — and it shall surely be — that if I again catch you talking such nonsense, I will either forfeit my own head and be no more called father of my son, or I will take you, strip away from you all respect, and whip you out of the assembly till you go blubbering back to the ships."

Then he beat him with his staff about the back and shoulders till he dropped and fell weeping. The golden scepter raised a bloody bruise on his back, so he sat down frightened and in pain, looking foolish as he wiped the tears from his eyes.

The people were sorry for him, yet they laughed heartily, and one would turn to his neighbor saying,

"Odysseus has done many a good thing before this in fight and council, but never did he do the Argives a better service than when he stopped this man's mouth from prating further. He will give the kings no more of his insolence."

That is what people said.

(Homer Iliad 2. 1-277 passim)

Hector, the Trojans' greatest champion, encounters his wife on the walls of Troy

[390] When Hector had gone through the city and had reached the Scaean gates through which he would go out on to the plain, his wife came running towards him, Andromache, daughter of great Eetion who ruled in Thebe under the wooded slopes of Mount Plakos, and was king of the Cilicians. His daughter had married Hektor, and now came to meet him with a nurse who carried his little child in her bosom, a mere babe. Hektor's darling son, and lovely as a star. Hektor had named him Scamandrios, but the people called him Astyanax, for his father stood alone as chief protector of Ilion. Hektor smiled as he looked upon the boy, but he did not speak, and Andromache stood by him weeping and taking his hand in her own.

[407] "Dear husband, your valor will bring you to destruction! Think about your infant son, and on my hapless self who before long will be your widow! For the Achaeans will attack you in a group and kill you. It would be better for me, should I lose you, to lie dead and buried, for I shall have nothing left to comfort me when you are gone, except only sorrow. I have neither father nor mother now. Achilles slew my father when he sacked Thebe, the goodly city of the Cilicians. He slew him, but out of respect did not despoil him. … I had seven brothers in my father's house, but they all went within the house of Hades on the same day, when Achilles killed them. He captured my mother, who had been queen of all the land under Mount Plakos, and brought her here with the spoil, and ransomed her for a great sum. No, Hektor, it is you now are my father, mother, brother, and dear husband! Have mercy on me. Stay here upon this wall. Do not make your child fatherless and your wife a widow!"

And Hektor answered,

[440] "Dear wife, I too have thought on all this. But how could I face the Trojans, men or women, if I shirked battle like a coward? I cannot do so: I know nothing save to fight

bravely in the forefront of the Trojan host and win renown for both my father and myself. Well do I know that the day will surely come when mighty Troy shall be destroyed together with Priam and Priam's people. But I grieve for none of these—not even for Hecuba, nor King Priam, nor for my brothers many and brave who may fall in the dust before their foes—for none of these do I grieve as much as I grive for you. The day shall come when some Achaean will rob you for ever of your freedom, and bear you weeping away. It may be that you will have to ply the loom in Argos at the bidding of a mistress, or to fetch water from the springs Messeis or Hypereia, treated brutally by some cruel task-master. Then will one say who sees you weeping, 'She was wife to Hektor, the bravest warrior among the Trojans during the war before Troy.' On this your tears will break forth anew for him who should have kept the day of captivity away from you. May I lie dead under the mound that is heaped over my body before I hear your cry as they carry you into slavery."

[466] He stretched his arms towards his child, but the boy cried and shrank into his nurse's bosom, frightened at the sight of his father's armor, and at the horse-hair plume that nodded fiercely from his helmet. His father and mother laughed to see this, but Hektor took the helmet from his head and laid it all gleaming upon the ground. Then he took his darling child, kissed him, and fondled him in his arms, praying over him the while to Zeus and to all the gods.

"Zeus, grant that this child of mine may be even as myself, chief among the Trojans; let him be not less excellent in strength, and let him rule Ilion with his might. Then may one say of him as he comes from battle, 'The son is far better than the father.' May he bring back the blood-stained spoils of him whom he has laid low, and let his mother's heart be glad."

With this he laid the child again in the arms of his wife, who took him to her own soft bosom, smiling through her tears. As her husband watched her his heart yearned towards her and he caressed her fondly, saying,

"My sweet wife, do not take these things too bitterly to heart. No one can hurry me down to Hades before my time. But if a man's hour is come, whether he be brave or he be a coward, there is no escape for him when he has once been born. Go home, then, and busy yourself with your daily duties, your loom, your distaff, and the ordering of your servants; for war is man's matter, and mine above all others of them that have been born in Ilion."

He took his plumed helmet from the ground, and his wife went back again to her house, weeping bitterly and often looking back towards him. When she reached her home she found her maidens within, and bade them all join in her lament; so they mourned Hektor in his own house though he was yet alive, for they felt that they would never see him return safe from battle, and from the furious hands of the Achaeans.

(Homer Iliad 6. 237-502)

The social economy of the Heroic Age

[290] The Trojans and brave Hektor would not have been able to break down the gates and the great bar, except Zeus turned his son Sarpedon against the Argives as a lion against a herd of

horned cattle. Before him he held his shield of hammered bronze, that the smith had beaten so fair and round, and had lined with ox hides which he had made fast with rivets of gold all round the shield. This he held in front of him, and brandishing his two spears came on like some lion of the wilderness, who has been long famished for want of meat and will dare break even into a well-fenced homestead to try and get at the sheep. He may find the shepherds keeping watch over their flocks with dogs and spears, but he is unwilling to be driven from the fold till he has had a try for it; he will either spring on a sheep and carry it off, or be hit by a spear from strong hand. That was how Sarpedon was inclined to attack the wall and break down its battlements. Then he said to Glaukos son of Hippolokhos,

[310] "Glaukos, why is it that we receive special honor in Lycia with respect to our place at the table? Why are the choicest portions served to us and our cups are kept brimming? and why do men look up to us as though we were gods? Moreover, we hold large estates by the banks of the river Xanthos, fair with wide orchards and wheat-growing land. It becomes us, therefore, to take our stand at the head of all the Lycians and bear the brunt of the fight, that one may say to another, 'Our princes in Lycia eat the fat of the land and drink best of wine, but they are fine men; they fight well and are ever at the front in battle.' My good friend, if, when we were once out of this battle, we could escape old age and death afterwards and for ever, I would neither press forward myself nor bid you do so. Death in ten thousand shapes hangs ever over our heads, and no man can escape it. Therefore let us go forward and either win glory for ourselves, or yield it to another."

Glaukos heeded his saying, and the pair forthwith led on the host of Lycians, … [420] who pressed close round Sarpedon, who was their king's counsellor. The Argives on their part got their men in fighting order within the wall, and there was a deadly struggle between them. The Lycians could not break through the wall and force their way to the ships, nor could the Danaans drive the Lycians from the wall now that they had once reached it. As two men, measuring-rods in hand, quarrel about their boundaries in a field that they own in common, and argue for their rights though it may be for a mere strip, even so did the battlements now serve as a bone of contention, and they beat one another's round shields for their possession.

Hephaistos makes a shield for Achilles

Hephaistos went to his bellows, turning them towards the fire and bidding them do their duty. Twenty bellows blew upon the melting-pots, and they blew blasts of every kind, some fierce to help him when he had need of them, and others less strong as Hephaistos willed it in the course of his work. He threw tough copper into the fire, and tin, with silver and gold; he set his great anvil on its block, and with one hand grasped his mighty hammer while he took the tongs in the other.

First he shaped the shield so great and strong, adorning it all over and binding it round with a gleaming circuit in three layers; and the baldric was made of silver. He made the shield in five thicknesses, and with many a wonder did his cunning hand enrich it.

He wrought the earth, the heavens, and the sea; the moon also at her full and the untiring sun, with all the constellations that glorify the face of heaven: the Pleiads, the Hyads, huge Orion, and the Bear, which men also call the Waggon and which turns round ever in one place, facing Orion, and alone never dips into the stream of the Ocean.

He also wrought two cities, fair to see and busy with the hum of men. In the one were weddings and wedding-feasts, and they were going about the city with brides whom they were escorting by torchlight from their chambers. Loud rose the cry of Hymen, and the youths danced to the music of flute and lyre, while the women stood each at her house door to see them.

[497] Meanwhile the people were gathered in assembly, for there was a quarrel, and two men were wrangling about the blood-price for a man who had died, the one claiming to the assembly that he had the right to pay off the damages in full, and the other refusing to accept anything. Each was seeking a limit, in the presence of an arbitrator, and the people took sides, each man backing the side that he had taken; but the heralds kept them back, and the elders sat on their seats of stone in a solemn circle, holding the staves which the heralds had put into their hands. Then they rose and each in his turn gave judgment, and there were two measures of gold laid down, to be given to him whose judgment should be deemed the fairest.
…

He wrought also a fair fallow field, large and thrice ploughed already. Many men were working at the plough within it, turning their oxen to and fro, furrow after furrow. Each time that they turned on reaching the headland a man would come up to them and give them a cup of wine, and they would go back to their furrows looking forward to the time when they should again reach the headland. The part that they had ploughed was dark behind them, so that the field, though it was of gold, still looked as if it were being ploughed: very wonderful to behold.

He wrought also a field of harvest grain, and the reapers were reaping with sharp sickles in their hands. Swathe after swathe fell to the ground in a straight line behind them, and the binders bound them in bands of twisted straw. There were three binders, and behind them there were boys who gathered the cut grain in armfuls and kept on bringing them to be bound: among them all the owner of the land stood by in silence and was glad. The servants were getting a meal ready under an oak, for they had sacrificed a great ox, and were busy cutting him up, while the women were making a porridge of much white barley for the laborers' dinner.

He wrought also a vineyard, golden and fair to see, and the vines were loaded with grapes. The bunches overhead were black, but the vines were trained on poles of silver. He ran a ditch of dark metal all round it, and fenced it with a fence of tin; there was only one path to it, and by this the vintagers went when they would gather the vintage. Youths and maidens all blithe and full of glee, carried the luscious fruit in plaited baskets; and with them there went a boy who made sweet music with his lyre, and sang the Linus-song with his clear boyish voice.

He wrought also a herd of horned cattle. He made the cows of gold and tin, and they lowed as they came full speed out of the yards to go and feed among the waving reeds that grow by the banks of the river. Along with the cattle there went four shepherds, all of them in gold, and their nine fleet dogs went with them. Two terrible lions had fastened on a bellowing bull that was with the foremost cows, and bellow as he might they haled him, while the dogs and men gave chase: the lions tore through the bull's thick hide and were gorging on his blood and bowels, but the herdsmen were afraid to do anything, and only hounded on their dogs; the dogs dared not fasten on the lions but stood by barking and keeping out of harm's way.

The god wrought also a pasture in a fair mountain dell, and large flock of sheep, with a homestead and huts, and sheltered sheepfolds.

Furthermore he wrought a meadow, like that which Daedalus once made in Knossos for lovely Ariadne. In it was a dance of youths and maidens, whom all would woo, all with their hands on one another's wrists. The maidens wore robes of light linen, and the youths well woven shirts that were slightly oiled. The girls were crowned with garlands, while the young men had daggers of gold that hung by silver baldrics; sometimes they would dance deftly in a ring with merry twinkling feet, as it were a potter sitting at his work and making trial of his wheel to see whether it will run, and sometimes they would go all in line with one another, and many people were gathered joyously about the dancing place. There was a bard also to sing to them and play his lyre, while two tumblers went about performing in the midst of them when the man struck up with his tune.

All round the outermost rim of the shield he set the mighty stream of the river Okeanos.

Then when he had fashioned the shield so great and strong, he made a breastplate also that shone brighter than fire. He made a helmet, close fitting to the brow, and richly worked, with a golden plume overhanging it; and he made greaves also of beaten tin.

Lastly, when the famed lame god had made all the armor, he took it and set it before the mother of Achilles; whereon she darted like a falcon from the snowy summits of Olympus and bore away the gleaming armor from the house of Hephaistos.

The death of Hector: Fate and Hades

[131] Then Achilles came up to Hector as it were Ares himself, plumed lord of battle. From his right shoulder he brandished his terrible spear of Pelian ash, and the bronze gleamed around him like flashing fire or the rays of the rising sun. Fear fell upon Hektor as he beheld him, and he dared not stay longer where he was but fled in dismay from before the gates, while Achilles darted after him at his utmost speed. As a mountain falcon, swiftest of all birds, swoops down upon some cowering dove—the dove flies before him but the falcon with a shrill scream follows close after, resolved to have her—even so did Achilles make straight for Hektor with all his might, while Hektor fled under the Trojan wall as fast as his limbs could take him. …

[157] Good was the man that fled, but better far was he that followed after, and swiftly indeed did they run, for the prize was no mere beast for sacrifice or bullock's hide, as it might be for a common foot-race, but they ran for the life [psukhê] of Hektor. As horses in a chariot race speed round the turning-posts when they are running for some great prize at the games in honor of some dead hero, so did these two run full speed three times round the city of Priam.

All the gods watched them, and the sire of gods and men was the first to speak.

"Alas, my eyes behold a man who is dear to me being pursued round the walls of Troy; my heart is full of pity for Hektor, who has burned the thigh-bones of many a heifer in my honor, at one while on the of many-vall-eyed Ida, and again on the citadel of Troy; and now I see noble Achilles in full pursuit of him round the city of Priam. What say you? Consider among yourselves and decide whether we shall now save him or let him fall, valiant though he be, before Achilles, son of Peleus."

[177] Then Athena said,

"Father, wielder of the lightning, lord of cloud and storm, what do you mean? Would you pluck this mortal whose doom has long been decreed out of the jaws of death? Do as you will, but we others shall not be of a mind with you."

And Zeus answered,

"My child, Trito-born, take heart. I did not speak in full earnest, and I will let you have your way. Do as your mind tells you, without letting up, without hindrance."

Thus did he urge Athena who was already eager, and down she darted from the topmost summits of Olympus.

Achilles was still in full pursuit of Hektor, … [209] and then the father of all balanced his golden scales and placed a doom in each of them, one for Achilles and the other for Hektor. As he held the scales by the middle, the doom of Hektor fell down deep into the house of Hades. Then Phoebus Apollo left him. Thereon Athena went close up to the son of Peleus and said,

[215] "Noble Achilles, favored of heaven, I think in my mind we two shall surely take back to the ships a triumph for the Achaeans by slaying Hektor, for all his lust of battle. Do what Apollo may as he lies groveling before his father, aegis-bearing Zeus, Hektor cannot escape us longer. Stay here and take breath, while I go up to him and persuade him to make a stand and fight you."

Thus spoke Athena. Achilles obeyed her gladly, and stood still, leaning on his bronze-pointed ashen spear, while Athena left him and went after Hektor in the form and with the voice of his brother Deiphobos. She came close up to him and said,

[224] "Dear brother, I see you are hard pressed by Achilles who is chasing you at full speed round the city of Priam. … But let us two make a stand and fight, and let there be no keeping our spears in reserve, [245] that we may learn whether Achilles shall kill us and bear off our spoils to the ships, or whether he shall fall before you."

Thus did Athena trick him by her cunning, and when the two were now close to one another great Hektor was first to speak.

"I will no longer flee you, son of Peleus, as I have been doing hitherto. Three times have I fled round the mighty city of Priam, without daring to withstand you, but now, let me either slay or be slain, for I am in the mind to face you. Let us, then, give pledges to one another by our gods, who are the fittest witnesses and guardians of all covenants; let it be agreed between us that if Zeus grants me the longer stay and I take your life, I am not to treat your dead body in any unseemly fashion, but when I have stripped you of your armor, I am to give up your body to the Achaeans. And do you likewise."

[260] Achilles glared at him and answered,

"Fool, prate not to me about covenants. There can be no covenants between men and lions. Wolves and lambs can never be of one mind, but hate each other through and through. Therefore there can be no understanding between you and me, nor can there be any covenants between us, till one or other shall fall and glut grim Ares with his life's blood. Be mindful of all your valour; you have need now to prove yourself indeed a bold warrior and fighter. You have no more chance, and Pallas Athena will immedialy vanquish you by my spear: you shall now pay me in full for the grief you have caused me on account of my comrades whom you have killed in battle."

He took his spear as he spoke and hurled it. Hektor saw it coming and avoided it; he watched it and crouched down so that it flew over his head and stuck in the ground beyond; Athena then snatched it up and gave it back to Achilles without Hektor's seeing her. Then Hektor said to the son of Peleus,

"You have missed your aim, Achilles, peer of the gods, and Zeus has not yet revealed to you the hour of my doom, though you made sure that he had done so. You were a false-tongued liar when you deemed that I should forget my valor and tremble before you."

He poised his spear as he spoke and hurled it. [290] His aim was true for he hit the middle of Achilles' shield, but the spear rebounded from it, and did not pierce it. Hektor was angry when he saw that the weapon had sped from his hand in vain, and stood there in dismay for he had no second spear. With a shout he called Deiphobos and asked him for one, but there was no man; then he saw the truth and said to himself,

"Alas! the gods have lured me on to my destruction. I deemed that the hero Deiphobos was by my side, but he is within the wall, and Athena has tricked me; death is now indeed very near and there is no way out of it—for thus have Zeus and his son Apollo the far-darter willed it, though before this they have been ever ready to protect me. My doom has come upon me; let me not then die ingloriously and without a struggle, but let me first do some great thing that shall be told among men hereafter."

As he spoke he drew the keen blade that hung so great and strong by his side, and gathering himself together be sprang on Achilles like a soaring eagle which swoops down from the clouds on to some lamb or timid hare. [245] Even so did Hektor draw his sword and spring upon Achilles. Achilles mad with rage rushed towards him.... He eyed Hector's fair flesh to see where he could best wound it, but all was protected by his excellent armor that Hektor had stripped from Patroklos after he had killed him, save only the throat where the collar-bones divide the neck from the shoulders, and this is the.quickest place for the life to escape. Here then did Achilles strike him as he was coming on towards him, and the point of his spear went right through the fleshy part of the neck, but it did not sever his windpipe so that he could still speak.

Hektor fell headlong, and Achilles vaunted over him saying,

"Hektor, you deemed that you should come off unpunished when you were spoiling Patroklos, and did not think of me, who was not with him. Fool that you were: for I, his comrade, mightier far than he, was still left behind him at the ships, and now I have laid you low. The Achaeans shall give him all due funeral rites, while dogs and vultures shall work their will upon yourself."

Then Hektor said, as his life ebbed out of him,

[337] "I pray you by your life and knees, and by your parents, let not dogs devour me at the ships of the Achaeans, but accept the

rich treasure of gold and bronze which my father and mother will offer you, and send my body home, that the Trojans and their wives may give me my dues of fire when I am dead."

Achilles glared at him and answered,

"Dog, do not speak to me of knees nor parents; would that I could be as sure of being able to cut your flesh into pieces and eat it raw, for the ill have done me, as I am that nothing shall save you from the dogs. You shall not be ransomed, even if they bring ten or twenty-fold ransom and weigh it out for me on the spot, with promise of yet more hereafter. Even if Priam son of Dardanos should offer me your weight in gold, even so your mother shall never lay you out and make lament over the son she bore. No, the dogs and vultures shall devour you completely."

[355] Hektor with his dying breath then said,

"I know you what you are, and was sure that I would not be able to move you, for your heart is hard as iron. But see to it that I bring not heaven's anger upon you on the day when Paris and Phoebus Apollo, valiant though you be, shall slay you at the Scaean gates."

When he had thus said the shrouds of death's final outcome enfolded him, whereon his life went out of him and flew down to the house of Hades, lamenting its sad fate that it should enjoy youth and strength no longer. But Achilles said, speaking to the dead body,

"Die; for my part I will accept my fate whensoever Zeus and the other gods see fit to send it."

As he spoke he drew his spear from the body and set it on one side; then he stripped the blood-stained armor from Hektor's shoulders while the other Achaeans came running up to view his wondrous strength and beauty; and no one came near him without giving him a fresh wound. Then would one turn to his neighbor and say,

"It is easier to handle Hektor now than when he was flinging fire on to our ships"

and as he spoke he would thrust his spear into him anew.

Achilles finished despoiling Hektor of his armor and [395] then pierced the sinews at the back of both his feet from heel to ankle and passed thongs of ox-hide through the slits he had made: thus he made the body fast to his chariot, letting the head trail upon the ground. Then when he had put the goodly armor on the chariot and had himself mounted, he lashed his horses on and they flew forward. The dust rose from Hektor as he was being dragged along, his dark hair flew all abroad, and his head once so comely was laid low on earth, for Zeus had now delivered him into the hands of his foes to do him outrage in his own land.

Thus was the head of Hektor being dishonored in the dust. His mother tore her hair, and flung her veil from her with a loud cry as she looked upon her son. His father made piteous moan, and throughout the city the people fell to weeping and wailing. It was as though the whole of frowning Ilion was being smirched with fire. Hardly could the people hold Priam back in his hot haste to rush without the gates of the city. He groveled in the mire and besought them, calling each one of them by his name.

Adapted from Samuel Butler, *Homer. The Iliad of Homer* (Longmans, Green and Co.: London, 1898).

READING 1B: HESIOD, *WORKS AND DAYS*

The next great poet of Greek literature was Hesiod, circa 700 B.C. Later Greeks considered him a contemporary of Homer, and he was even credited with triumphing over Homer in a singing contest. Unlike the Homeric poems, the Works and Days is set in the present, and so provides more direct historical testimony. Hesiod sings in the voice of a farmer in Boeotia, a region in central Greece. In this work, he offers advice for living an honest and hard-working life, and he cautions against an existence of idleness, greed, and corruption. The poem may be autobiographical or fictional. In the poem, Hesiod's advice is directed to his brother Perses, who bribed local chiefs into awarding him a greater share of their late father's estate. Some of this sermon relates to family, religion, and social relations, but most of the advice relates to agriculture and the best way to tend to a farm. This section of the poem reads like a farmer's almanac and even includes a summary of the days of the month which are favorable or unfavorable for certain farming activities

The Works and Days also contains a mythological explanation of the history of mankind. This history is divided into five ages starting with the Golden, Silver, and Bronze ages, continuing to the Heroic Age of the Trojan war and ending with the Iron Age: the age of Hesiod. In each successive age mankind is less pure, with the exception of the heroic age, and the Iron Age is the most immoral and degenerate of all. Hesiod describes his own era in negative terms as he expounds on the greed, dishonour, and violence of the times, in violation of the laws of Zeus, causing Dike, goddess of justice, to quit the earth in disgust. Hesiod lived in an age when the chiefdoms described by Homer were just beginning to transform into the hoplite citizen-societies of the Greek polis (city-state or citizen-state). Hesiod may be read as voicing the values and worldview of the smallholder farmers who become the hoplite-citizens of the polis, and we find expressed in his poems the tensions that characterized the rise of the polis: social tensions between different social classes and in the relationship between the community of common men and their leaders. Hesiod offers a critique of his society and calls for a moral and social order of equitable shares in the social, political, and economic life of the community.

Consider:
- What are the conditions of the society depicted in the poems?
- What conflicts, tensions, and problems are present in the society?

Hesiod, *Works and Days*

Muses of Pieria who give glory through song, come hither, tell of Zeus your father and chant his praise. Through him mortal men are famed or unfamed, sung or unsung alike, as great Zeus wills. [5] For easily he makes strong, and easily he brings the strong man low; easily he humbles the proud and raises the obscure, and easily he straightens the crooked and blasts the proud — Zeus who thunders aloft and has his dwelling most high. Attend thou with eye and ear, and make judgments straight with righteousness. [10] And, Perses, I would tell of true things.

....

Perses, lay up these things in your heart, and do not let that Strife who delights in mischief hold your heart back from work, while you peep and peer and listen to the wrangles of the court-house. [30] He who has not a year's victuals laid up for himself has no time for quarrels and courts. When you have got plenty of that, you can raise disputes and strive to get another's goods. But you shall have no second chance [35] to deal so again: nay, let us settle our dispute here with true judgment which is of Zeus and is perfect. For we had already divided our inheritance, but you seized the greater share and carried it off, greatly swelling the glory of our bribe-swallowing lords who love to judge such a cause as this. [40] Fools! They know not how much more the half is than the whole, nor what great advantage there is in a poor man's bread.

For the gods keep hidden from men the means of life. Otherwise you would easily do work enough in a day to supply you for a full year even without working; [45] soon would you put away your rudder over the smoke, and the fields worked by ox and sturdy mule would run to waste. But Zeus in the anger of his heart hid it, because crafty Prometheus deceived him; therefore he planned sorrow and mischief against men. [50] Zeus hid fire. But that the noble son of Iapetus, Prometheus, stole it again for men from Zeus the counsellor, hiding it in a hollow fennel-stalk, so that Zeus who delights in thunder did not see it. But afterwards Zeus who gathers the clouds said to him in anger: 'Son of Iapetus, surpassing all in cunning, [55] you are pleased with yourself for having outwitted me and stolen fire — a great plague to you yourself and to men that shall be. But I will give an evil thing to men as the price for fire, a thing in which they may all be glad of heart while they embrace their own destruction.' So said the father of men and gods, and laughed aloud.

[60] Then he instructed famous Hephaestus to make haste and mix earth with water and to put in it the voice and strength of humankind, and fashion a sweet, lovely maiden-shape, like to the immortal goddesses in face. He instructed Athena to teach her needlework and the weaving of the varied web; [65] and golden Aphrodite, to shed grace upon her head and cruel longing and cares that weary the limbs. And he charged Hermes the guide, the Slayer of Argus, to put in her a shameless mind and a deceitful nature. So he ordered. And they obeyed the lord Zeus the son of Cronos. [70] At once the famous Lame God molded clay in the likeness of a modest maid, as the son of Cronos planned. And the goddess bright-eyed Athena girded and clothed her, and the divine Graces and queenly Persuasion put necklaces of gold upon her, [75] and the rich-haired Hours crowned her head with spring flowers. And Pallas Athena bedecked her form with all manner of finery. Also the Guide, the Slayer of Argus, contrived within her lies and crafty words and a deceitful nature at the will

of loud thundering Zeus, [80] and the Herald of the gods put speech in her. And he called this woman Pandora, because all they who dwelt on Olympus gave each a gift, a plague to men who eat bread.

But when he had finished this total, pitiless trap, the Father sent glorious Argus-Slayer, [85] the swift messenger of the gods, to take it to Epimetheus as a gift. And Epimetheus did not think on what Prometheus had said to him, bidding him never take a gift of Olympian Zeus, but to send it back for fear it might prove to be something harmful to men. But he took the gift, and afterwards, when the evil thing was already his, he understood.

[90] For before this the tribes of men lived on earth remote and free from the ills and hard toil and heavy sicknesses that bring the Fates upon men — for in misery men now grow old quickly. But the woman took off the great lid of the jar with her hands [95] and scattered all these, and her thought caused sorrow and mischief for men. Only Hope stayed within the great jar, remaining behind in an unbreakable home. Hope did not fly out from the door, for before it could, the lid of the jar stopped it, by the will of Aegis-holding Zeus who gathers the clouds. [100] But the rest, countless plagues, wander amongst men; for earth is full of evils, and the sea is full. Of themselves diseases come upon men continually by day and by night, bringing mischief to mortals silently; for wise Zeus took away speech from them. [105] So is there no way to escape the will of Zeus.

Or if you will, I will sum you up another tale well and skilfully — and do you lay it up in your heart — how the gods and mortal men sprang from one source. First of all [110] the deathless gods who dwell on Olympus made a golden race of mortal men who lived in the time of Cronos when he was reigning in heaven. And they lived like gods [115] without sorrow of heart, remote and free from toil and grief: miserable age rested not on them, but with legs and arms never failing they made merry with feasting beyond the reach of all evils. When they died, it was as though they were overcome with sleep, and they had all good things, for the fruitful earth on its own bore them fruit abundantly and without stint. They dwelt in ease and peace upon their lands with many good things, [120] rich in flocks and loved by the blessed gods.

But after the earth had covered this generation … then those who dwell on Olympus created a second generation made of silver and less noble by far. It was like the golden race neither in body nor in spirit. [130] A child was brought up at his good mother's side a hundred years, an utter simpleton, playing childishly in his own home. But when they were full grown and were come to the full measure of their prime, they lived only a little time and that in sorrow because of their foolishness, for they could not keep from sinning and [135] from wronging one another, nor would they serve the immortals, nor sacrifice on the holy altars of the blessed ones as it is right for men to do wherever they dwell. Then Zeus the son of Cronos was angry and put them away, because they would not give honor to the blessed gods who live on Olympus.

[140] But when earth had covered this generation, too … Zeus the Father made a third generation of mortal men, a race of bronze, sprung from ash-trees. It was in no way equal to the silver age, [145] but was terrible and strong. They loved the lamentable works of Ares and deeds of violence; they ate no bread, but were hard of heart like adamant, fearful men. Great was their strength and unconquerable the arms which grew from their shoulders on their strong limbs. [150] Their armor was of bronze,

and their houses of bronze, and of bronze were their implements: there was no black iron. These were destroyed by their own hands and passed to the dank house of chill Hades, and left no name: terrible though they were, [155] black Death seized them, and they left the bright light of the sun.

But when earth had covered this generation also, Zeus the son of Cronos made yet another, the fourth, upon the fruitful earth, which was nobler and more righteous, a god-like race of hero-men who are called [160] demi-gods, the race before our own, throughout the boundless earth. Grim war and dread battle destroyed a part of them, some in the land of Cadmus at seven-gated Thebes when they fought for the flocks of Oedipus, and some, when it had brought them in ships over the great sea [165] to Troy for rich-haired Helen's sake: there death's end enshrouded a part of them. But to the others father Zeus the son of Cronos gave a living and an abode apart from men, and made them dwell at the ends of earth. [170] And they live untouched by sorrow in the islands of the blessed along the shore of deep-swirling Ocean, happy heroes for whom the grain-giving earth bears honey-sweet fruit flourishing thrice a year, far from the deathless gods, and Cronos rules over them; for the father of men and gods released him from his bonds. And these last equally have honor and glory.

And again far-seeing Zeus made yet another generation of men, the fifth, who now live upon the bounteous earth. How I wish that I were not among the men of the fifth generation! [175] Would that I either had died before or been born afterwards! For now truly is a race of iron, and men never rest from labor and sorrow by day, and from perishing by night; and the gods shall lay sore trouble upon them. But, notwithstanding, even these shall have some good mingled with their evils. [180] And Zeus will destroy this race of mortal men also when they come to have grey hair on the temples at their birth. The father will not agree with his children, nor the children with their father, nor guest with his host, nor comrade with comrade; nor will brother be dear to brother as before. [185] Men will dishonor their parents as they grow quickly old, and will carp at them, chiding them with bitter words, hard-hearted they, not knowing the fear of the gods. They will not repay their aged parents the cost of their nurture, for might shall be their right: and one man will sack another's city. [190] There will be no favor for the man who keeps his oath or for the just or for the good; but rather men will praise the evil-doer and his violent dealing. Strength will be right, and reverence will cease to be; and the wicked will hurt the worthy man, speaking false words against him, and will swear an oath upon them. [195] Envy, foul-mouthed, delighting in evil, with scowling face, will go along with wretched men one and all. [200] And then Righteousness and Shame, with their sweet forms wrapped in white robes, will go from the wide-pathed earth and forsake mankind to join the company of the deathless gods: and bitter sorrows will be left for mortal men, and there will be no help against evil.

·········

But you, Perses, listen to right and do not foster violence; for violence is bad for a poor man. [215] Even the prosperous cannot easily bear its burden, but is weighed down under it when he has fallen into delusion. The better path is to go by on the other side towards Justice; for Justice beats Outrage when she comes at length to the end of the race. But only when he has suffered does the fool learn this. For Oath keeps pace with wrong judgments. [220] There is a noise when Justice is being dragged in the way where those who devour bribes and give sentence with crooked judgments, take her. And she, wrapped in mist, follows to the city and haunts of the people, weeping, and bringing mischief to men, even to such as have driven her forth in that they did not deal fairly with her. [225] But those who give straight judgments to strangers and to the men of the land, and go not aside from what is just, their city flourishes, and the people prosper in it: Peace, the nurse of children, is abroad in their land, and all-seeing Zeus never decrees cruel war against them. [230] Neither famine nor disaster ever haunt men who do true justice, but light-heartedly they tend the fields which are all their care. The earth bears them food in plenty, and on the mountains the oak bears acorns upon the top and bees in the middle. Their woolly sheep are weighed-down with fleeces; [235] their women bear children like their parents. They always flourish with good things, and do not travel on ships, for the grain-giving earth bears them fruit.

But for those who practice violence and cruel deeds far-seeing Zeus, the son of Cronos, ordains a punishment. [240] Often even a whole city suffers for a bad man who sins and devises presumptuous deeds, and the son of Cronos lays great trouble upon the people, famine and plague together, so that the men perish away, and their women do not bear children, and their houses become few, [245] through the contriving of Olympian Zeus. And again, at another time, the son of Cronos either destroys their wide army, or their walls, or else makes an end of their ships on the sea. You princes, mark well this punishment, you also, for the deathless gods are near among men; and [250] mark all those who oppress their fellows with crooked judgments; and heed not the anger of the gods. For upon the bounteous earth Zeus has thrice ten thousand spirits, watchers of mortal men, and these keep watch on judgments and deeds of wrong [255] as they roam, clothed in mist, all over the earth. And there is virgin Justice, the daughter of Zeus, who is honored and revered among the gods who dwell on Olympus, and whenever anyone hurts her with lying slander, she sits beside her father, Zeus the son of Cronos, [260] and complains about men's wicked heart, until the people pay for the mad folly of their princes who, evilly minded, pervert judgment and give sentence crookedly. Keep watch against this, you princes, and make straight your judgments, you who devour bribes; put crooked judgments altogether from your thoughts. [265] He does harm to himself who does harm to another, and evil planned harms the plotter most.

The eye of Zeus, seeing all and understanding all, beholds these things too, if so he will, and fails not to mark what sort of justice is this that the city keeps within it. [270] Now, therefore, may neither I myself be righteous among men, nor my son — for then it is a bad thing to be righteous — if indeed the unrighteous shall have the greater right. But I think that all-wise Zeus will not yet bring that to pass. But you, Perses, lay up these things within your heart and [275] listen now to right, ceasing altogether to think of violence. For the son of Cronos has ordained this law for men, that fishes and beasts and winged fowls should devour one another, for justice is not among them; but to mankind he gave justice, which proves [280] far the best. For whoever knows what is right and is ready to speak it, far-seeing Zeus gives him prosperity; but whoever deliberately lies in his witness and perjures himself, and so hurts Justice and sins beyond repair, that man's generation is left obscure thereafter. [285] But the generation of the man who swears truly is better in the future.

To you, foolish Perses, I will speak good sense. Badness can be got easily and in abundance; the road to her is smooth, and she lives very near us. But between us and Goodness the gods have placed the sweat of our brows; [290] long and steep is the road that leads to her, and it is rough at the first; but when a man has reached the top, then is she easy to reach, though before that she was hard.

....

But do you at any rate, always remembering my charge, work, high-born Perses, that Hunger [300] may hate you, and venerable Demeter richly crowned may love you and fill your barn with food; for Hunger is altogether a fitting comrade for the sluggard. Both gods and men are angry with a man who lives idle, [305] for in nature he is like the stingless drones who waste the labor of the bees, eating without working. Let it be your care to order your work properly, that in the right season your barns may be full of victual. Through work men grow rich in flocks and substance, and when working they are much better loved by the immortals. [311] Work is no disgrace: it is idleness which is a disgrace. But if you work, the idle will soon envy you as you grow rich, for fame and renown attend on wealth. And whatever be your lot, work is best for you, [315] if you turn your misguided mind away from other men's property to your work and attend to your livelihood as I bid you.

An evil shame is the needy man's companion, shame which both greatly harms and prospers men: shame is with poverty, but confidence with wealth. [320] Wealth should not be seized: god-given wealth is much better; for if a man takes great wealth violently and perforce, or if he steals it through his tongue, as often happens when gain deceives men's sense and dishonor tramples down honor, [325] the gods soon blot him out and make that man's house low, and wealth attends him only for a little time. Alike with him who does wrong to a suppliant or a guest, or who goes up to his brother's bed and commits unnatural sin in lying with his wife, [330] or who shamelessly offends against fatherless children, or who abuses his old father at the cheerless threshold of old age and attacks him with harsh words, truly Zeus himself is angry, and at the last lays on him a heavy requital for his evil doing.

[335] You must turn your foolish heart completely away from these things, and, as far as you are able, sacrifice to the deathless gods purely and cleanly, and burn rich meats also, and at other times propitiate them with drink-offerings and incense, both when you go to bed and when the holy light has come back, [340] that they may be gracious to you in heart and spirit, and so you may buy another's property and not another yours.

Call your friend to a feast, but leave your enemy alone. And especially call him who lives near you: for if any mischief happens in the place, [345] neighbors come unarmed at once, but kinsmen take time to arm themselves. A bad neighbor is as great a plague as a good one is a great blessing; he who enjoys a good neighbor has a precious possession. Not even an ox will stray away if you have a watchful neighbor. Take fair measure from your neighbor and pay him back [350] fairly with the same measure, or better, if you can; so that if you are in need afterwards, you will have a true friend.

Shun evil profit: evil profit is as bad as ruin. Be friends with the friendly, and visit him who visits you. Give to one who gives, but do not give to one who does not give. [355] A man gives to the generous, but no one gives to the close-fisted. Give is a good girl, but Take is bad and she brings death. For the man who gives willingly, even though he gives a great thing, rejoices in his gift and is glad in heart; but whoever gives way to shamelessness and takes something himself, [360] even though it is a small thing, it freezes his heart.

He who adds to what he has, will keep off bright-eyed hunger; for if you add only a little to a little and do this often, soon that little will become great. What a man has by him at home does not trouble him: [365] it is better to have your stuff at home, for whatever is abroad may mean loss.

·········

Do not let a flaunting woman coax and cozen and deceive you: she is after your barn. The man who trusts women trusts cheats.

[375] There should be an only son to feed his father's house, for so wealth will increase in the home; but if you leave a second son you should die old. Yet Zeus can easily give great wealth to a greater number.

······

[405] First of all, get a house, and a woman and an ox for the plough — a slave woman and not a wife, to follow the oxen as well — and make everything ready at home, so that you may not have to ask of another. For if he refuses you, and then, because you are in lack, the season passes by, your work will come to nothing. [410] Do not put your work off till tomorrow and the day after; for a sluggish worker does not fill his barn, nor one who puts off his work: industry makes work go well, but a man who puts off work is always at hand-grips with ruin.

·········

But if desire for uncomfortable sea-faring seize you when the Pleiades plunge into the misty sea [620] to escape Orion's rude strength, then truly gales of all kinds rage. Then keep ships no longer on the sparkling sea, but be sure to till the land as I instruct you. Haul up your ship upon the land and pack it closely with stones [625] all round to keep off the power of the winds which blow damply, and draw out the bilge-plug so that the rain of heaven may not rot it. Put away all the tackle and fittings in your house, and stow the wings of the sea-going ship neatly, and hang up the well-shaped rudder over the smoke. [630] Wait until the season for sailing is come, and then haul your swift ship down to the sea and stow a convenient cargo in it, so that you may bring home profit, even as your father and mine, foolish Perses, used to sail on shipboard because he lacked sufficient livelihood. And one day he came to this very place, crossing over a great stretch of sea; [635] he left Aeolian Cyme and fled, not from riches and substance, but from the wretched poverty that Zeus imposes on men, and he settled near Helicon in a miserable hamlet, [640] Ascra, which is bad in winter, sultry in summer, and good at no time.

But you, Perses, remember all works in their season but sailing especially. Admire a small ship, but put your freight in a large one; for the greater the load, the greater will be your piled gain, [645] if only the winds will keep back their harmful gales.

If ever you turn your misguided heart to trading and wish to escape from debt and joyless hunger, I will show you the measures of the loud-roaring sea, though I have no skill in sea-faring nor in ships; [650] for never yet have I sailed by ship over the wide sea, but only to Euboea from Aulis where the Achaeans once stayed through much storm when they had gathered a great host from divine Hellas for Troy, the land of fair women. [655] Then I crossed over to Chalcis, to the games of wise Amphidamas where the sons of the great-hearted hero proclaimed and appointed prizes. And there I boast that I gained the victory with a song and carried off a handled tripod which I dedicated to the Muses of Helicon, in the place where they first set me in the way of clear song. [660] Such is all my experience of man-made ships; nevertheless I will tell you the will of Zeus who holds the aegis; for the Muses have taught me to sing in marvelous song.

Fifty days after the solstice, when the season of wearisome heat is come to an end, [665] is the right time for men to go sailing. Then you will not wreck your ship, nor will the sea destroy the sailors, unless Poseidon the Earth-Shaker decides upon it, or Zeus, the king of the deathless gods, wishes to slay them; for the issues of good and evil alike are with them. [670] At that time the winds are steady, and the sea is harmless. Then trust in the winds without care, and haul your swift ship down to the sea and put all the freight on board. But return home again as quickly as you can, and do not wait until the time of the new wine and the autumn rain and [675] the oncoming storms with the fierce gales of Notus, which accompanies the heavy autumn rain of Zeus and stirs up the sea and makes it dangerous.

Another time for men to go sailing is in spring when a man first sees leaves on the topmost shoot of a fig-tree as large as the foot-print that a crow makes; [680] then the sea is passable, and this is the spring sailing time. For my part I do not praise it, for my heart does not like it. Such a sailing is quickly stolen, and you will hardly avoid mischief. Yet in their ignorance [685] men do even this, for wealth means life to poor mortals; but it is fearful to die among the waves. But I bid you consider all these things in your heart as I say. Do not put all your goods in hollow ships; [690] leave the greater part behind, and put the lesser part on board; for it is a bad business to meet with disaster among the waves of the sea, as it is bad if you put too great a load on your wagon and break the axle, and your goods are spoiled. Observe due measure: and proportion is best in all things.

[695] Bring home a wife to your house when you are of the right age, while you thirty years old, give or take a few; this is the right age for marriage. Let your wife have been grown up four years, and marry her in the fifth. Marry a maiden, so that you can teach her careful ways, [700] and especially marry one who lives near you, but look well about you and see that your marriage will not be a joke to your neighbors. For a man wins nothing better than a good wife, and, again, nothing worse than a bad one, a greedy soul who [705] roasts her man without the help of fire, strong though he may be, and brings him to a raw old age.

....

[760] Do all of this, but especially avoid the talk of men. For Talk is mischievous, light, and easily raised, but hard to bear and difficult to be rid of. Talk never wholly dies away when many people voice her: even Talk is in some ways divine.

Mark the days which come from Zeus, duly telling your slaves of them, and that the thirtieth day of the month is best for one to look over the work and to deal out supplies. For these are days which come from Zeus the all-wise, when men discern aright. To begin with, the first, the fourth, and the seventh — [770] on which Leto bore Apollo with the blade of gold — each is a holy day. The eighth and the ninth, two days at least of the waxing month, are especially good for the works of man. Also the eleventh and twelfth are both excellent, [775] alike for shearing sheep and for reaping the kindly fruits; but the twelfth is much better than the eleventh, for on it the airy-swinging spider spins its web in full day, and then the Wise One, gathers her pile. On that day a woman should set up her loom and get forward with her work. [780] Avoid the thirteenth of the waxing month for beginning to sow: yet it is the best day for setting plants. The sixth of the mid-month is very unfavorable for plants, but is good for the birth of males, though unfavorable for a girl either to be born at all or to be married. [785] Nor is the first sixth a fit day for a girl to be born, but a kindly one for gelding kids and sheep and for fencing in a sheep cote. It is favorable for the birth of a boy, but such will be fond of sharp speech, lies, cunning words, and stealthy conversation. [790] On the eighth of the month geld the boar and loud-bellowing bull, but hard-working mules on the twelfth. On the great twentieth, in full day, a wise man should be born. Such a one is very sound-witted. The tenth is favorable for a male to be born; but, for a girl, the fourth day [795] of the mid-month. On that day tame sheep and shambling, horned oxen, and the sharp-fanged dog and hardy mules to the touch of the hand. But take care to avoid troubles which eat out the heart on the fourth of the beginning and ending of the month; it is a day very fraught with fate. [800] On the fourth of the month bring home your bride, but choose the omens which are best for this business. Avoid fifth days: they are unkindly and terrible. On a fifth, they say, the Erinyes assisted at the birth of Horcus (Oath) whom Eris (Strife) bore to trouble the accursed. [805] Look about you very carefully and throw out Demeter's holy grain upon the well-rolled threshing floor on the seventh of the mid-month. Let the woodman cut beams for house building and plenty of ships' timbers, such as are suitable for ships. On the fourth day begin to build narrow ships. [810] The ninth of the mid-month improves towards evening; but the first ninth of all is quite harmless for men. It is a good day on which to beget or to be born both for a male and a female: it is never a wholly evil day. Again, few know that the twenty-seventh of the month is best [815] for opening a wine jar, and putting yokes on the necks of oxen and mules and swift-footed horses, and for hauling a swift ship of many thwarts down to the sparkling sea; few call it by its right name. On the fourth day open a jar. The fourth of the mid-month is a day holy above all. And again, few men know that the fourth day after the twentieth is best while it is morning: [820] towards evening it is less good.

These days are a great blessing to men on earth; but the rest are changeable, luckless, and bring nothing. Everyone praises a different day but few know their nature. Sometimes a day is a stepmother, sometimes a mother. [825] That man is happy and lucky in them who knows all these things and does his work without offending the deathless gods, who discerns the omens of birds and avoids transgression.

Adapted from Hugh G. Evelyn-White, *Hesiod. Works and Days* (William Heinemann Ltd.: London, 1914).

Chapter 2:
Tyranny, Oligarchy, Democracy

READING 2A. HERODOTUS: THE TYRANNY OF CYPSELUS

Tyranny is one of the most distinctive but also poorly understood phenomena of Greece in the Archaic period. In the Classical period, when the polis, or city-state, and its community of free citizens who shared in self-government had emerged decisively as the dominant form of society in Greece, the tyrant was regarded with horror. Tyranny came to be seen as the antithesis of the polis, viewed as the personal autocracy of one man, imposed by force on his fellow citizens and depriving them of their freedom and political equality.

Most of our sources for Archaic tyranny (including Herodotus and Aristotle) come from the Classical period and reflect this highly negative perspective. At the same time, they include contradictory elements, seemingly earlier traditions going back to the Archaic period that treat the tyrant positively, as a popular leader who defends the interests of the people and contributes to the growth of the polis. This positive attitude seems to be more strongly associated with the first tyrant in any dynasty (although negative views attach to them too), while their descendants are regarded more negatively. Whatever the original source and popularity of the tyrant, it is a consistent characteristic of Archaic Greek tyrannies that they were short-lived and that rather than developing into a stable system of autocratic or monarchical rule, they were overthrown in the second or third generation to be replaced by the collective political participation of the polis. By the Classical period, no major area of Greece was ruled by tyrants.

Explanations for the divided tradition about tyrants that we get from our sources remain uncertain and much debated. It does seem, however, that tyrants rose in response to social tensions. From the end of the Dark Age, Greek societies grew and became less homogenous. In place of villages, with homogenous populations sharing common conditions of life, larger city-states formed whose members did not all have direct contact with each other and among whom there were increasing differences in wealth and lifestyle. As overall wealth grew it also became more unequally distributed and gaps developed between the interests and circumstances of different people in the community. Yet, unlike the societies of the Near East when they experienced similar growth, Greece did not develop hierarchical, class-based societies. Instead the Greeks invented a new form of society and government: the polis. In the polis, rather than there being a king or centralized state, power was shared among citizens. These citizens were mainly independent farmers, owning their own land and controlling their own product rather than paying taxes to or having their production controlled by (as in Mycenaean Greece of the Near East) landowners or a government.

All farmers above a certain minimum line of property ownership formed a broad group (representing maybe around 30 to 50% of the population) who, as they controlled their own goods, also made their own political decisions, coming together to govern themselves as a community of citizens. They also came together to fight for themselves. Rather than the fighting role, and the power that went with it, being given to professional state army, or to a particular social class (like the knights and nobles of the Middle Ages), these men came together to fight for themselves in a citizen militia. This was 'hoplite warfare', which was fought by a militia of heavy infantry (with a particular 'panoply' of arms and armour), that developed in this period as a distinctively Greek way of fighting. In principle, all those included in this group of hoplite farmers were self-governing equals (while the landless poor were excluded, along with women and slaves).

It seems, however, that in different times and places, there were developments in opposition to this model and toward social and political hierarchy. For example, we hear of small farmers falling into debt, losing their land and even being enslaved, which would suggest a move toward a concentration of wealth and power in the hands of an elite class. And within the polis system of government there could similarly be class tension over how much power would be exercised by the citizens as a whole and how much would be given to particular officials who tended to be drawn from the elite. Tyrants seem to have emerged in the context of such class tension in Greek societies, perhaps representing the people and the polis against moves by the elite to concentrate too much power exclusively in their own hands. Later, though, it may be that tyrants began to be seen not as leaders of the people but as autocrats who were themselves keeping power for themselves and their children. This is one possible interpretation but the question remains open and, as is generally the case for the Archaic period, the evidence is patchy.

The city of Corinth, which was strategically situated to dominate both the trade routes into the Peloponnese and the shipping routes which linked the Aegean to the Corinthian Gulf, was a great commercial centre. By the middle of the seventh century, the wealth produced by this trade seems to have concentrated in the hands of a small group who also monopolized power. A tyrant named Cypselus arose, seemingly in opposition to this group, overthrowing them. This resulted in three generations of tyranny, as first Cypselus, then his son Periander, and finally his grandson Psammetichus controlled Corinth (c. 658-c. 585 B.C). Cypselus came to power through his position as an army commander, which won him great popularity and yielded military support for his new political faction. Cypselus was also known for his consideration and sound judgements which endeared him to the citizens of Corinth. The Greek historian Herodotus provides an account of his rise to power and the subsequent tyranny of his son Periander.

Herodotus, known variously as the "Father of History" or the "Father of Lies," was the first Greek historian. His lived in the fifth century B.C. (c.448-420) and wrote about the great conflict between the Greeks and Persians in a work called The Histories (or, more truly to his own words, The Inquiries). In trying to understand the nature of this great war, he wrote about the history, ethnography, and geography of both Greece and the Persian Empire. He was born in Halicarnassus, a Greek city in Caria which was then situated within the Persian Empire. He travelled extensively around the Mediterranean conducting his *historia* ('inquiry' or 'research'), making use of oral, literary, epigraphic, and archaeological sources. Much of his writing made heavy use of anecdotal stories and legends, the veracity of which is often debated by scholars.

While you read this and the following readings, try to define tyranny and explain how this method of government generally came about in Greece.

Herodotus, *Histories*, 5.92

[92] Such was the address of the Spartans. Most of the allies listened politely but were not persuaded. The only person who dared to speak out was the Corinthian delegate, Sosicles. He said:

[92a] "Surely heaven and earth will soon change places, with the earth up and the sky down, and men will soon live in the sea, with fish taking their place on the dry land, if you, the Lacedaemonians, propose to replace the rule of equality in the cities of Greece with tyrannies! Nothing in the whole world is more unjust, or more blood-soaked, than a tyranny. If, however, you Spartans think it is a good thing for cities to be under despotic rule, begin by installing a tyrant over your own state, and only then install them in other places. As things stand now, you know nothing of tyrants, and you have always been careful that Sparta has never submitted to one. You are embarking on a course that will abuse your allies' rights. If you knew as much as we do about the true nature of tyranny, you would be better positioned to make a decision.

[92b] "The government at Corinth was once an oligarchy—a single clan, called the Bacchiadae, administered the state. In order to keep power to themselves they intermarried only one another. It happened that one of them, Amphion, had a daughter, Labda, who was lame. When none of the Bacchiadae were willing to marry her, she was married to Eëtion, son of Echecrates, a man of the village of Petra. He was not one of the Bacchiadae, but instead was descended from the Lapithae and Caenidae. Because Eëtion was unable to have children, either with this wife or any other, he went to Delphi to consult the oracle. Barely had he entered the temple when the Priestess greeted him with these words:

'No one honours you now, Eëtion, though you are worthy of honour; Labda will soon conceive, and her offspring will be a rock, which one day will fall on the kingly race, and dispense justice in the city of Corinth.'

"Somehow news of the Eëtion's oracle reached the ears of the Bacchiadae. Up to this point they had been unable to understand the meaning of an earlier oracle concerning Corinth, which prophesied the same event as Eëtion's oracle. It ran as follows:

'An eagle gives birth among the rocks to a lion—a savage meat-eater—he shall shake the legs out from beneath many. Think hard about this, men of Corinth, who dwell near fair Pirene and in the city of Corinth with its rocky heights.'

[92c] "The Bacchiadae had known this oracle for some time, but they had no idea what it meant until they heard the response given to Eëtion. Then, however, they immediately guessed its meaning, since the two fit so well together.

"Although the meaning of the first prophecy was now clear, they bided their time, but nonetheless decided to put the child that Eëtion was expecting to death. As soon as the baby was born, they sent ten of their number to the village where Eëtion lived, with orders to do away with the baby. So the men came to Petra, and went into Eëtion's house, and asked if they might see the child. Labda, who knew nothing of their plan, assumed that their request arose from their friendly feelings towards her husband. She brought the child and gave it to one of them. On their way to the house they had agreed that whoever first got hold of the child should dash it against the ground. Fate, however, intervened. When Labda put the baby into the man's arms, the baby smiled at him, and when he saw the smile, he was touched with pity, and could not bring himself to kill it. He therefore passed the baby to the second man, who gave it to the third. And so the baby was passed, hand to hand, through all ten without anyone being willing to kill it. The mother took the baby back, and the men left the house. As soon as they left, they began to argue, blaming one another and especially criticizing the man who had been the first to hold the child in his arms, because he had not fulfilled his part of the agreement. At last, after a long argument, they decided to re-enter the house and cooperate in the murder.

[92d] "It was fated, however, that evil should come upon Corinth from a child of Eëtion, and so Labda happened to be standing near the door and heard the entire argument. Fearful that they might change their mind and return to kill her baby, she took it and hid it where they seemed least likely to look, in a 'cypsel' or corn-bin. She knew that if they came back to look for the child, they would search her entire house. And they did, but were unable to find the child after looking everywhere. They finally decided to leave, and to declare to those who had sent them that they had carried out their orders. And so that was their story when they returned home.

[92e] "Eëtion's son was given the name Cypselus, after the corn-bin, recalling the danger from which he had escaped. When he grew to manhood, he went to Delphi and consulted the oracle and received a puzzling response. It was the following:

'Lo! Coming into my dwelling is Cypselus, son of Eëtion, king of glorious Corinth. He is a man much favoured by fate, and his children too, but not his children's children.'

"Such was the oracle, and Cypselus seized power and became master of Corinth. Once he acquired power, however, he showed himself a harsh ruler—many Corinthians he drove into exile, many others he deprived of their property, and a still greater number he deprived of their lives.

[92f] "After he had ruled for thirty years, and prospered right to the end of his life, he left Periander, his son, as ruler. At the beginning of his reign, Periander was a milder ruler than his father, but after he exchanged messengers with Thrasybulus, the tyrant of Miletus, his rule became even more blood-stained than his father's. On this occasion he sent a herald to Thrasybulus to ask what form of administration was safest to set up in order to govern best. Thrasybulus led the messenger outside the city-gates, and took him into a field of corn. As he began to walk through it, he continually asked the herald about his journey from Corinth. As he went along, whenever he saw an ear of corn growing above the rest, he broke it off and threw it away. In this way he went through the whole field and destroyed all the best and strongest parts of the crop. Then, without an explanation, he sent the messenger back. On the return of the messenger to Corinth, Periander was eager to know what Thrasybulus had said. The messenger, however, reported that he had given no advice, and he wondered aloud why Periander had sent him to such a strange man, who seemed to have lost his senses, since he did nothing but destroy his own property. Then he told what Thrasybulus had done.

[92g] "Periander knew what the action meant—that Thrasybulus' advice was to destroy his city's most eminent citizens. And from this time forth he treated his subjects with the utmost ruthlessness. In cases where his father Cypselus had been merciful, and had neither put men to death nor banished them, Periander completed what his father had left unfinished.

"One day he stripped all the women of Corinth stark naked, for the sake of his own wife Melissa (whom he had earlier murdered). He had sent messengers to Thesprotia, on the banks of the Acheron river, in order to consult the oracle of the dead concerning a treasure that a stranger had entrusted to him. Melissa appeared, but refused to tell where the treasure was. She was cold and naked, she said, because the garments that had been buried with her were useless, since they had not been burnt. The proof that she spoke the truth (she said) was a secret message to Periander—'the oven was cold when he baked his loaves in it'.

"When this message was brought him, Periander understood it and he immediately made a proclamation that all the women of Corinth should go to the temple of Hera. (He had, you see, been convinced by her message, because he had slept with her after she was dead.) So, the women put on their finest clothes and went forth assuming that they were going to a festival. Periander stationed his guards there and stripped them all—regardless of whether they were free or slave. Then, taking their clothes to a pit, he called on the name of Melissa, and burnt the whole heap. Then he sent a second messenger to the oracle. Melissa's ghost told him where he would find the stranger's treasure.

"That, my Lacedaemonian friends, is what tyranny is, and such are the deeds that come from it. We Corinthians were dumb-founded to hear that you sent for Hippias. Now it surprises us still more to hear you speak as you do. We beg you, by the common gods of Greece, do not plant tyrants in her cities. If, however, you are determined to do so—if you persist, against all justice, in seeking to restore Hippias—know, at least, that the Corinthians will not approve your conduct."

Adapted from A. D. Godley, *Herodotus, with an English translation* (Cambridge. Harvard University Press, 1920).

Reading 2b. Herodotus: The Pisistratids

While many Greek city-states experienced tyranny in the seventh and early sixth centuries, Athens was not controlled by a tyrant until the middle of the sixth century. Attempts had been made by leaders such as Solon (594-593 B.C.) to ease some of the economic and political tensions of the city, which partially satisfied for a time the people's desire to reform. Eventually Athenians turned to a tyrant in order to solve their enormous social and economic problems. As with Cypselus, it was the military successes of Pisistratus (sometimes spelled 'Peisistratos') and his championing of the poorer classes which allowed him to assume the leadership of Athens briefly in 561. But it was not until 546 B.C. that he was able to maintain permanent control of the government of Athens. He ruled until his death in 527 B.C. and was succeeded by his sons Hippias and Hipparchus. Two different readings, one from Herodotus and a second from the Greek philosopher Aristotle, offer insight into the tyranny of Pisistratus.

Herodotus, *Histories* 1.59-64

[59] At that time the Athenians were held in subjection and divided into factions by Pisistratus, who was tyrant of the Athenians. He was the son of Hippocrates, who was still a private citizen when a great marvel happened to him when he was at Olympia to see the games: when he had offered the sacrifice, the vessels, standing there full of meat and water, began to boil over although there was no fire underneath them. Chilon the Lacedaemonian, who happened to be there and who saw this marvel, advised Hippocrates not to marry a woman who could bear children, and if he had a wife already, to send her away, and if he had a son, to disown him. Hippocrates refused to follow the advice of Chilon; and afterward Pisistratus was born to him.

Later, when there was a feud between the Athenians of the coast under Megacles son of Alcmaeon and the Athenians of the plain under Lycurgus son of Aristolaides, Pisistratus created a third faction, since he was thinking about tyranny. He collected partisans and pretended to champion those of the hills, and the following was his plan. Wounding himself and his mules, he drove his wagon into the marketplace, with a story that he had escaped from his enemies, who would have killed him (so he said) as he was driving into the country. So he implored the people to give him a guard: and indeed he had won a reputation in his command of the army against the Megarians, when he had taken Nisaea and performed other great exploits. [5] The Athenian people, having been deceived by this in this way, granted him a bodyguard. Pisistratus made them clubmen instead of spearmen: for the retinue that followed him carried wooden clubs. These rose with Pisistratus and seized the Acropolis.

Pisistratus ruled the Athenians, disturbing in no way the order of offices nor changing the laws, but governing the city according to its established constitution and arranging all things fairly and well.

[60] After a short time, however, the partisans of Megacles and of Lycurgus cooperated with each other and drove him out. In this way Pisistratus first took Athens and lost it, since he held a tyranny that was not yet firmly rooted.

Before long, however, his enemies who had co-operated to drive him out began to feud once more. Then Megacles, harassed by factional strife, sent a message to Pisistratus offering him his daughter to marry and the tyranny, too. When this offer was accepted by Pisistratus, who agreed on these terms with Megacles, they devised a plan to bring Pisistratus back which, to my mind, was so exceptionally foolish that it is strange (since from old times Greeks have always been distinguished from foreigners by their greater cleverness and their freedom from silly foolishness) that these men should devise such a plan to deceive Athenians, said to be the cleverest of the Greeks.

There was in the Paeanian deme a woman called Phya, three fingers short of six feet, four inches in height, and otherwise, too, well-formed. This woman they equipped in full armor and put in a chariot, giving her all the paraphernalia to make the most impressive spectacle, and so drove into the city; heralds ran before them, and when they came into town proclaimed as they were instructed:

"Athenians, give a hearty welcome to Pisistratus, whom Athena herself honors above all men and is bringing back to her own acropolis."

So the heralds went about proclaiming this; and immediately the report spread in the demes that Athena was bringing Pisistratus back, and the townsfolk, believing that the woman was the goddess herself, worshipped this human creature and welcomed Pisistratus."

[61] Having re-acquired his tyranny in the manner which I have described, Pisistratus married Megacles' daughter according to their agreement. But since he already had young sons, and since the Alcmaeonid family were said to be under a curse, he had no wish that his newly-wedded wife bear him children, and so lay with her, but not in the ordinary manner. At first the woman hid the fact: but soon she told her mother (whether interrogated or not, I do not know) and the mother told her husband. Megacles was very angry to be dishonored by Pisistratus in this way, and in his anger he patched up his quarrel with the other faction. Pisistratus, learning what was going on, fled from the country, and came to Eretria where he deliberated with his sons. It was the opinion of Hippias that prevailed, that they should recover the tyranny, and so they began collecting contributions from all the cities that owed them anything. Many of these cities gave great amounts, the Thebans more than any other. In the course of time, everything was ready for their return: for they brought Argive mercenaries from the Peloponnese. In addition they were joined by a man of Naxos called Lygdamis, who was most keen in their cause and brought them money and men.

[62] So after ten years they set out from Eretria and returned home. The first place in Attica which they took and held was Marathon: and while encamped there they were joined by their partisans from the city, and by others who flocked to them from the country—demesmen who loved the rule of one more than freedom. These, then, assembled; but the Athenians in the city, who while Pisistratus was collecting money and afterwards when he had taken Marathon took no notice of it, did now, and when they learned that he was marching from Marathon against Athens, they set out to attack him. They came out with all their force to oppose the returning exiles. Pisistratus' men encountered the enemy when they had reached the temple of Pallenian Athena in their march from Marathon towards the city, and encamped opposite them. There (by the providence of heaven) Pisistratus met Amphilytus the Acarnanian, a diviner, who came to him and prophesied as follows in hexameter verses:

"The cast is made, the net spread; the tunny-fish shall flash in the moonlit night."

[63] This is what Amphilytus said, being inspired; Pisistratus understood him and, saying that he accepted the prophecy, led his army against the enemy. The Athenians of the city had by this time had breakfast, and after breakfast some were dicing and some were sleeping; they were attacked by Pisistratus' men and put to flight. So they fled, and Pisistratus devised a very subtle plan to keep them scattered and prevent them assembling again: he had his sons mount their horses and ride forward; they overtook the fugitives and spoke to them as they were instructed by Pisistratus, telling them to take heart and each to depart to his home.

[64] The Athenians did, and by this means Pisistratus gained Athens for the third time, buttressing his tyranny with many mercenaries and with revenue collected both from Athens and from the district of the river Strymon. He also took hostage the sons of the Athenians who remained and did not leave the city at once, and placed these in Naxos. (He had conquered Naxos too and put Lygdamis in charge.) And besides this, he purified the island of Delos in response to certain oracles, and this is how he did it: he removed all the dead that were buried in ground within sight of the temple and conveyed them to another part of Delos. So Pisistratus was tyrant of Athens: and as for the Athenians, some had fallen in the battle, and some, with the Alcmeonids, became exiles from their native land.

Adapted from A. D. Godley, *Herodotus, with an English translation* (Cambridge. Harvard University Press, 1920).

Reading 2c. Aristotle: The Pisistratids

The second excerpt comes from a work entitled ***The Constitution of the Athenians*** written by Aristotle, a Greek philosopher. Aristotle (384-322 B.C.) studied under Plato in the Academy at Athens, and in his turn was one of the tutors of Alexander the Great of Macedonia. He was a prolific writer on diverse subjects such as philosophy (including ethics and metaphysics), rhetoric, politics, and natural science. His method of study entailed extensive recording of experiences and observations, and his wide range of inquiry reveals his very productive and curious intellect. In his political writings, Aristotle reveals the basic tension running through the Classical view of the tyrant as a bad figure, an autocrat who deprives citizens of their freedom, yet also reflecting positive views of Pisistratus passed down from the Archaic Age, stressing the beneficial aspects of his rule and calling his tyranny a "golden age".

Aristotle, *Constitution of the Athenians*

14. Peisistratus, being thought to be an extreme advocate of the people, and having won great fame in the war against Megara, inflicted a wound on himself with his own hand and then gave out that it had been done by the members of the opposite factions, and so persuaded the people to give him a bodyguard, the resolution being proposed by Aristophon. He was given the retainers called Club-bearers, and with their aid he rose against the people and seized the Acropolis, in the thirty-second year after the enactment of his laws, in the archonship of Comeas. [2] It is said that when Peisistratus asked for the guard, Solon opposed the request and said that he was wiser than some men and braver than others—he was wiser than those who did not know that Peisistratus was aiming at tyranny, and braver than those who knew it but held their tongues. But as he failed to carry them with him by saying this, he brought his armor out in front of his door and said that for his part he had come to his country's aid as far as he could (for he was now a very old man), and that he called on the others also to do the same. [3] Solon's exhortations on this occasion had no effect. Peisistratus, having seized the government, proceeded to carry on the public business in a manner more constitutional than tyrannical. But before his government had taken root the partisans of Megacles and Lycurgus made common cause and expelled him, in the sixth year after his first establishment, in the archonship of Hegesias. [4] In the twelfth year after this Megacles, being harried by party faction, made overtures again to Peisistratus, and on terms of receiving his daughter in marriage brought him back, in an old-fashioned and extremely simple manner. Having first spread a rumor that Athena was bringing Peisistratus back, he found a tall and beautiful woman, according to Herodotus a member of the Paeanian deme, but according to some accounts a Thracian flower-girl from Collytus named Phye, dressed her up to look like the goddess, and brought her to the city with him, and Peisistratus drove in a chariot with the woman standing at his side, while the people in the city marvelled and received them with acts of reverence.

15. This is how his first return took place. In the seventh year later, he was expelled a second time; he did not maintain his hold for long, but came to be afraid of both factions owing to his unwillingness to live with the daughter of Megacles as his wife, and secretly withdrew. [2] First he settled at a place near the Gulf of Thermae called Rhaecelus, but from there he

went on to the neighborhood of Pangaeus, from where he got money and hired soldiers, and in the eleventh year went again to Eretria, and now for the first time set about an attempt to recover his power by force, being supported in this by a number of people, especially the Thebans and Lygdamis of Naxos, and also the knights who controlled the government of Eretria. [3] Winning the battle of Pallenis, he seized the government and disarmed the people; and now he held the tyranny firmly, and he took Naxos and appointed Lygdamis ruler. [4] The way in which he disarmed the people was this: he held an armed muster at the Temple of Theseus, and began to hold an Assembly, but he lowered his voice a little, and when they said they could not hear him, he told them to come up to the forecourt of the Acropolis, in order that his voice might carry better; and while he used up time in making a speech, the men designated for this purpose gathered up the arms, locked them up in the neighboring buildings of the Temple of Theseus, and came and informed Peisistratus. [5] He, when he had finished the rest of his speech, told his audience not to be surprised at what had happened about their arms, and not to be dismayed, but to go away and occupy themselves with their private affairs, while he would attend to all public business.

16. This was the way, therefore, in which the tyranny of Peisistratus was originally set up and this is a list of the changes that it underwent. [2] Peisistratus's administration of the state was, as has been said, moderate, and more constitutional than tyrannic; he was kindly and mild in everything, and in particular he was merciful to offenders, and moreover he advanced loans of money to the poor for their industries, so that they might support themselves by farming. [3] In doing this he had two objects, to prevent their stopping in the city and make them stay scattered about the country, and to cause them to have a moderate competence and be engaged in their private affairs, so as not to desire nor to have time to attend to public business. [4] And also the land's being thoroughly cultivated resulted in increasing his revenues; for he levied a tithe from the produce. [5] And for this reason he organized the Local Justices, and often went to the country on circuit in person, inspecting and settling disputes, in order that men might not neglect their agriculture by coming into the city. [6] For it was when Peisistratus was making an expedition of this kind that the affair of the man on Hymettus cultivating the farm afterwards called Tax-free Farm is said to have occurred. He saw a man at farm-work, digging mere rocks, and because of his surprise ordered his servant to ask what crop the farm grew; and the man said, "All the aches and pains that there are, and of these aches and pains Peisistratus has to get the tithe." The man did not know who it was when he answered, but Peisistratus was pleased by his free speech and by his industry, and made him free from all taxes. [7] And in all other matters, too, he gave the multitude no trouble during his rule, but always worked for peace and safeguarded tranquillity, so that men were often to be heard saying that the tyranny of Peisistratus was the Golden Age of Cronos; for it came about later when his sons had succeeded him that the government became much harsher. [8] And the greatest of all the things said of him was that he was popular and kindly in temper. For he was willing to administer everything according to the laws in all matters, never giving himself any advantage; and once in particular when he was summoned to the Areopagus to be tried on a charge of murder, he appeared in person to make his defence, and the issuer of the summons was frightened and left. [9] Owing to this he remained in his office for a long period, and every time that he was thrown out of it he easily got it back again. For both the notables and the men of the people were most of them willing for him to govern, since he won over

the former by his hospitality and the latter by his assistance in their private affairs, and was good-natured to both. [10] And also the laws of Athens concerning tyrants were mild at those periods, among the rest particularly the one that referred to the establishment of tyranny. For they had the following law: 'These are the ordinances and ancestral principles of Athens: if any persons rise in insurrection in order to govern tyrannically, or if any person assists in establishing the tyranny, he himself and his family shall be disfranchised.'

17. Peisistratus, therefore, grew old in office, and died of disease in the archonship of Philoneos, having lived thirty-three years since he first established himself as tyrant, but the time that he remained in office was nineteen years, as he was in exile for the remainder. [2] Therefore the story that Peisistratus was a lover of Solon and that he commanded in the war against Megara for the recovery of Salamis is clearly nonsense, for it is made impossible by their ages, if one reckons up the life of each and the archonship in which he died. [3] When Peisistratus was dead, his sons held the government, carrying on affairs in the same way. He had two sons by his wedded wife, Hippias and Hipparchus, and two by his Argive consort, Iophon and Hegesistratus surnamed Thettalus. [4] For Peisistratus married a consort from Argos, Timonassa, the daughter of a man of Argos named Gorgilus, who had previously been the wife of Archinus, a man of Ambracia of the Cypselid family. This was the cause of Peisistratus's friendship with Argos, and a thousand Argives brought by Hegesistratus fought for him in the battle of Pallenis. Some people date his marriage with the Argive lady during his first banishment, others in a period of office.

18. Affairs were now under the authority of Hipparchus and Hippias, owing to their station and their ages, but the government was controlled by Hippias, who was the elder and was statesmanlike and wise by nature; whereas Hipparchus was fond of amusement and love-making, and had literary tastes: it was he who brought to Athens poets such as Anacreon and Simonides, and the others. [2] Thettalus was much younger, and bold and insolent in his mode of life, which proved to be the source of all their misfortunes. For he fell in love with Harmodius, and when his advances were continually unsuccessful he could not restrain his anger, but displayed it bitterly in various ways, and finally when Harmodius's sister was going to be a Basket-carrier in the procession at the Panathenaic Festival he prevented her by uttering some insult against Harmodius as being effeminate; and the consequent wrath of Harmodius let him and the Aristogeiton to enter on their plot with a number of accomplices. [3] At the Panathenaic Festival on the Acropolis they were already keeping a watch on Hippias (who happened to be receiving the procession, while Hipparchus was directing its start), when they saw one of their partners in the plot conversing in a friendly way with Hippias. They thought that he was giving information, and wishing to do something before their arrest they went down and took the initiative without waiting for their confederates, killing Hipparchus as he was arranging the procession by the Leocoreum. [4] This played havoc with the whole plot. Of the two of them Harmodius was at once dispatched by the spearmen, and Aristogeiton died later, having been taken into custody and tortured for a long time. Under the strain of the tortures he gave the names of a number of men that belonged by birth to families of distinction, and were friends of the tyrants, as fellow conspirators. For they were not able immediately to find any trace of the plot, but the current story that Hippias separated the people in the procession from their arms and searched for those that retained their daggers is not true, for in those days they did not walk

in the procession armed, but this custom was instituted later by the democracy. [5] According to the account of people of democratic sympathies, Aristogeiton accused the tyrants' friends in order to make his captors commit an impiety and weaken themselves at the same time by making away with men who were innocent and their own friends. Others say, however, that his accusations were not fictitious but that he disclosed his actual accomplices. [6] Finally, in order to hasten his own death he offered to give information against many more, and induced Hippias to give him his right hand as a pledge of good faith, and when he grasped it he taunted him that he was giving his hand to his brother's murderer. This so enraged Hippias that in his anger he could not control himself but drew his dagger and made away with him.

19. After this it began to come about that the tyranny was much harsher; for Hippias's numerous executions and sentences of exile in revenge for his brother led to his being suspicious of everybody and embittered. [2] About four years after Hipparchus's death the state of affairs in the city was so bad that he set about fortifying Munychia, with the intention of moving his establishment there. While engaged in this he was driven out by the king of Sparta, Cleomenes, as oracles were constantly being given to the Spartans to put down the tyranny, for the following reason. [3] The exiles headed by the Alcmeonidae were not able to effect their return by their own unaided efforts, but were always meeting reverses; for besides the other plans that were complete failures, they built the fort of Leipsydrion in the country, on the slopes of Parnes, where some of their friends in the city came out and joined them, but they were besieged and dislodged by the tyrants, owing to which afterwards they used to refer to this disaster in singing their catches:

"Faithless Dry Fountain! Lackaday,
What good men's lives you threw away!
True patriots and fighters game,
They showed the stock from which they came!"

[4] So as they were failing in everything else, they contracted to build the temple at Delphi, and so acquired a supply of money for the assistance of the Spartans. And the Pythian priestess constantly uttered a command to the Spartans, when they consulted the oracle, to liberate Athens, until she brought the Spartiates to the point, although the Peisistratidae were strangers to them; and an equally great amount of incitement was contributed to the Spartans by the friendship that subsisted between the Argives and the Peisistratidae. [5] As a first step, therefore, they dispatched Anchimolus with a force by sea; but he was defeated and lost his life, because the Thessalian Cineas came to the defence with a thousand cavalry. Enraged at this occurrence, they dispatched their king Cleomenes by land with a larger army; he won a victory over the Thessalian cavalry who tried to prevent his reaching Attica, and so shut up Hippias in the fortress called the Pelargicum and began to lay siege to it with the aid of the Athenians. [6] While he was sitting down against it, it occurred that the sons of Peisistratidae were caught when trying secretly to get away; and these being taken they came to terms on the condition of the boys' safety, and conveyed away their belongings in five days, surrendering the Acropolis to the Athenians; this was in the archonship of Harpactides, and Peisistratus's sons had retained the tyranny for about seventeen years after their father's death making when added to the period of their father's power a total of forty-nine years.

Adapted from H. Rackham (1868-1944), *The Athenian Constitution* (London: William Heinemann Ltd., 1952).

Reading 2d. Herodotus: The Persian Debate

Democracy, meaning the rule (kratos) of the people (demos), began to develop in Athens at the end of the sixth century B.C, following the expulsion of Pisistratids and a popular rising against a new want-to-be tyrant, Isagoras. Following the expulsion of Isagoras and his Spartan supporters from the city, the people gained a stronger voice in government, as able to decide and act for themselves, as a collective citizenry, rather than only through elite leaders. The Athenian system of democracy, termed a direct democracy, is different from our modern representative or parliamentary democracies, in that all adult male citizens sat in the assembly which passed its laws, participating in direct self-government rather than electing representatives to rule on their behalf. Through Athenian influence and example, democracy spread to other Greek citizen-states in the fifth century B.C. Yet in many Greek cities, hoplite citizen-farmers guarded their exclusive right to participate in government, rejecting the inclusion of the poor and landless in political power, and aristocratic families, as a still smaller group within the citizen body, defended their claim to take the lead in government. These cities remained oligarchies. Athens' championing of democracy was opposed by Sparta's championing of oligarchy. Thus there was ideological division in Greece, between oligarchic and democratic cities, and, within individual cities, between oligarchs and democrats.

In his history, Herodotus reports a debate that summarizes and compares the three main types of government: democracy, oligarchy, and monarchy. In the debate, the favorable and unfavorable features for each system are examined. This debate supposedly took place not in Greece, but in the Persian Empire at a time of instability following the death of the king Cambyses, when the Persian nobles came together to debate and decide on a new government. In the context of this debate, three Persian noblemen each proposed a system of government, arguing its good points and pointing out the weaknesses of other systems. In the end Darius, the supporter of monarchy, took charge and became the new king of the Persians (522-486). It must be stressed that the tone and the substance of the speeches given is Greek. For all that Herodotus, anticipating criticism, protests that the debate did take place as he describes, the speeches summarize Greek attitudes to and understanding of these rival systems of government. It is impossible to believe that the Persian nobility ever contemplated instituting even oligarchic, let alone democratic, citizen government in Persia.

Some questions:

- Summarize the three types of government in the reading by Herodotus.
- What are the good and bad points for each system as presented by the speakers?
- Compare ancient and modern democracy.

Herotodus, *Histories*, 3.80-83

[80] Five days passed after the assassination of the King and the confusion settled. The conspirators then met to discuss the entire political situation. Many Greeks deny that the following speeches were really made, but they were in reality made.

Otanes recommended that the government should be entrusted to all Persians. "In my opinion," he said, "we should no longer be ruled by a monarch—the rule of one is neither good nor pleasant. Your have surely not forgotten how outrageous the tyranny of Cambyses became, and you have experienced for yourselves the insolence of the Magian. How can monarchy possibly be a suitable institution? It allows someone to do whatever he likes without being answerable. Give this much power to even the most worthy man in the world, and it will deprive him of his good character. The good things he has will immediately make him arrogant, and jealousy is such a natural instinct that it will inevitably arise. Together, pride and envy produce every wicked vice—both of them leading on to deeds of savage violence. It is true that kings, because they possess everything they desire, ought to be free of envy. The opposite is true, however, in their actions towards their subjects. They become jealous of their most virtuous subjects and wish them dead. And they enjoy the company of the most wicked criminals, always being ready to listen to the slanders of these liars. More than anyone else, a king is inconsistent. Pay him respect in moderation, and he is angry because you do not revere him more deeply; show him profound reverence, and he is again offended and claims you fawn on him. But the worst of all is that he sets aside the laws of the land, puts men to death without trial, and subjects women to violence. By contrast, the rule of the many has, in the first place, the most beautiful of names—isonomy, 'equal laws'. It is also free from all those outrages that a king is accustomed to commit. In a democracy, position is given by lot, a magistrate is answerable for what he does, and the rules depend on the common people. I vote, therefore, that we do away with monarchy, and raise the people to power. For the people are all in all."

[81] This was the opinion of Otanes. Megabyzus spoke next, and he advised setting up an oligarchy. "I agree with everything that Otanes has said to persuade you to abolish the monarchy. But his recommendation that we should give power to the people is not the best advice. An unwieldy mob is more lacking in understanding and more impetuous than any other group. It would be foolish for men to try to escape a tyrant because of his lack of restraint, and then surrender themselves to the uneducated whims of an unruly mob. At least a tyrant knows what is he doing in all his actions. But a mob is completely devoid of knowledge. For how can there be any knowledge in a rabble? It is untaught and has no natural sense of what is right and proper. It rushes without thinking into political decisions with all the fury of a stream swollen in the winter, and confuses everything. Let the enemies of the Persians be ruled by democracies. We Persians, however, should choose from amongst ourselves our worthiest citizens and put the government into their hands. This will accomplish two things. First, we ourselves shall be among the rulers; second, the best political decisions will normally be taken with power entrusted to the best men."

[82] This was the advice that Megabyzus gave. Darius came forward next and spoke as follows. "Everything that Megabyzus said against democracy was correct, I think. But his remarks on oligarchy are not prudent. Take

these three forms of government—democracy, oligarchy, and monarchy—and let each be at its best. I maintain that monarchy is far better than the other two. Who can possibly govern better than the very best man in the whole state? The plans of such a man are like himself, and so he governs the mass of the people to their satisfaction. At the same time, his actions against wrong-doers are kept more secret than in other states. In oligarchies, by contrast, men compete with each other in the service of the state, and fierce animosities are bound to arise between men, since each wants to be leader and to introduce his own measures. This leads to violent quarrels, which leads to open conflict, often ending in bloodshed. This inevitably leads to monarchy. Again we see how much better this system of government is than any other. In a democracy, however, it is inevitable that there will be corruption: such corruption, however, does not lead to enmities, but to close friendships among those engaged in it, since they must conspire together in order to continue their crimes. This will continue until someone comes forward to act as champion of the common people and puts an end to the corruption. Immediately everyone admires him for doing such a great service to the public, and this admiration soon results in him being appointed monarch. So, here too, it is clear that monarchy is the best form of government. Finally, to sum up my whole argument in a few words: from where, I ask you, did we get the freedom that we enjoy? Did democracy give it us, or oligarchy, or a monarch? Since a single man restored to us our freedom, my opinion is that we keep the rule of one. Even apart from this, we should not change the laws of our forefathers when they work well: to do that is not good."

[83] These were the three opinions brought forward at this meeting; the four other Persians voted in favour of the last.

Adapted from A. D. Godley, *Herodotus, with an English translation* (Cambridge. Harvard University Press, 1920).

Reading 2e. The Old Oligarch

The Old Oligarch is a modern term applied to the author of a political pamphlet written on the nature of the constitution of fifth century Athens. While the author of this pamphlet is unknown, he was likely a member of the Athenian elite who favored an oligarchical system of government. The work presents a hostile view of the democratic government of Athens, and criticizes the extensive power of the people. It was composed in the manner of a political speech most likely at the end of the fifth century (perhaps in the 420s) during the Peloponnesian War. The speech condemns the Athenian Empire and disapproves of democracy as the rule of the 'worst sort', the common masses, who rule in their class interest, at the expense of the 'better sort', and whose rule is productive of loose morality and disorderly license. The Old Oligarch instead proposes that government should remain in the hands of wealthy, well-born, well educated men (aristoi), yet admits that this would be difficult to bring about since democracy is highly effective at providing for the dominance of the masses, in the exercise of political power to their own ends.

While you read this consider these questions:

- What, in the Old Oligarch's view, is so bad about democratic government?
- Why is it bad, if at the same time it is highly effective?

The Old Oligarch, On the Constitution of the Athenians

[1.1] Regarding the constitution of the Athenians, I do not approve of their choice of this type of constitution. For in making this choice they have decided that the poor should fare better than good citizens. This then is why I do not approve. However, since this is their decision, I shall demonstrate how well they preserve their constitution, and how well they are acting where the rest of Greece thinks that they are going wrong.

[2] First of all, then, I shall say that at Athens it is just that the poor and common men have the advantage over the well-born and the wealthy. For it is the commons that mans the fleet and has won power for the city. It is the steersmen and the shipmates and the shipmasters and the lookout-men, as well as the ship-builders who have brought the state her power, rather than hoplites and the well-born and the good citizens. Since this is so, it is only fair that the commons should have a share in offices filled by lot or by election, and that any citizen who wishes should be allowed to speak. [3] On the other hand, there are offices which bring security to the whole commons if they are in the hands of good citizens, but danger if not. The people do not insist on having a share through the lot in the supreme command or in the command of the cavalry, for the commons realizes that it reaps greater benefit in not having these offices in its own hands, but in allowing men of standing to hold them. The commons, however, does seek to hold all those offices that bring pay and private profit.

[4] Secondly, some people are surprised that everywhere they give the advantage to the lowly, the poor, and democrats rather than to good citizens. In this, however, it can be seen that they are preserving the democracy. For if the poor and the common folk and the worse

elements do well, the growth of these classes will strengthen the democracy; whereas if the rich and the good citizens are treated well, the democrats are strengthening their own opponents.

[5] In every land the best element is opposed to democracy. The best elements are by far less likely to lack self-control and indulge in injustice, and are very discriminating as to what is worthy. Among the commons, by contrast, there is complete ignorance, disorderliness and mischief; for poverty tends to lead them to what is disgraceful, as does lack of education and the ignorance which befalls some men because of their lack of means.

[6] It may be said that the Athenians ought not to allow just anyone to make speeches or sit on the Council, but only those of the highest capability and quality. But in allowing even the poor to speak, they are also very well advised. For if good citizens make speeches and join in deliberations, good will result to those like themselves and ill to the democrats. As it is, anyone who wants can get up and make a speech and propose what is to the advantage of himself and those like him, even a good-for-nothing fellow maybe. [7] Someone might ask how such a person would know what is advantageous to himself or to the commons. The Athenians realize that this man's ignorance, depravity and goodwill are more beneficial to them than the good citizen's who is ill-disposed, despite his virtue and wisdom.

[8] This is not the way to create the best city, but this is the best way to preserve the democracy. For the commons does not care whether the state is well governed if it means that the commons itself is in subjection; instead, it wants that the commons should have its freedom and be in control; disorder is of little consequence to it. What you consider disorder results in the strength and the liberty of the commons itself. [9] If on the other hand you seek good order, the first thing that you realize is that the laws are made by the most capable men; then good citizens can keep the poor in check and deliberate on matters of state, refusing to allow madmen to sit on the Council or make speeches or attend the general assemblies. An excellent system like that, though, would very soon throw the commons into complete subjection.

[10] The freedom allowed to slaves and foreigners at Athens is extreme. It is forbidden to strike a slave there; nor will a slave make way for you. I shall explain why the city allows this. For if it were legal for a freeman to strike a slave or an alien or a freedman, Athenians would often be struck after being mistaken for a slave; for the commons there does not dress any better than the slaves and the aliens, and their general appearance is not at all better. [11] If anyone is surprised then that they allow slaves, or at least some of them, to live luxuriously and magnificently, here too the Athenians are acting rationally. In a naval state slaves often have to work for hire so that their owners can make profit from their labor, and we must later let them go free.... [12] This then is why we make slaves equal with free men; and we have also placed aliens on a footing of equality with citizens because the state has need of aliens, owing to the number of skilled trades and because of the fleet. For this reason, then, we were right to place even the aliens on a footing of equality.

[13] The commons also condemns the practice of athletics and music in Athens. It considers such activities inferior, largely because that common people are unable to succeed at these pursuits. In the provision of dramatic choruses or athletic contests, however, or in providing equipment for warships, they know that it is

the rich who provide choruses while the commons has men to work the choruses; that it is the rich who subsidize athletic contests and the equipping of warships, while the commons provides the men. At any rate in these activities the commons demands pay for singing, running, dancing and sailing, in order that it becomes wealthier and the rich become less rich. In the law-courts they pay less attention to justice than to their own gain. ...

[II 18] The Athenians also do not allow comedians to mock or criticize the commons; otherwise they would have to endure hearing themselves being criticized. They do, however, allow you to mock any individual you wish to. They well know that generally the man who is mistreated by comedians in this way is not of the commons or of the crowd, but someone rich or well born or influential. They know that few of the poor and democrats are criticized, and they only because they are busy-bodies and try to rise above their station. Consequently they are not angry when such men are mocked either.

[19] It is clear to me, then, that the Athenian commons knows who the good citizens are and who the poor are. Despite this knowledge, however, they favour those who are friendly and useful to them, even if they are poor, and they hate the good citizens. For they do not believe that these mens' virtues exist for the good of the commons, but for its ill. ... [20] I pardon the commons itself for its support of democracy, for it is understandable that everyone should seek his own interest. But the man who is not of the commons yet chooses to live in a democratic rather than in an oligarchical state seeks opportunity for wrongdoing, and realizes that his wickedness is more likely to go unnoticed in a democracy than in an oligarchy.

[III 1] I do not approve of the type of constitution that the Athenians practice, but given that they saw fit to be a democracy, my opinion is that they preserve their democracy well by employing the means I have pointed out.

In addition, I notice that some criticize the Athenians because sometimes the Council or Assembly are unable to deal with a man, even if he waits around for a year. [2] This happens at Athens simply because they are so busy that it is impossible for them to deal with everyone before sending them away. Why is this? First of all because they have more festivals to celebrate than any other Greek state, and during these festivals less state business can be performed. Secondly, they have more private and public law-suits and official audits to decide than all the rest of the world put together. In addition to this the Council has to deliberate on much relating to war, revenue, legislation, current happenings at home and among the allies. It also has to receive the tribute and look after the dock-yards and the temples. Is it therefore any wonder that with so much going on they are unable to deal with everyone? ...

[8] Given that this is the way that matters stand, I maintain that the state of things at Athens cannot be different than it is at present, unless it is possible to make small changes to this and that. It is not possible to make many changes without robbing the democracy of power.

[9] There are many ways in which the constitution could be improved, but to leave the democracy in existence and still find ways to improve their government is not easy, unless, as I said just now, it is by way of small changes.

Adapted from H. G. Dakyns, *The Works of Xenophon* (Macmillan and Co., 1897).

Chapter 3:

Athens and Sparta

READING 3A. THUCYDIDES: THE SPARTAN DEBATE

The two leading Greek citizen-states of the fifth century B.C. were Athens and Sparta. Both were strong military powers: Athens' strength lay in its navy and empire, while Sparta's strength was its strong standing army and Peloponnesian alliance. Sparta's conquest of neighboring Messenia in the seventh century, allowed the Spartans to live on the labour of their Messenian helot serfs. At the same time, to ensure the ongoing subjugation of the helots, the Spartans turned themselves into a collective of hard, disciplined, obedient full-time soldiers. Thus the Spartans became the most effective hoplites and most powerful state in Archaic Greece, forming an alliance of the citizen-states of the Peloponnese (southern Greece) under their leadership. In the fifth century, however, democratic Athens rose as a rival power to Sparta. She took over from Sparta the leadership of the Greek cause against Persia in the aftermath of the second Persian War, as head of the new Delian League, a naval alliance formed to defend against the Persian threat. Increasingly Athenian leadership turned into Athenian domination, and the league became in practice an Athenian empire. Allied contributions to a league navy became tribute that paid for an Athenian navy. Wealth flowed into Athens as the centre of a maritime, commercial empire. Imperial wealth flowed to the Athenian people and paid for the deepening of their democracy. In turn, the people, in their government, favoured the expansion of empire. Democracy at home and empire abroad rose in tandem. By the middle of the fifth century B.C., Sparta feared that Athens' imperialism would destabilize her own league, and the Greek world found itself divided between two rival alliances.

In 432 B.C. a critical debate took place in Sparta which was recorded by Thucydides in his History of the Peloponnesian War. At this time a series of speeches were given by ambassadors from Corinth, Athens, and by the Spartan leaders. These speeches reveal the political tone of the times, the build-up of hostility and aggression, and the great differences between Athens and Sparta politically and culturally. Athenian imperialism is attacked by Corinth and justified by Athens, while Spartan isolationism and procrastination is criticized. The debate resolved none of the differences and problems between Athens and Sparta and their allies, and ultimately war was declared.

Thucydides (c. 460-400 B.C.) was an Athenian general during the Peloponnesian war, which lasted between 431-404 B.C. As a participant he was in a position to provide an eye-witness account of some events during the war, and to interview contemporaries who were present during campaigns or speeches. His precision and his insistence on finding the "truth" behind events have led many to view Thucydides as the first scientific and objective historian. At the same time, his history is a grand tragedy, exploring the limits of man's ability to control his own fate, subject as he is, not to the gods, but to the great, impersonal forces of history (see also the notes accompanying Reading 4A in this coursepack).

While you are reading this, keep in mind the following questions:

- How might the different political and social systems of Sparta and Athens have contributed to the relative positions they find themselves in at this time, with respect to material resources and national character?
- What sort of picture do the Athenians paint of the real motives and essential nature of states?

Thucydides describes his project (*Histories* 1.1)

1. THUCYDIDES, an Athenian, wrote the history of the war in which the Peloponnesians and the Athenians fought against one another. He began to write when they first took up arms, believing that this war would be greater and more memorable than any previous war. For he concluded that both states were then at the full height of their military power, and he saw that the rest of the Greeks either sided with one or the other of them or intended to do so. [2] No crisis ever affected Greece more deeply than it did; its effect was shared by many of the Barbarians, and might be said even to affect the world at large. [3] The character of the events which preceded, whether immediately or in more remote antiquity, owing to the lapse of time cannot be made out with certainty. But, judging from the evidence which I am able to trust after most careful enquiry, I should imagine that former ages were not great either in their wars or in anything else.

The Spartan debate (1. 66-88)

66. The causes of hostility which at this time existed between the Athenians and Peloponnesians were as follows. The Corinthians complained that the Athenians were blockading their colony of Potidaea, which was occupied by a Corinthian and Peloponnesian garrison; the Athenians responded that the Peloponnesians had stirred up a revolt in a state which

was an ally and tributary of theirs, and that they had now openly joined the Potidaeans, and were fighting on their side. The Peloponnesian war, however, had not yet broken out; the peace still continued; for thus far the Corinthians had acted alone.

67. But now, seeing Potidaea besieged, the Corinthians began to act more earnestly. Corinthian troops were shut up within the walls, and they were afraid of losing the town; so without delay they invited the allies to meet at Sparta. There they railed against the Athenians, whom they accused of having broken the treaty and of having wronged the Peloponnesians.... The Megarians alleged, among other grounds of complaint, that they were excluded from all harbors within the Athenian empire and from the Athenian market, contrary to the treaty. The Corinthians waited until the other allies had stirred up the Lacedaemonians; at length they came forward, and, last of all, spoke as follows:

68. "The spirit of trust, Lacedaemonians, which animates your own political and social life makes you distrust others who, like ourselves, have something unpleasant to say. This habit of mind, although it gives you a reputation for fairness, too often leaves you in ignorance of what is going on outside your own country. Time after time we have warned you of the mischief which the Athenians would do to us, but instead of taking our words to heart, you chose to suspect that we spoke only from selfish motives. And this is the reason why you have brought the allies to Sparta, too late, not before but after the injury has been inflicted, and when they are smarting under the sense of it. Who then can speak with more authority than ourselves, who have the most serious accusations to make, since we are outraged by the Athenians, and neglected by you? If the crimes which they are committing against Greece were being done in a corner, then you might be ignorant, and we should have to inform you of them; but now, what need is there of many words? Some of us, as you see, have already been enslaved; they are at this moment plotting against others, notably against allies of ours; and long ago they had made all their preparations in expectation of war. Else why did they seduce the island of Corcyra from its allegiance, which they are still occupying in defiance of our complaints? And why are they blockading Potidaea, the latter a most advantageous base for the controlling the Thracian peninsula? And is not Corcyra a great naval power which might have assisted the Peloponnesians?

69. "The blame for all this rests on you; for you originally allowed them to fortify their city after the Persian War, and then to build their Long Walls. By doing this you are allowing them not only to strip their unfortunate subjects of liberty, but now to take it away from your own allies, too. For the true destroyer of a people's liberty is he who can put an end to their slavery, but does not bother; and all the more, if he be reputed the champion of liberty in Greece. And so we finally meet in assembly! But with what difficulty! and even now we have no clear proposal about a course of action. By this time we ought to have been considering, not whether we have been wronged, but how we are to exact revenge. The aggressor is not now threatening, but advancing; he has made up his mind, while we have decided nothing. And we know too well how the Athenians encroach upon their neighbors by slow degrees and with stealthy steps. They are quite careful when they merely think that you are too stupid to notice; but, once they realize that you overlook their aggressions on purpose, they will strike you mercilessly. Of all the Greeks, Lacedaemonians, you are

the only people who never do anything; you are content to defend yourselves against enemies not by acts, but by intentions, and seek to oppose them, not at the start when they are weak but when their strength has doubled. How did you come to be considered safe? That reputation of yours was never justified by facts. We all know that the Persians made their way from the ends of the earth almost to the Peloponnesus before you encountered him in a worthy manner. And now you are blind to the doings of the Athenians, who are not far away, like the Persians were, but close at hand. Instead of attacking your enemy, you wait to be attacked! And so you increase the risks in a war which has been delayed until his power is doubled. And you know that the Persians failed chiefly through their own errors, and that we have more often been delivered from these very Athenians by blunders of their own than by any help from you. Some allies have already been ruined because of the hopes which you inspired in them; they trusted you so completely that they took no precautions themselves. These things we say in no accusing or hostile spirit—let that be understood—but by way of constructive advice. For men advise with erring friends; they bring accusations against enemies who have done them a wrong.

70. "And surely if any one ever had a right to find fault with our neighbors, we do. There are important interests at stake which, as far as we can see, you are ignoring. And you have never considered what kind of men these Athenians are. You will have to fight them soon, and they are completely unlike yourselves. They are revolutionary, equally quick in the conception and in the execution of every new plan; you by contrast are conservative—careful only to keep what you have, originating nothing, and not acting even when action is most necessary. They are bold beyond their strength; they run risks which prudence would condemn; and in the middle of misfortune they are full of hope. It is your nature, on the other hand to act feebly although you are stong; when your plans are most prudent, to distrust them most; and when calamities come upon you, to think that you will never be delivered from them. They are impetuous, and you are dilatory; they are always abroad, and you are always at home. For they hope to gain something by leaving their homes; but you are afraid that any new enterprise may imperil what you have already. When they are victorious, they pursue their victory to the utmost; when defeated, they fall back the least. Their bodies they devote to their country as if they belonged to other men; their true self is in their mind, which is most truly their own when employed in her service. When they do not carry out an intention which they have formed, they seem to have sustained a personal bereavement; when an enterprise succeeds, they have gained a mere instalment of what is to come. If they fail, however, they at once conceive new hopes and so fill up the void. With them alone to hope is to have, for they lose not a moment in the execution of an idea. This is the lifelong task, full of danger and toil, which they are always imposing upon themselves. None enjoy their good things less, because they are always seeking for more. To do their duty is their only holiday, and they deem the quiet of inaction to be as disagreeable as the most tiresome business. If a man should say about them, in a word, that they were born neither to have peace themselves nor to allow peace to other men, he would simply speak the truth.

71. "In the face of such an enemy, Lacedaemonians, you persist in doing nothing. You

do not see that peace is best secured by those who use their strength justly and whose attitude shows that they have no intention of submitting to wrong. Justice with you seems to consist in giving no annoyance to others and in defending yourselves only against positive injury. But this policy would hardly be successful, even if your neighbors were like yourselves; and in the present case, as we pointed out just now, your ways compared with theirs are old-fashioned. And, as in the arts, so also in politics, the new must always prevail over the old. In settled times the traditions of government should be observed; but when circumstances are changing and men are compelled to meet them, much originality is required. Which is also the reason why the Athenian customs, through much experience, are more new to you than yours are to them.

"The time has come to bring your procrastination to an end; send an army at once into their territory and assist your allies, especially the Potidaeans, to whom your word is pledged. Do not allow friends and family to fall into the hands of their worst enemies, or drive us in despair to seek the alliance of others; in taking such a course we should be doing wrong either before the gods who are witnesses of our oaths or before men whose eyes are upon us. For the true breakers of treaties are not only those who, when forsaken, turn to others, but those who forsake allies whom they have sworn to defend. We will remain your friends if you choose to take action; for we should be guilty of an impiety if we deserted you without cause; and we shall not easily find allies that we like as much. Take heed then; you have inherited the leadership of Peloponnesus from your fathers; see to it that her greatness is not lessened at your hands."

72. This is what the Corinthians said. By chance an Athenian delegation which had come on other business happened to be staying at Lacedaemon. When they heard what the Corinthians had said, they felt compelled to go before the Lacedaemonian assembly, not so much to answer the accusations brought against them by the cities, but to put before the Lacedaemonians the whole question, and make them understand that they should take time to deliberate and not be rash. They also wanted to declare the greatness of their city, reminding the elder generation of what they knew, and informing the younger of what lay beyond their experience, expecting that their words would sway the Lacedaemonians in the direction of peace. So they came and said that, if they might be allowed, they too would like to address the people. The Lacedaemonians invited them to come forward, and they spoke as follows:

73. "We were not sent here to argue with your allies, but on a special mission; we noticed, however, that no small outcry has arisen against us, so we have come forward, not to answer the accusations which they bring (for you are not judges before whom either we or they have to plead), but to prevent you from listening too readily to their bad advice and so make the wrong decision about a very serious question. We will also argue, in reply to the wider charges which are raised against us, that we have every right to possess what we have acquired.

"There is no reason for us to speak of the ancient deeds reported by tradition and which no one who hears us ever saw. But we must speak about the Persian war and the other events which you yourselves remember, even though we have brought them up so often that the repetition has become disagreeable to us. When we faced those perils we did so for the common benefit; you shared in these achievements and in the glory, and whatever benefit there may be in that, we would not be wholly deprived. Our words are not designed to soften anyone's hostility, but to declare clearly the character of the city with which, unless you are careful, you will soon be at war. We want to remind you that we, first and alone, dared to engage with the barbarians at Marathon, and that, when they returned, being too weak to defend ourselves by land, we and our whole people took to our ships and shared with the other Greeks in the victory of Salamis. Because of this the enemy was prevented from sailing to the Peloponnesus and ravaging city after city. For how could you have helped one another against such a strong fleet? The Persian king himself is the best witness of our words; for when he was once defeated at sea, he felt that his power was gone and quickly retreated with the greater part of his army.

74. "This event proved undeniably that the fate of Greece depended on her navy. And the three most important elements of success were our contributions: the greatest number of ships, the most capable general, and the most devoted patriotism. The entire fleet numbered about four hundred ships, and our own contingent amounted to nearly two-thirds of them. Everyone admits that our victory was due to the decision to fight in the narrows, which is attributed to the influence of Themistocles, our general; and for this achievement you yourselves honored him above any foreigner who ever visited you. Thirdly, we displayed the most extraordinary courage and devotion; there was no one to help us by land; those who lay in the enemy's path were already enslaved all the way up to our border; because of this we decided to leave our city and sacrifice our homes. Even though we were hard pressed, we still refused to desert the cause of allies who were still resisting the enemy; nor did we make ourselves useless to them by dispersing. Instead, we manned our ships and fought, taking no offense at your failure to assist us sooner. We maintain then that we did you a good deed at least as great as you did for us. The cities from which you came to help us were still habitable, and you might hope to return to them; your concern was for yourselves and not for us; at any rate, you remained at a distance while we had anything to lose. We on the other hand set forth from a city which was no more, and fought for one for which there was only a small hope. And yet we saved ourselves, and did our part in saving you. If, in order to preserve our land, like other states, we had defected to the Persians at first, or afterward had not ventured to set sail because our ruin was already complete, it would have been useless for you with your weak navy to fight at sea, but everything would have gone quietly just as the Persian king desired.

75. "Considering, Lacedaemonians, the energy and wisdom that we displayed at that time, do we deserve to be so bitterly hated by the other Greeks merely because we have an empire? That empire was not acquired by force. No, the allies came of their own accord and asked us to be their leaders when you would not stay and make an end of the barbarian enemy. The subsequent development of our power was originally forced upon us by circumstances; fear was our first motive; afterward ambition, and then self-interest stepped in. And when we had incurred the hatred of most of our allies, and some of them had already revolted and been subjugated, and you were no longer the friends to us which you once had been, but suspicious and ill-disposed, how could we without great risk relax our hold? For the cities as fast as they fell away from us would have gone over

to you. And no man is to be reproached who seizes every possible advantage when the danger is so great.

76. "In any case, Lacedaemonians, we may respond to you that you, in the exercise of your supremacy of the Peloponnesus, manage its cities to suit your own interest. If it had been you, and not we, who had remained in the command of the allies long enough to be hated, you would have been quite as hateful to them as we are, and would have been compelled, for the sake of your own safety, to rule with a strong hand. An empire was offered to us: are you surprised that, acting as human nature always will, we accepted it? or that we have refused to give it up again, constrained by three all powerful motives—ambition, fear, interest? We are not the first who have aspired to rule; the world has ever held that the weaker must be kept down by the stronger. And we think that we are worthy of power; and there was a time when you thought so too. Now, however, you talk about justice when you mean expediency. Did justice ever deter any one from taking by force everything possible? Men who indulge the natural ambition of empire deserve credit if they are in any degree more careful of justice than they need be. If others took our place as rulers, it would very quickly become clear how moderately we have ruled; indeed, our very moderation should be something that we are praised for, rather than being unjustly turned into a criticism.

77. "Our critics accuse us of being litigious because in our legal disputes with our allies, which are regulated by treaty, we do not even stand upon our rights, but instead have instituted the practise of deciding disputes at Athens under laws that are equal to both. None of our opponents bothers to see why other powers exercising dominion over others escape this criticism even though they are less moderate in their dealings with their subjects than we are. Why is it? Because those who practise violence have no longer any need of law. We, by contrast, are in the habit of meeting our allies on terms of equality. Because of this, if our allies, contrary to their own ideas of right, suffer even a little bit through some legal decision of ours, or through our exercise of our imperial power they are not grateful at our moderation in leaving them so much. They are far more offended at their trifling loss than if we had from the first plundered them in the face of day and had completely ignored the law. For then they would themselves have admitted that the weaker must give way to the stronger. People typically resent injustice more than violence, because the one seems to be an unfair advantage taken by an equal, the other is the irresistible force of a superior. They were patient under the yoke of the Persians, who inflicted on them far more grievous wrongs; but now our dominion is odious in their eyes. This is not a surprise: the ruler of the day is always hated by his subjects. And if your empire ever replaces ours, won't you inevitably lose the good-will which you owe to the fear of us? You certainly will lose it if you show the same temper that you gave an example of when, for a short time, you led the alliance against the Persians. For the institutions under which you live are incompatible with those of foreign states; and further, when any of you goes abroad, he respects neither these nor any other Hellenic laws.

78. "You should take care, then, not to rush your decision about this important matter; and do not, by listening to the misrepresentations and complaints of others, bring trouble upon yourselves. You also should recognize, while it is still possible, that war

is unpredictable by its very nature. Indeed, if a war becomes protracted its result usually becomes a mere matter of chance over which neither side can have any control. Its outcome will be equally unknown and equally hazardous to both sides. The unlucky thing is that in their hurry to go to war, men begin with blows, and when they suffer a reverse in fortune, only then do they turn to words. You, however, have not yet made this mistake; nor have we. Therefore while we both can still choose the wiser course, we urge you not to break the peace or violate your oaths. Let our differences be determined by arbitration, according to the treaty. If you refuse, we call to witness the gods by whom you have sworn that you are the authors of the war; and we will do our best to strike in return."

79. When the Lacedaemonians had heard the charges brought by the allies against the Athenians, and their rejoinder, they ordered everybody but themselves to withdraw, and deliberated alone. The majority were agreed that there was now a clear case against the Athenians, and that they must fight at once. But Archidamus their king, who was held to be both an able and a prudent man, came forward and spoke as follows:

80. 'At my age, Lacedaemonians, I have had experience of many wars, and I see several of you who are as old as I am, and who will not, as men too often do, desire war because they have never known it, or in the belief that it is either a good or a safe thing. Any one who calmly reflects will find that the war that you are now considering is likely to be a very great one. When we go to war with our neighbours in the Peloponnese, their mode of fighting is like ours, and they are all within a short march. It is different when we have to fight against men whose country is a long way off, and who are excellent seamen and thoroughly provided with the means of war. They are wealthy both privately and publicly; they have ships, horses, infantry, and a population larger than is to be found in any other Greek city; in addition they have the numerous allies who pay them tribute. Is this a people against whom we can lightly take up arms or plunge into a contest unprepared? In what are we putting our trust? In our navy? In that we are inferior; and it will take time to exercise and train ourselves until we are their equals. In our money? Not at all, since in that we are weaker still; we have no money kept in a common treasury, nor are we ever willing to contribute out of our private means.

81. 'Perhaps someone may be encouraged by the superior equipment and numbers of our infantry, which will enable us regularly to invade and ravage their lands. But their empire extends to distant countries, and they will be able to import their supplies by sea. We could, of course, try to stir up revolts among their allies. But their allies are mostly islanders, so to defend them we shall have to employ a fleet, as well as to defend ourselves. How then shall we wage this war? For if we can neither defeat them at sea, nor deprive them of the revenues by which their navy is maintained, we shall lose. And if we have gone so far, we shall no longer be able even to make peace with honour, especially if we are believed to have begun the war. We must not flatter ourselves for one moment with the idea that the war will end if we do nothing but invade their country. No, I fear that we shall bequeath this land to our children; for the Athenians are proud and will never trade their liberty to save their land, or be terrified like novices at the sight of war.

82. 'Not that I expect you to shut your eyes to their plans or to stop unmasking them, or tamely to allow them to injure our allies. But do not take up arms yet. Let us first send and

negotiate with them: we do not need to let them know positively whether we intend to go to war or not. In the meantime we can begin our own preparations; we can seek for allies wherever we can find them, whether in Greece or among the Barbarians, who can make up our shortcomings in ships and money. Those who are exposed to Athenian machinations, like ourselves, cannot be blamed if in self-defence they seek the the help not of Greeks only, but also of Barbarians. And we must develop our own resources to the maximum extent possible. If they listen to our ambassadors, fine; but, if not, in two or three years' time we shall be in a stronger position, if we then decide to attack them. Perhaps, too, when they begin to see that we are getting ready, and that our words are to be interpreted by our actions, they may be more likely to yield; for their fields will be still untouched and their property unharmed, and it will be in their power to save them by their decision. Think of their land as if it were simply a hostage, the better it is cultivated, the more valuable it is; you should spare it as long as you can, and not by reducing them to despair make their resistance more obstinate. For if we allow ourselves to be goaded into premature action by the reproaches of our allies, and invade Attica before we are ready, we shall only involve the Peloponnesus in greater difficulty and disgrace. Accusations brought by cities or persons against one another can be satisfactorily dealt with; but when a great alliance, in order to satisfy private grudges, undertakes a war of which no man can foresee the issue, it is not easy to terminate it with honour.

83. 'And let no one think that there is any lack of courage in so many cities hesitating to attack a single one. The allies of the Athenians are no less numerous, and they pay them tribute, too. War is not only an affair of arms, but also of money which gives to arms their use, and which is needed above all things when a land-based power is fighting against a maritime power: let us find money first, and then we may safely allow our minds to be stirred up by the speeches of our allies. We, on whom the future responsibility, whether for good or evil, will chiefly fall, should calmly reflect on the consequences that may follow.

84. 'Do not be ashamed of the slowness and procrastination with which they are so fond of accusing you; if you begin the war in haste, you will end it more slowly because you took up arms without sufficient preparation. Remember that we have always been citizens of a free and famous state, and that for us the policy which they condemn may well be the very best good sense and discretion. It is a policy which has saved us from growing arrogant in prosperity or quitting under adversity, as other men do. We are not lured by flattery into dangerous courses of which we disapprove; nor are we goaded by offensive charges into compliance with anyone's wishes. Our disciplined habits make us both brave and wise; brave, because our spirit of loyalty quickens the sense of honour, and our sense of honour inspires courage; wise, because we are not so highly educated that we have learned to despise the laws, and are trained too severely and have too loyal a spirit to disobey them. We are not that useless overly-clever type which makes a man an excellent critic of an enemy's plans, but paralyses him in the moment of action. We think that our enemies are as intelligent as we are, and that the element of fortune cannot be forecast in words. Let us assume that they have carefully planned for themselves, and let our preparations be, not words, but deeds. Our hopes ought not to rest on the hope that they will make mistakes, but on our own caution and foresight. We should remember that one man is much the same as another, and that he is best who is trained in the severest school.

85. 'These are the principles that our fathers have handed down to us, and that we keep to

our lasting benefit; we must not lose sight of them, and when many lives and much wealth, many cities and a great name are at stake, we must not be hasty, or make up our minds in a few short hours; we must take time. We can afford to wait, when others cannot, because we are strong. And now, send to the Athenians and argue with them about Potidaea first, and also about the other wrongs that your allies are complaining about. They say that they are willing to have the matter heard before judges. If someone offers to submit to justice, you must not proceed against them until his case has been heard. While that is going on, prepare for war. That would be the approach that will be best for you and the most formidable to your enemies.'

This is what Archidamus said. Finally, Sthenelaidas, at that time one of the Ephors, came forward and addressed the Lacedaemonians as follows:

86. 'I do not know what the long speeches of the Athenians mean. They have been loud in their own praise, but they do not pretend to say that they are dealing honestly with our allies and with the Peloponnesus. If they behaved well in the Persian War and are now behaving badly to us they ought to be punished twice, because they were once good men and have become bad. But we are the same now as we were then, and if we allow our allies to be mistreated we shall not be doing our duty; nor can we delay, for they cannot put off their troubles. Other powers may have money and ships and horses, but we have brave allies and we must not betray them to the Athenians. If they were suffering in word only, their wrongs might be redressed by words and legal processes; but now not a moment to lose, and we must help them with all our strength. Let no one tell us that we should take time to think when we are suffering injustice. No. We say that those who intend to commit injustice are the ones who should take a long time to think. In light of this, Lacedaemonians, we must prepare for war as the honour of Sparta demands. Stand up to the growing power of Athens! Let us not betray our allies, but, with the Gods on our side, let us attack the evil-doer.'

87. Once Sthenelaidas had spoken he, as Ephor, immediately put the question to the Lacedaemonian assembly himself. Their custom is to signify their decision by shouts and not by voting. But he claimed that he was unable to tell which side had the louder shout, and wishing to elicit a demonstration that might encourage the warlike spirit, he said, 'Whoever of you, Lacedaemonians, thinks that the treaty has been broken and that the Athenians are in the wrong, let him rise and go yonder' (pointing to a particular spot), 'and those who think otherwise to the other side.' So the assembly rose and divided, and it was determined by a large majority that the treaty had been broken. The Lacedaemonians then called the allies back in and told them that in their judgment the Athenians were guilty, but that they wished to hold a general assembly of the allies and take a vote from them all; then the war, if they approved of it, might be undertaken by common consent. Having accomplished their purpose, the allies returned home; and the Athenian envoys, when their errand was done, also returned home. ...

88. In arriving at this decision and resolving to go to war, the Lacedaemonians were influenced not so much by the speeches of their allies, as by the fear of the Athenians and of their increasing power. For they saw that more than half of Greece already subject to them.

Adapted from Benjamin Jowett, *Thucydides translated into English* (Oxford. Clarendon Press. 1881).

Reading 3b. Thucydides: Pericles' Funeral Oration

This is Thucydides' famous report of the speech delivered by Pericles at the end of the first year of the Peloponnesian war (431 B.C.). While it is presented by Thucydides as Pericles' words, it should not be regarded as a transcript of the speech he actually gave, but rather as Thucydides' summary paraphrase of the speech. Pericles was Athens' leading politician and general in the mid-fifth century, a champion of democracy at home and empire abroad. He delivered this speech on the occasion of a public funeral for those Athenian citizen-soldiers who had fallen in the first year of the war. He exhorts the audience to follow their example of dedicated service to the city. It is the democratic Athenian way, he says, to respect each man's freedom to manage his own, individual affairs as he chooses, but at the same time to expect each citizen in public affairs to rise above narrow, private interest and to participate to the best of their ability in the government of the city and to serve the city in the common interest of all. He praises Athens, offering an ideal view in which there is a perfect harmony between individual freedom and collective solidarity, where everyone realizes their self-interest in serving the common, public interest. He contrasts this to Sparta's warrior-collective in which solidarity and dedication to public service are achieved by the complete subordination of the individual to the collective, where citizens are indoctrinated in discipline, conformity, and unquestioning obedience to the laws and traditions of the city. The balance of personal liberty and public commonality, Pericles declares, is the secret of Athens' energy, resourcefulness, striving, and ambition. It has been the motor of her rise to power and prosperity.

While you read, ask yourself:

What are the relative strengths and weaknesses of the Spartan and Athenian models of the polis? What does Sparta gain, relative to Athens, by the maintenance of a small, exclusive body of citizens rigorously schooled in the subordination of self to society, in total solidarity and collective homogeneity? What kind of society, with what characteristics, does this produce? On the other hand, what does Athens gain, relative to Sparta, by a much broader and more diverse citizenry, whose differences and individual perspectives are respected, but who are at the same time expected to freely put aside private interest in the service of the public good? What kind of society, with what characteristics, does this produce? How might you expect the two societies to compare with respect, on the one hand, to order and stability, and, on the other hand, to adaptability and growth?

Pericles' funeral oration (2. 34-47)

34. In the same winter the Athenians gave a funeral at the public cost to those who had first fallen in the war. It was a custom of their ancestors, and it was performed in the following manner. Three days before the ceremony, the bones of the dead are laid out in a tent which has been set up; and their friends bring to their relatives such offerings as they please. In the funeral procession cypress coffins are borne on carts, one for each tribe; the bones

of the deceased being placed in the coffin of their tribe. Among these is carried one empty bier decked for the missing, that is, for those whose bodies could not be recovered following the battle. Any citizen or stranger who pleases, joins in the procession: and the female relatives are there to wail at the burial. The dead are laid in the public sepulchre in the beautiful suburb of the city, in which those who fall in war are always buried. (Those who fell at Marathon are an exception to this: because of their singular and extraordinary valour they were buried on the spot where they fell.) After the bodies have been laid in the earth, a man chosen by the state, of approved wisdom and eminent reputation, pronounces over them an appropriate speech of praise, after which everyone leaves. Such is the manner of the burying; and throughout the whole of the war, whenever the occasion arose, the established custom was observed. Meanwhile these were the first that had fallen, and Pericles, son of Xanthippus, was chosen to pronounce their eulogy. When the proper time arrived, he advanced from the sepulchre to an elevated platform in order to be heard by as many of the crowd as possible, and spoke as follows:

35. "Most of my predecessors in this place have commended the man responsible for the law that made this speech part of the law, asserting that it is a good thing that a speech should be delivered at the burial of those who fall in battle. In my view, the virtues which had been displayed in deeds would be best recognized by honours that also were shown by deeds—such as you now see in this funeral prepared at the public cost. I would have preferred that the reputations of many brave men were not to be entrusted to the mouth of a single individual, to stand or fall according as he spoke well or not. For it is difficult to speak properly upon a subject where it is hard to convince your hearers that you are speaking the truth. On the one hand, the friend who is familiar with every detail of a story may think that some point has not been set forth with that fullness which he wishes and knows it to deserve; on the other, a stranger to the matter may be led by envy to suspect exaggeration if he hears anything that sounds superior his own nature. For men can endure to hear others praised only so long as they can persuade themselves of their own ability to equal the actions recounted: when this point is passed, envy arises and with it comes incredulity. Our ancestors, however, have stamped this custom with their approval, and so it becomes my duty to obey the law and to try to satisfy your different wishes and opinions as best I may.

36. "I shall begin with our ancestors: it is both just and proper that they should have the honour of the first mention on an occasion like the present. Our ancestors dwelt in the country without break in the succession from generation to generation, and handed it down free to the present time by their bravery. And if our distant ancestors deserve praise, our own fathers do even more, since they added to their inheritance the empire which we now possess, and spared no pains to be able to leave their acquisitions to the present generation. Finally, there are few parts of our empire that have not been augmented by those of us here, who are still more or less in the prime of life. Indeed, our mother city has been furnished by us with everything that can enable it to depend on its own resources both for war and for peace. That part of our history which tells of the military achievements which gave us our different possessions, or of the bravery with which either we or our fathers stemmed the tide of Greek or foreign aggression, is a theme too familiar to my hearers for me to dwell on, and I shall therefore pass it by. But what was the road by which we reached our position? what was the form of government under which our

greatness grew? what were the national habits out of which it sprang? These are questions which I may try to answer before I proceed to my eulogy of these men; since I think this is a subject that is proper to consider on the present occasion, and which the whole assembly, whether citizens or foreigners, may hear with advantage.

37. "Our form of government does not copy the laws of neighbouring states; indeed, we are a pattern to others more than imitators of them. Our policies favour the many instead of the few; this is why it is called a democracy. If you look at our laws, they afford equal justice to all in their private disagreements; advancement in public life falls to reputation for capacity, not social standing; class considerations are not allowed to interfere with merit; nor again does poverty bar the way. If a man is able to serve the state, he is not hindered by low origins.

The freedom which we enjoy in our government extends also to our private lives. Far from exercising a jealous surveillance over each other, we do not feel called upon to be angry with our neighbour for doing what he likes. Indeed, we do not even indulge in those injurious looks which cannot fail to be offensive, although they inflict no positive penalty. But although we are easygoing in our private relations, this does not make us lawless as citizens. Our chief safeguard against lawlessness is that we are taught to obey the magistrates and the laws, especially those involving the protection of the injured, whether they are actually among the laws already passed, or belong to that code which, although unwritten, cannot be broken without shame.

38. "In addition, we provide many ways to refresh ourselves mentally from business. We publicly celebrate games and sacrifices all the year round, and these, together with the elegance of private celebrations, form a daily source of pleasure and help to relieve weary spirits. Also, the magnitude of our city draws the produce of the world into our harbour, so that to the Athenian the fruits of other countries are as familiar a luxury as those of his own.

39. "If we turn to our military policy, there also we differ from our antagonists. Our city is open to the world, and we never have banished foreigners to prevent them from learning our ways or observing our actions, although the eyes of an enemy may occasionally profit through our openness. We rely less on system and policy than on the native spirit of our citizens; while in education, where our rivals from their very cradles seek manliness though painful discipline, at Athens we live exactly as we please, and yet are just as ready to encounter every legitimate danger as they are. As proof of this it may be noticed that the Lacedaemonians do not invade our country alone, but bring with them all their allies; while we Athenians advance unsupported into the territory of a neighbour, and fighting upon a foreign soil usually vanquish with ease men who are defending their homes. Nor has any enemy yet encountered our whole unified strength, since we have to attend to our marine and to send our citizens by land upon a hundred different services simultaneously; because of this, wherever they engage with some such fraction of our strength, they magnify a success against a detachment into a victory over the nation, and a defeat into a reverse suffered at the hands of our entire people. And yet, since we are still willing to encounter danger with habits not of labour but of ease, and courage not of art but of nature, we have a double advantage: first of escaping the experience of anticipating hardships before they happen, but also of facing

them in the hour of need as fearlessly as those who are never free from them.

"Nor are these the only points in which our city is worthy of admiration. 40. We cultivate the beautiful without extravagance and knowledge without a loss of manliness; we employ wealth more for real use than for ostentatious show, and assign the real disgrace of poverty not to the fact itself but to any failure to the struggle against it. Our public figures have their private affairs to attend to in addition to politics, and our ordinary citizens, though occupied with the pursuits of industry, are still fair judges of public matters. For we Athenians, unlike other peoples, regard someone who takes no part in public duties not as unambitious but as useless, because individuals are able to judge even if we cannot originate. Indeed, instead of looking on discussion as an obstacle to action, we think of it as an indispensable first step to any wise action at all. For we outdo others in this, too: as much as anyone else we are daring in our undertakings, and yet examine what we do carefully. With other men, it is ignorance that makes them daring, and consideration makes them hesitate. But a reputation for courage is most fairly accorded to those who are never tempted to shrink from danger even though they fully know the difference between hardship and pleasure. In generosity, too, we are also unique. We acquire our friends by conferring favours, not by receiving them. Yet, of course, the doer of the favour is the firmer friend of the two, because he wants to keep the recipient in his debt through continued kindness. The debtor is less keen because he knows that returning a favour is more like a payment than a free gift. It is only the Athenians, who, fearless of consequences, bestow favours not from calculations of advantage, but out of the confidence that liberality brings.

41. "In short, I say that as a city we are the school of Greece, and that that the individual Athenian in his own person is able to adapt himself to the greatest variety of forms of action with the greatest degree of versatility and grace. This is no mere boast that I've concocted for the occasion. No, it is a plain matter of fact, as is proven by the power that our state has obtained through these practices. For, out of all contemporary powers, only Athens is found to be greater than her reputation when a crisis comes. Athens is the only city whose enemies are not embarrassed to be defeated by. We are the only city whose subjects make no complaint about our worthiness to rule. Far from it. The present and succeeding generations will always admire us, since we have not left our empire without witness and have shown it by irrefutable arguments. We have no need of a Homer to record our achievements, or some other poet whose verses might give temporary pleasure, only for their impression to melt at the touch of fact. Instead, we have forced every sea and land to be the highway of our daring, and thereby have left imperishable monuments behind us everywhere, whether for the harm done to our enemies or for the good done to our friends. Such is the city for which these men bravely fought and died; they could not bear the thought that Athens might be taken from them; and every one of us who survive should gladly toil on her behalf.

42. "If I have dwelt at some length upon the character of our country, it has been to show that our stake in the struggle is not the same as those who have no such blessings to lose. It has also been to show that the praise of the men over whom I am now speaking is established by definite proofs. My speech is now in a great measure complete; for the Athens that I have celebrated is only what the heroism of these and those like them have made her — men whose fame, unlike that of most Greeks, will

be found to be only equal to what they deserve. Surely a death such as theirs provides a true measure of a man's worth; it may be the first revelation of a man's virtues, but it is on any reckoning their final proof. For there is justification in the statement that a man's steadfastness in his country's battles is like a cloak that covers his other imperfections, since his good action have eclipsed the bad, and his merits as a citizen more than outweighed any failings as an individual. None of these men were weakened by wealth; nor did they hesitate to resign the pleasures of life. The poor among them did not avoid death in the hope, natural to poverty, that a man, though poor, might one day become rich. No, holding that vengeance upon their enemies was more to be desired than any personal blessings, and thinking that this was the most glorious of dangers, they joyfully decided to accept the risk, to make sure of their vengeance, and to let their own desires wait. They committed their unknown chance of happiness to hope, and decided to act boldly in the business before them and to trust in themselves. In this way they chose to die resisting, rather than to live submitting. The only thing that they fled was dishonour. They met danger face to face, and in one brief moment, while at the height of their fortune, they ascended, not from their fear, but from their glory.

43. "Such was the end of these men; they were worthy of Athens. You, their survivors, must decide to be as unfalteringly brave in the field, even if you pray to meet a happier fate. The value of such bravery is not to be expressed in words. Anyone can speak to you at length about the advantages of a brave defence, which you know already. But instead of listening to him I encourage you to fix your eyes upon the greatness of Athens continually, until you become filled with the love of her. And when you are impressed by the spectacle of Athens' glory, reflect that this empire has been won by men who knew their duty and had the courage to do it, and who in the hour of conflict keenly felt the fear of dishonour. If they ever failed in an enterprise, they would not allow their virtues to be lost to their country, but instead freely gave their lives to her as the fairest offering which they could offer....

44. "I have comfort to offer, therefore, not condolence, to the parents of the dead who may be here. You know that the life of man is subject to numberless risks. You also know that they may be judged the most fortunate who have gained most honour, whether through an honourable sorrow like yours or an honourable death like theirs, whose days have been so ordered that the term of their happiness is likewise the term of their life.

Still I know that it is a hard thing to ask, especially when you will constantly be reminded of the departed by seeing in the homes of others the blessings that you too once enjoyed. For grief is felt not so much because we sense that something is missing that we have never known, but because of the loss of something that we had been used to for a long time. You who are still young enough to have children must bear up in the hope of having other children to replace these; not only will they help you to forget what you have lost, but they will become both a reinforcement and a security for our city. For those who do not have children are less likely to give give good counsel to the state, since they will not have children to be be exposed to any potential dangers. As for you that are past having of children, you must congratulate yourselves with the thought that the best part of your life was fortunate, and that the brief span that remains will be cheered by the fame of the departed. For the love of honour never grows old; and honour it is, not gain, as some would have it, that rejoices the heart of age and helplessness.

45. "Turning to the sons or brothers of the dead, I see an arduous struggle before you to emulate them. For all men praise the dead, and, no matter how outstanding your virtue may be, you can hardly expect to be considered in the same league as them, much less their equal.

The living, too, have envy to contend with, while those who are no longer among us are honoured with a goodwill into which rivalry does not enter.

"On the other hand, if I must say something on the subject of female excellence to those of you who will now be widows, it will be summed up in this brief exhortation. Great will be your glory if you do not show more weakness than is your natural character; and the greatest honour will be hers who is least talked of among the men, whether for good or for bad.

46. "My task is now finished. I have performed it to the best of my ability, and in word, at least, the requirements of the law are now satisfied. The tribute of deeds has been paid in part; for the dead have been honourably interred, and it remains only that their children should be maintained at the public charge until they are fully grown: this is the solid prize with which Athens crowns her sons living and dead, after a struggle like theirs. And where the rewards for merit are greatest, there are found the best citizens. And now that you have finished your lamentations for your relatives, you may depart."

47. Such was the funeral that took place during this winter, with which the first year of the war came to an end.

Adapted from Benjamin Jowett, *Thucydides translated into English* (Oxford: Clarendon Press, 1881).

Chapter 4
The Peloponnesian War

READING 4A. THE REVOLT AT MYTILINE

In his introduction to his History of the Peloponnesian War, Thucydides explains both the reason he undertook to write the history of this war and the methods he used to gather and analyze the sources for the work. As he contends, his methods differ greatly from other researchers, like Herodotus, whose approach of artful, appealing storytelling he scorned. Instead, Thucydides turns an unblinking, clinical eye to hard facts in order to give an objective diagnosis of the human condition, challenging the readers' expectations and beliefs, confronting them with perplexity and demanding that they re-examine what they think they know and wrestle with difficult questions. He explains that the Peloponnesian War was the "greatest disturbance in the history of the Greeks, affecting also a large part of the non-Greek world, and indeed ... the whole of mankind." For Thucydides, the disturbance of the normal order of things and the subjection of states to extreme pressures and changing circumstances revealed the underlying causes of things: the real motivations and drives of people and states, how human nature operates in different conditions, how people respond to change and reason, and how they reach decisions. He is also interested in how the mechanics of society and politics operate and how the social order is affected in different circumstances. For this reason he chose to write a history of this war so that future leaders could learn from the events, understanding not just the course of the Peloponnesian War but also the general forces and principles that underlie human life and history. At the same time, he asserts that the Peloponnesian War inflicted the greatest suffering upon the Greeks, and even as he rejects storytelling, his is a tragic history that exposes the paradoxes of human nature, the fragility of human prosperity and human reason and the reversals of fortune to which the power and greatness of peoples and states are subject as they are caught up in the flow of history.

Thucydides concludes that the underlying cause of the war was "the growth of Athenian power and the fear which this caused in Sparta." The Athenian Empire united Aegean Greece in a political and commercial alliance, and while Athens was the main beneficiary of this empire, the subjugated city-states also received some of the benefits of security and prosperity. They could not, however, be reconciled to the loss of liberty, and in the Peloponnesian War, as before, some of these cities revolted from Athens' rule in an attempt to reclaim their liberty. In 428 B.C. the city of Mytilene, located on the island of Lesbos in the Aegean, withdrew its allegiance and stopped its tribute payments. This action was encouraged by the Spartans, who promised to support the revolt and accept the Mytilenians into their own alliance. The following year, after Athens compelled Mytilene to submit, the Athenians debated in the assembly how Mytilene should be punished. It was decided that Mytilene was to be destroyed, and a fleet was sent to carry out the order. The next day, however, the debate was reopened (a rare occurence), and the decision was reversed. In the end, the Mytilenians were spared by a fast-rowing trireme that was able to reach Mytilene just prior to the judgment being carried out.

- Consider the picture Thucydides is painting here of Athenian democratic decision-making, as effected through competitive public debate with rival speakers competing to persuade the people.
- Do the speakers offer clear, rational arguments?
- What motivates their choice of how to their argue their case, what arguments to present?
- What psychological forces operate in competitive persuasion, driving both the speakers and the audience?
- Is this a good way to make public policy?

The Mytilenian Debate (Thucydides 3.36-50)

[35] On returning to Lesbos, the Athenian commander Paches reduced Pyrrha and Eresus, and finding Salaethus, the Lacedaemonian governor, concealed in Mytilene, sent him to Athens. ... [36] When the captives arrived at Athens the Athenians instantly put Salaethus to death, although he made various offers, and among other things promised to arrange the withdrawal of the Peloponnesians from Plataea which was still blockaded. Concerning the other captives a debate was held, and in their indignation the Athenians determined to put to death not only the men then at Athens, but all adult citizens of Mytilene, and to enslave the women and children; the actions of the Mytilenaeans seemed unforgivable, because they were not subjects like the other states which had revolted, but free. That Peloponnesian ships should have dared to make their way to Ionia and assist the rebels only increased their anger, and besides showed that the revolt had been a premeditated affair planned over a long time.

So they sent a ship to their commander announcing their determination, and ordered him put the Mytilenaeans to death at once. ...

But on the following day a kind of remorse seized them; they began to reflect that a decree which doomed to destruction not only the guilty, but a whole city, was cruel and monstrous. The Mytilenaean envoys who were at Athens perceived the change of feeling, and they and the Athenians who were in their interest prevailed on the magistrates to bring the question again before the people; this they were the more willing to do, because they saw themselves that the majority of the citizens were anxious to get an opportunity to reconsider their decision. An assembly was again summoned, and different opinions were expressed by different speakers.

The speech of Cleon

In the former assembly, Cleon the son of Cleaenetus had proposed the decree condemning the Mytilenaeans to death, which had passed. He was the most violent of the citizens, and at that time exercised by far the greatest influence over the people. And now he came forward a second time and spoke as follows:

[37] "I have remarked again and again that a democracy cannot manage an empire, but never more than now, when I see you regretting your condemnation of the Mytilenaeans. Having no fear or suspicion of one another in daily life, you deal with your allies with the same assumptions, and you do not consider that when you yield to them out of pity or are misled by their specious tales, you are guilty of a weakness dangerous to yourselves, and receive no thanks from them. You should remember that your empire is a despotism exercised over unwilling subjects, who are always conspiring against you; they do not obey in return for any kindness which you do them to your own injury, but because you are their masters; they have no love of you, but they are held down by force. Besides, what can be more irksome than to be perpetually changing our minds? We forget that a state in which the laws, though imperfect, are inviolable, is better off than one in which the laws are good but ineffective. Dullness and modesty are a more useful combination than cleverness and licence; and the more simple sort generally make better citizens than the more clever. For clever people desire to be thought wiser than the laws; they want to be always getting their own way in public discussions; they think that they can nowhere have a finer opportunity of displaying their intelligence. Their foolishness ususally ends in the ruin of their country. Ordinary folk, mistrusting their own capacity, admit that the laws are wiser than themselves: they do not pretend to criticise the arguments of a great speaker; and being impartial judges, not ambitious rivals, they hit the mark. That is the spirit in which we should act; not suffering ourselves to be so excited by our own cleverness in a war of wits as to advise the Athenian people contrary to our own better judgment.

[38] "I myself think as I did before, and I am surprised at those who have brought forward the case of the Mytilenaeans again, since they are imposing a delay which is in the interest of the wrong-doer. For after a time the anger of the sufferer diminishes, and he pursues the offender with less keenness; but the vengeance which follows closest upon the wrong is most adequate to it and exacts the fullest retribution. And again I wonder who will answer me, and whether he will attempt to show that the crimes of the Mytilenaeans are a benefit to us, or that when we suffer, our allies suffer with us. Clearly he must be someone who has such confidence in his powers of speech as to contend that you never adopted what was most certainly your resolution; or else he must be someone who, under the inspiration of a bribe, elaborates an overly clever speech in the hope of diverting you from the point.

In rhetorical contests the city gives away the prizes to others, while it takes the risk upon itself. In this it is you who are to blame, for you establish these contests. Speeches are to be heard, but you treat them like some kind of spectacle; and where actions are needed, you trust your ears; you estimate the desirability of proposed action from the eloquence of an orator, but when it comes to established facts, instead of accepting the proof of your own eyes, you believe only what clever speakers tell you. No one is easier to dupe, sooner deceived by novel notions, or slower to follow approved advice. You despise what is familiar, while you are worshippers of every new extravagance. There is not a man among you would not would choose to be an orator if he could;

if someone cannot speak himself, his next wish is to rival those who can speak by seeming to understand their ideas by applauding every point almost before it is made, and by being as quick in catching an argument as you are slow in foreseeing its consequences. You are always hankering after an ideal state, but you do not give your minds even to what is right before you. In a word, you are at the mercy of your own ears, and sit like spectators attending a performance of sophists, and are very unlike counsellors of a state.

[39] "Let us not waste time with such quibbling. I say to you that no single city has ever injured us so deeply as Mytilene. I can excuse those who find our rule too heavy to bear, or who have revolted because the enemy has compelled them.

But these rebels possessed an island with fortifications; the only way our enemies could threaten them was by sea, but they had their own force of warships to protect against that; they were independent and held in the highest honor by you. What these rebels have done is not revolt—revolt implies oppression. They have instead rebelled and entered the ranks of our bitterest enemies and have conspired with them to seek our ruin. This is surely far worse than if they had been led by motives of ambition to take up arms against us on their own account. They learned nothing from the misfortunes of their neighbours who had already revolted and been subdued by us; nor, apparently, did the happiness which they were enjoying make them hesitate to risk destruction. They trusted recklessly in the future. They chose to cherish hopes which, if less than their wishes, were greater than their powers. They went to war, preferring might to right. No sooner did they seem likely to win than they attacked us, although we were doing them no wrong. Too swift and sudden a rise is apt to make cities insolent and, in general, ordinary good fortune is safer than extraordinary. Humans apparently find it easier to drive away adversity than to retain prosperity. We should from the beginning have made no difference between the Mytilenaeans and the rest of our allies, and then their insolence would never have risen to such a height; for men naturally despise those who court them, but respect those who do not give way to them. Yet it is not too late to punish these people as their crimes deserve. And do not absolve the common people while you throw the blame upon the oligarchs. For they were all of one mind when we were to be attacked. Had the people deserted the oligarchs and come over to us, they might at this moment have been reinstated in their city; but they considered that their safety lay in sharing the dangers of the oligarchy, and therefore they joined in the revolt. Consider: if you impose the same penalty upon those of your allies who wilfully rebel and upon those who are constrained by the enemy, which of them will not revolt upon any pretext however trivial? Why won't he think that, if he should succeed, he will be free, and, if he should fail, he would suffer no irreparable harm? In the meantime we shall have to risk our lives and our fortunes against all of them in turn. Even if we defeat them, we shall recover only a ruined city, and, for the future, the revenues which are our strength will be lost to us. If we fail, however, the number of our adversaries will increase. We ought to be spending our time repelling our enemies; instead we shall be wasting time in fighting against our own allies.

[40] "We must not therefore give our allies hope of pardon, either winnable by words or purchasable by money, as if their errors were of the kind that are commonly found among men. Their attack was not unplanned, which

might have been an excuse for them. They knew what they were doing. This was my original argument, and I still maintain that you should abide by your former decision, and not be misled by the three failings most fatal to empire—mercy, sentiment, and leniency. Mercy should be reserved for the merciful, and not thrown away upon those who will have no compassion on us, and who must by the force of circumstances always be our enemies.

And for the rhetoricians that delight you with their orations, let them play their prizes in matters that are less critical than these and on which the city will not pay so dearly for its brief pleasure in listening to them, while they for a good speech get a good fee. Lastly, forgiveness is naturally shown to those who, being reconciled, will continue friends, and not to those who will always remain what they were enemies who will give up none of their enmity. In one word, if you do as I say, you will do what is just to the Mytilenaeans, and also what is expedient for yourselves. If, however, you take the opposite course of action, they will not be grateful to you, and you will be self-condemned. For, if they were right in revolting, you must be wrong in maintaining your empire. But if, right or wrong, you are resolved to rule, then rightly or wrongly they must be punished for your good. Otherwise you must give up your empire, and, when virtue is no longer dangerous, you may be as virtuous as you please. Punish them as they would have punished you; let not those who have escaped appear to have less feeling than those who conspired against them. Consider what they would and would not have done if they had conquered? especially since they were the aggressors. For those who recklessly attack others always rush into extremes, and sometimes, like these Mytilenaeans, to their own destruction. They know the fate reserved for them by an enemy who survives: when a man is injured without cause he is more dangerous if he escapes than an enemy who has only suffered what he has inflicted. Be true then to yourselves, then, and recall as vividly as you can what you felt at the time; think how you would have given the world to crush your enemies, and now take your revenge. Do not be soft-hearted at the sight of their distress, but remember the danger that was just now hanging over your heads. Punish them as they deserve, and set an example to your other allies that rebellion will be punished with death. If this is made quite clear to them, your attention will no longer be diverted from your enemies by wars against your own allies."

The speech of Diodotus

[41] Such were the words of Cleon. In the previous assembly, the chief opponent of the decree which condemned the Mytilenaeans was Diodotus the son of Eucrates, who now came forward again and spoke as follows:

[42] "I do not all criticize those who invite us to reconsider our sentence upon the Mytilenaeans, nor do I approve of the criticism that has been made against the practice of deliberating more than once about matters so critical. In my opinion the two things most harmful to proper consideration of issues are haste and passion. Haste is often a mark of foolishness; passion, of vulgarity and narrowness of mind. When a man insists that words ought not to be our guides in action, he is either lacking in sense or lacking in honesty: he is lacking in sense if he does not see that there is no other way in which we can throw light on the unknown future; and he is not honest if, seeking to get a discreditable measure passed, and knowing that he cannot speak well in a bad cause, he decides that he can slander well and terrify his

opponents and his audience by the audacity of his insults. Worst of all are those who, in addition to other words of abuse, declare that their opponent is hired to make an eloquent speech. If someone is accused of stupidity after having failed to win an argument, he might go on his way having lost his reputation for sense but not for honesty. But when someone is accused of dishonesty, even if he succeeds, he is viewed with suspicion, and if he fails he is thought to be both fool and rogue. And so the city suffers; for it is robbed of its counsellors by fear. Happy would a city be if such citizens could not speak at all, for then the people would not be misled! The good citizen should prove his superiority as a speaker, not by trying to intimidate those who are to follow him in debate, but through fair argument; and the wise city ought not to give more honour to its best counsellor, any more than it will deprive him of what he already has. The best path, then, is not only that there be no punishment for those whose proposals are rejected, but that they should also be free from all reproach. That way, he who succeeds will not say pleasant things against his better judgment in order to gain a still higher place in popular favour, and he who fails will not be striving to attract the multitude to himself by similar compliances.

[43] "This is not our way; and, besides, the moment that a man is suspected of giving advice, however good, from corrupt motives, we feel such a grudge against him for the gain that we suppose (perhaps erroneously) he will receive that we deprive the city of an undeniable advantage.

It has come to this, that the best advice when offered in plain terms is as much distrusted as the worst. The end result is that it is not only he who wishes to lead the multitude into the most dangerous courses who must deceive the people, but also the one who gives sound advice. In this city, and in this city only, to do good openly and without deception is impossible, because you are too suspicious; and, when a man confers an unmistakeable benefit on you, he is rewarded by a suspicion that he is getting more than he gives through some trickery. But, whatever you may suspect, when great interests are at stake, we orators ought to look further and weigh our words more carefully than you whose perspective is more limited. And you should remember that we are accountable for our advice to you, but you who listen are accountable to nobody. If he who gave and he who followed evil counsel suffered equally, you would be more reasonable in your ideas. Now, however, whenever you suffer a setback, you are led away by the passion of the moment to punish the individual who advised for his error of judgment, but your own error you condone, if the judgments of many agreed with it.

[44] "I do not come forward either as an advocate of the Mytilenaeans or as their accuser; the question for us rightly considered is not, what are their crimes? but, what is in our interest? If I prove them completely guilty, I will not on that account advise you to put them to death, unless it is expedient. Similarly, if there is by chance some degree of excuse for them, I would not advise that you spare them unless it is clearly for the good of the state. For in my opinion we are now concerned not with the present, but with the future. Cleon insists that inflicting death is the expedient course and will protect you against revolt in the future. I agree with him that future expediency must be our primary aim, but stoutly maintain the opposite point. Do not be misled by the apparent justice of his proposal and reject the solid advantages of mine. You are angry with the Mytilenaeans, and his argument may for the moment attract you as having greater justice; but we are not in

court with them, and do not need to be told what is just; we are considering a question of policy, and need to know how to make the Mitylenians useful to Athens.

[45] "In the past states have imposed the punishment of death on offences that are less serious than the Mitylenians have committed; nevertheless hope still leads men to risk their lives. No one would ever set out on a risky enterprise if they knew that they would fail. So, what city has begun to revolt without thinking that its resources, whether its own or obtained from allies, were great enough to justify the attempt? Everyone makes mistakes both in public and in private life; this is part of nature, and no law will prevent it. People have tried out a whole catalogue of penalties in the hope that, by increasing their severity, they might suffer less at the hands of wrong-doers. In early times punishments, even of the worst offences, were naturally milder; but as time went on and mankind continued to transgress, they often went all the way to death. And still there are transgressors. Some greater terror then must be discovered: clearly death is no deterrent. For poverty will always add boldness to necessity; and wealth, will add covetousness to pride and contempt. Moreover, the various conditions of human life, as they in turn fall under the sway of some mighty and fatal power, lure men through their passions to destruction. Desire and hope are never absent: the one leads, the other follows; the one plans the enterprise, the other suggests that fortune will be kind. Because desire and hope are unseen, they are all the more dangerous than the dangers which are seen. Luck, too, strengthens the illusion, for it often appears unexpectedly and causes states as well as individuals to run additional risks, regardless of whether their means are adequate. States are more susceptible to these risks than individuals, because the stakes are higher—freedom or empire—and because when a man has a whole people acting with him, he magnifies himself out of all proportion. In a word then, it is impossible and simply absurd to suppose that human nature can be restrained either by the strength of law or by any other terror once it has decided upon some favourite project.

[46] "We ought not to act hastily out of a mistaken reliance on the security which the penalty of death affords. Nor should we drive our rebellious subjects to despair; they must not think that there is no place for repentance, or that they may not at any moment give up their mistaken policy. Consider this. At present if a city has revolted, if it becomes conscious of its weakness it will surrender and still be able to defray the cost of the war and to pay tribute for the future. If we become too severe, will not the citizens make better preparations, and, when besieged, resist to the very end, knowing that it is all the same whether they come to terms early or late? Will that not mean that we ourselves suffer? For we shall waste more money by beseiging a city which refuses to surrender; when the place is taken it will be a mere wreck, and we shall in future lose the revenues derived from it; and in these revenues lies our military strength. Do not then weigh offences with the severity of a judge, when you will only be injuring yourselves. Rather, keep an eye to the future; let the penalties which you impose on rebellious cities be moderate, and then their wealth will be undiminished and at your service. Do not hope to find a safeguard in the severity of your laws, but only in the vigilance of your administration. At present we too often do just the opposite. A free people under a strong government will always revolt in the hope of independence; and when we have conquered them we think that they cannot be punished too severely. But instead of inflicting

extreme penalties on free men who revolt, we should practise extreme vigilance before they revolt, and never allow such a thought to enter their minds. After we have been compelled to put down a rebellion, however, we ought to extenuate their crimes as much as possible.

[47] "You must consider another problem that will befall you if you listen to Cleon. At present the democrats are everywhere our friends. Either they refuse to join with the oligarchs, or, if compelled to do so, they are always ready to turn against them when they start a revolt. This means that if you go to war with a rebellious state you have the mass of their population on your side. What will happen if you destroy the people of Mytilene who took no part in the revolt, and who voluntarily surrendered the city as soon as they got arms into their hands? By surrendering they did you a favour, and to slay them would be a crime. This will play into the hands of the oligarchic parties, who from this point onwards, in fomenting a revolt, will always have the people on their side: for you will have proclaimed to all that the innocent and the guilty will share the same fate. Even if they were guilty you should forgive their conduct, and not allow the only friends whom you have left to be converted into enemies. The maintenance of our empire will be easier in the future if you suffer wrong willingly sometimes; it will be more difficult if you put to death for the sake of justice those whom we had better spare. Cleon may speak of a punishment which is just and also expedient, but you will find that, in any proposal like his, the two cannot be combined.

[48] "Know then that what I advise is for the best. Do not give in either to pity or to leniency—for I am as unwilling as Cleon can be that you should be influenced by any such motives. Simply weigh the arguments which I have made and vote for my proposal: Pass sentence at your leisure on the Mytilenaeans whom Paches, deeming them guilty, has sent here; but leave the rest of the inhabitants where they are. This will be good policy for the future, and will strike present terror into your enemies. For wise counsel is really more formidable to an enemy than the severity of unreasoning violence."

The outcome

[49] Thus spoke Diodotus. two opinions thus expressed were the ones that most directly contradicted each other; and the Athenians, notwithstanding their change of feeling, now proceeded to a division, in which the show of hands was almost equal, although the motion of Diodotus carried the day. The Athenians immediately despatched another warship, hoping that, if the second could overtake the first, which had a start of about twenty-four hours, it might be in time to save the city. The Mytilenaean envoys provided wine and barley for the crew, and promised them great rewards if they arrived first. And such was their energy that they continued rowing whilst they ate their barley, kneaded with wine and oil, and slept and rowed by turns. Fortunately no adverse wind sprang up, and, the first of the two ships sailing in no great hurry on its unhappy errand, and the second hastening as I have described, the one did indeed arrive sooner than the other, but not much sooner. Paches had read the decree and was about to put it into execution, when the second appeared and prevented the massacre of the city. So near was Mytilene to destruction.

[50] The captives whom Paches had sent to Athens as being the most guilty numbered about a thousand, or rather more; these the Athenians, upon the motion of Cleon, put to death. They

tore down the walls of the Mytilenaeans and took away their fleet. Then, instead of imposing tribute on them, they divided the whole island, except for the territory of Methymna, into three thousand portions, of which they dedicated three hundred to the Gods; the remainder they divided among colonists taken from their own citizens, whom they chose by lot and sent to Lesbos. The citizens of Lesbos undertook to pay them a yearly rent of two minae for each portion and cultivated the land themselves. The Athenians also took possession of the towns on the mainland which the Mytilenaeans held, and these from that point onwards were subject to Athens. Thus ended the revolt of Lesbos.

Adapted from Benjamin Jowett, *Thucydides translated into English* (Oxford: Clarendon Press, 1881).

Reading 4b. The Melian Dialogue

During the Peloponnesian War, Athens not only prevented the withdrawal of subjugated city states from the alliance, but also actively sought to increase its power by subduing previously neutral territories. In 416 B.C. the island of Melos, located in the middle of the Aegean, was overpowered by an Athenian force after a six month siege. The island had remained neutral prior to the attack, but had originally been a colony of Sparta and thus had long-standing contacts with it.

In the reading, the Athenians demand the submission of Melos and turn a deaf ear to the Melians' appeals to justice and right. The Melians refuse to surrender, declaring their trust in the gods and in the commitments of the Spartans. This, however, was all in vain. The island was conquered and all the inhabitants were either killed or enslaved. The last minute mercy shown to the Mytilenians was denied to the Melians.

Some questions to consider:
- What sort of picture do the Athenians paint of human nature and of the real motives of states?
- What alternative picture of the interests of states do the Melians offer?
- Does the fact that the hopes of the Melians prove vain in the face of Athenian power politics mean that the Athenian view is vindicated, that this is the way things necessarily are, and that the Melians' view is always, in all cases, false?

The Melian Dialogue (Thucydides 5. 84-116)

[84] During the following summer [416 B.C.] … the Athenians made an expedition against the island of Melos with thirty ships of their own, six allied ships from Chios, and two from Lesbos, 1,200 hoplites and 300 archers besides twenty mounted archers of their own, and about 1500 hoplites furnished by their allies in the islands. The Melians are colonists of the Lacedaemonians, and they would not submit to Athens like the other islanders. At first they were neutral and took no part. But when the Athenians tried to coerce them by ravaging their lands, they were driven into open hostilities. The generals, Cleomedes the son of Lycomedes and Tisias the son of Tisimachus, encamped with the Athenian forces on the island. But before they did the country any harm they sent envoys to negotiate with the Melians. Instead of bringing these envoys before the people, the Melians wanted them to explain their mission to the city's magistrates and to the chief men. They spoke as follows:

[85] "We notice that we are not allowed to speak to the multitude. This is apparently because you fear that they might hear our persuasive and unanswerable arguments all at once in a continued oration and be convinced by them. For we know that this is the purpose of your bringing us to audience before the few. But you that sit here should make that point surer yet: give your answers point by point, not in a set speech, but presently interrupting us whenever anything said by us needs to be contradicted by you. And first

answer us whether you like this proposal or not?"

[86] The Melian representatives answered: "The quiet interchange of explanations is a reasonable approach, and we do not object to that. But your preparations for war, which is not a future fear but visible now before our very eyes, seems to undercut your words. We see that, although you may argue with us, you intend to be our judges; and that at the end of the discussion, if the Justice of our cause prevails and we refuse to yield, we may expect war; if we are persuaded by you, slavery awaits us."

[87] Athenians: No, but if you are only going to argue from hopes about the future, or if you meet us with any purpose other than that of looking your circumstances in the face and saving your city, we are done here; but if this is your intention we will proceed.

[88] Melians: It is an understandable and natural thing that men in our position should have much to say and should indulge in many hopes. But we admit that this meeting has gathered to discuss the question of our preservation; and therefore let the argument proceed in the manner which you propose.

[89] Athenians: Well, then, we Athenians will use no specious words; we will not go out of our way to prove at length that we have a right to rule, because we overthrew the Persians; or that we attack you now because we are suffering any injury at your hands. We should not convince you if we did; nor must you expect to convince us by arguing that, although a colony of the Lacedaemonians, you have taken no part in their expeditions, or that you have never done us any wrong. But you and we should say what we really think, and aim only at what is possible. For we both know that the question of justice only enters into the discussion about human affairs where the pressure of necessity is equal, and that the powerful exact what they can, and the weak give what they must.

[90] Melians: Well, then, since you set aside justice and invite us to speak of expediency, in our judgment it is certainly expedient that you should respect a principle that is for the common good, which is this: that men in danger should be able to appeal to what is fair and right and should be able to resort to arguments that are not strictly relevant to the current point. Your interest in this principle is quite as great as ours, inasmuch as you, if you fall, will incur the heaviest vengeance, and will thus become the most terrible example to mankind.

[91] Athenians: The fall of our empire, if it should fall, is not an event to which we look forward with dismay; for ruling states such as Sparta are not cruel to their vanquished enemies. And we are fighting not so much against the Lacedaemonians, as against our own subjects who may some day rise up and overcome their former masters. But this is a risk which you should leave to us. And we will now begin to demonstrate that we have come in the interests of our empire, and that in what we are about to say we are only seeking the preservation of your city. For we want to make you ours with the least trouble to ourselves, and it is in both your interest and ours that you should not be destroyed.

[92] Melians: It may be your interest to be our masters, but how can it be ours to be your slaves?

[93] Athenians: The advantage for you will be that by submission you will avert disaster; and we shall be all the richer for your preservation.

[94] Melians: But must we be your enemies? Will you not receive us as friends if we are neutral and remain at peace with you?

[95] Athenians: No, your enmity is not half so dangerous to us as your friendship; for your enmity is in the eyes of our subjects an argument of our power, the other of our weakness.

[96] Melians: But are your subjects really unable to distinguish between states in which you have no concern, and those which are mostly your own colonies, and in some cases have revolted and been subdued by you?

[97] Athenians: As far as right goes they think one has as much of it as the other, and that if any maintain their independence it is because they are strong, and that if we do not molest them it is because we are afraid. Because of this, your subjection will increase our security; it will also extend our empire. For we are masters of the sea. You who are islanders, and insignificant islanders too, must not be allowed to escape us.

[98] Melians: But do you not recognise another danger? For, once more, since you drive us from the plea of justice and press upon us your doctrine of expediency, we must show you what is in our interest, and, if it is in yours also, may hope to convince you: Will you not be making enemies of all those who are now neutral? When they see how you are treating us, will they not expect you some day to turn against them, too? And if so, are you not strengthening the enemies whom you already have, and bringing upon you others who, if they could help, would never dream of being your enemies at all?

[99] Athenians: We do not consider our really dangerous enemies to be any of the peoples inhabiting the mainland. For they are secure in their freedom, and may delay indefinitely any measures of precaution which they take against us. Our most danderous enemies are, firstly, islanders like you who happen to be independent, and secondly those who are already growing impatient with the necessity of submitting to our rule. These are our real enemies, for they are the most reckless and most likely to bring both themselves and us into a danger which they cannot help but foresee.

[100] Melians: Granted, you and your subjects are willing take all these risks, you to preserve your empire and they to be rid of it. But if that is so, it would be despicable and cowardly for us, who retain our freedom, to fail to do and suffer anything rather than become your slaves.

[101] Athenians: Not so, if you think about it dispationably. If you were fighting against equals, it is true that you could not yield without disgrace. Now, however, you are considering whether or not you will try to resist an overwhelming force. The question is not one of honour but of prudence.

[102] Melians: But we know that in war fortune is sometimes impartial, and not always on the side of numbers. If we yield now, all is over; but if we continue to fight, there is still hope that we may come out standing tall.

[103] Athenians: Hope is a good comfort in the hour of danger. When people have something else to depend upon, hope is hurtful, though not ruinous. But when the extravagent nature of hope has induced people to gamble everything, they do not see its true nature until the moment of their catastrophe. While the knowledge of this might enable them to be on their guard, fortune never fails until it is too late. You are weak and a single loss of a bet might be your ruin. Do not delude yourself in this way. Avoid the error that so many fall into. For although some might still be saved

if they would merely looked towards human means, when visible grounds of confidence forsake them, they turn towards to the invisible, to prophecies and oracles and the like. These destroy men through the hopes which they inspire in them.

[104] Melians: We know only too well how hard the struggle must be against your power, and against fortune, if it is not about to be impartial. Nevertheless we do not despair of fortune; for we hope to stand as high as you in the favour of heaven, because we are righteous. And we are struggling against you, who are unrighteous. We are satisfied that what we lack in resources will be compensated by the aid of our allies the Lacedaemonians; they cannot refuse to help us, if only because we are their kinsmen, and for the sake of their own honour. And therefore our confidence is not so utterly blind as you suppose.

[105] Athenians: As for the gods, we expect to have as much of their favour as you do: for we are not doing or claiming anything that goes beyond common opinion about the gods and the principles that govern men's behaviour. We believe that the gods by a law of their nature want to rule wherever they can, and we know that this is so of men. This law was not made by us, and we are not the first to have acted upon it. We have merely inherited this principle, and shall in turn leave it to others. We know that you and all mankind, if you were as strong as we are, would do as we do. In regards to the gods; we have told you why we expect to stand as high in their good opinion as you. With regards to the Lacedaemonians, however, when you imagine that they will come to help you because of shame, we admire the simplicity of your world view, but we do not envy you the folly of it. The Lacedaemonians are exceedingly virtuous among themselves, and according to their national standard of morality. But when it comes to their dealings with others, although many things might be said, a word is enough to describe them. Of all men whom we know they are the most known for confusing what is pleasant with what is honourable, and what is expedient with what is just. But their true character is completely inconsistent with your present blind hope of deliverance.

[106] Melians: That is the very reason why we trust them; they will look to their interest, and therefore will not be willing to betray the Melians, who are their own colonists, lest they should be distrusted by their friends in Greece and play into the hands of their enemies.

[107] Athenians: But do you not see that the path of expediency is safe, whereas justice and honour involve danger in practice, and such dangers the Lacedaemonians seldom care to face?

[108] Melians: On the other hand, we think that whatever perils may exist, the Lacedaemonians will be ready to face them for our sakes, and will consider danger less dangerous where we are concerned. For if they need to act we are close at hand, and they can better trust our loyal feeling because we are their kinsmen.

[109] Athenians: Yes, but what encourages men who are invited to join in a conflict is clearly not the good will of those who summon them to their side, but a clear superiority in real power. To this no men look more keenly than the Lacedaemonians; so little confidence have they in their own resources, that they only attack their neighbours when they have numerous allies, and therefore they are not likely to make their way by themselves to an island, when we are masters of the sea.

[110] **Melians:** But they may send their allies. In any case, the Cretan sea is a large place, so that those controlling it will have more difficulty in overtaking vessels attempting to escape than those who are being pursued will have in escaping. If the attempt should fail, they may invade Attica itself, or attack those allies of yours whom Brasidas did not reach. Then you will have to fight, not for the conquest of a land in which you have no concern, but nearer home, for the preservation of your confederacy and of your own territory.

[111] **Athenians:** Help may indeed come from Lacedaemon to you as it has come to others. But if you had had any actual experience of it, then you will know that never once have the Athenians retired from a siege through fear of a foe elsewhere. You told us that the safety of your city would be your first care, but we remark that, in this long discussion, not a word has been uttered by you which would give a reasonable man expectation of deliverance. Your strongest arguments are future hopes, and what power you have is not to be compared with that which has now already been arrayed against you. Unless after we have withdrawn you mean to come to a wiser conclusion (which is always possible), you are showing a great lack of sense. For surely you cannot dream of grasping that false sense of honour which has been the ruin of so many when danger and dishonour were staring them in the face. For many men, although they have foreseen what dangers they were entering, have nevertheless been so overcome by the powerful word dishonour that this idea has caused them to fall willingly into real and irretrievable calamities. Through their own folly they have incurred a worse dishonour than fortune would have inflicted upon them.

If you are wise you will not run this risk. You ought to see that there can be no disgrace in yielding to a great city that invites you to become her ally on reasonable terms, keeping your own land, and merely paying tribute. You ought also to realize that you will certainly gain no honour if, having to choose between two alternatives, safety and war, you obstinately prefer the worse. To maintain our rights against equals, to be politic with superiors, and to be moderate towards inferiors is the path of safety. Reflect once more when we have withdrawn, and say to yourselves over and over again that you are deliberating about your one and only country, which may be saved or may be destroyed by a single decision.

[112] The Athenians left the conference: the Melians, after consulting among themselves, resolved to persevere in their refusal, and answered as follows, "Men of Athens, our resolution is unchanged; and we will not in a moment surrender the liberty which our city has enjoyed undiminished since being founded 700 years ago; we will trust to the good fortune which, by the favour of the gods, has thus far preserved us, and for human help to the Lacedaemonians, and endeavour to save ourselves. We are ready, however, to be your friends. We want to be the enemies neither of you nor of the Lacedaemonians, and we ask you to leave our country when you have made such a peace as may appear to be in the interest of both parties."

[113] Such was the answer of the Melians; the Athenians, as they left the conference, spoke as follows, "Well, we must say, judging from your decision, that you are the only men who deem the future to be more certain than the present, and who regard doubtful possibilities as already realised. Be warned, however, that the more you depend on and trust in the Lacedaemonians and fortune, and hope, the more complete will be your ruin."

[114] The Athenian envoys returned to the army; and the generals, when they found that the Melians would not yield, immediately commenced hostilities. They surrounded the town of Melos with a wall, dividing the work among the several contingents. They then left troops of their own and of their allies to keep guard both by land and by sea, and retired with the greater part of their army; the remainder carried on the blockade....

[116] In the following winter ... the Melians managed to capture a part of the Athenian wall where the fortifications were insufficiently guarded. The Athenians, however, immediately sent fresh troops, under the command of Philocrates the son of Demeas. The place was now closely invested, and there was treachery among the citizens themselves. So the Melians were induced to surrender to the discretion of the Athenians, who then put to death all who were of military age, and made slaves of the women and children. They then colonised the island, sending 500 settlers of their own there.

Adapted from Benjamin Jowett, *Thucydides translated into English* (Oxford: Clarendon Press, 1881).

Chapter 5

The Hellenistic World

Reading 5a. Hellenism and Indigenous Cultures

In the following passage Plutarch exalts Alexander above the philosophers by the claim that he, unlike they, actually changed the world. In particular, he celebrates Alexander for bringing Greek civilization to barbarian peoples and so uniting the people of the world in one, common culture. In practice, while Greek cities, which had already been planted throughout the Mediterranean, were established across Asia following Alexander's conquests, their populations tended to remain somewhat separate from the indigenous population. Though there were important cultural exchanges, Hellenism remained to a significant degree, contrary to the impression given by Plutarch, the exclusive culture of the colonial rulers. Consider what attitudes are revealed in this passage concerning Greekness and non-Greeks.

The Hyrcanians, Arachosians, Sogdians, Susianians, Gedrosians, Bactrians, as well as Babylonians and Persians, are all Asian peoples. Alexandria, Seleuceia, Prophthasia, and Bucephalia are Greek cities that were established in Egypt and Asia.

Plutarch, On the Fortune and Virtue of Alexander the Great 1.328c-329d

But if you examine the results of Alexander's instruction, you will see that he educated the Hyrcanians to respect the marriage bond, and taught the Arachosians to till the soil, and persuaded the Sogdians to support their parents, not to kill them, and the Persians to revere their mothers and not to take them in wedlock. O wondrous power of philosophic instruction, that brought the Indians to worship Greek gods, and the Scythians to bury their dead, not to devour them! We admire Carneades' power, which made Cleitomachus, formerly called Hasdrubal, and a Carthaginian by birth, adopt Greek ways. We admire the character of Zeno, which persuaded Diogenes the Babylonian to be a philosopher. But when Alexander was civilizing Asia, Homer was commonly read, and the children of the Persians, of the Susianians, and of the Gedrosians learned to chant the tragedies of Sophocles and Euripides. And although Socrates, when tried on the charge of introducing foreign deities, lost his cause to the informers who infested Athens, yet through Alexander Bactria and the Caucasus learned to revere the gods of the Greeks. Plato wrote a book on the One Ideal Constitution, but because of its forbidding character he could not persuade anyone to adopt it; but Alexander established more than seventy cities among savage tribes, and sowed all Asia with Grecian magistracies, and thus overcame its uncivilized and brutish manner of living. Although few of us read Plato's Laws, yet hundreds of thousands have made use of Alexander's laws, and continue to use them. Those who were vanquished by Alexander are happier than those who escaped his hand; for these had no one to put an end to the wretchedness of their existence, while the victor compelled those others to lead a happy life. Therefore it is even more just to apply Themistocles' saying to the nations conquered by Alexander. For, when Themistocles in exile had obtained great gifts from Artaxerxes, [the Persian king], and had received three cities to pay him tribute, one to supply his bread, another his wine, and a third his meat, he exclaimed, "My children, we should be ruined now, had we not been ruined before." Thus Alexander's new subjects would not have been civilized, had they not been vanquished; Egypt would not have its Alexandria, nor Mesopotamia its Seleuceia, nor Sogdiana its Prophthasia, nor India its Bucephalia, nor the Caucasus a Greek city nearby; for by the founding of cities in these places savagery was extinguished and the worse element, gaining familiarity with the better, changed under its influence. If, then, philosophers take the greatest pride in civilizing and rendering adaptable the intractable and untutored elements in human character, and if Alexander has been shown to have changed the savage natures of countless tribes, it is with good reason that he should be regarded as a very great philosopher.

Moreover, the much-admired Republic of Zeno, the founder of the Stoic sect, may be summed up in this one main principle: that all the inhabitants of this world of ours should not live differentiated by their respective rules of justice into separate cities and communities, but that we should consider all men to be of one community and one polity, and that we should have a common life and an order common to us all, even as a herd that feeds together and shares the pasturage of a common field. This Zeno wrote, giving shape to a dream or, as it were, shadowy picture of a well-ordered and philosophic commonwealth; but it was Alexander who gave effect to the idea. For Alexander did not follow Aristotle's advice to treat the Greeks as if he were their leader, and other peoples as if he were their master; to have regard for the Greeks as for friends and kindred, but to conduct himself toward other peoples as though they were plants or animals; for to do so would have been to burden his leadership with numerous battles and banishments and festering seditions. But, as he believed that he came as a heaven-sent governor to all, and as a mediator for the whole world, those whom he could not persuade to unite with him, he conquered by force of arms, and he brought together into one body all men everywhere, uniting and mixing in one great loving-cup, as it were, men's lives, their characters, their marriages, their very habits of life. He bade them all consider as their fatherland the whole inhabited earth, as their stronghold and protection his camp, as akin to them all good men, and as foreigners only the wicked; they should not distinguish between Greek and foreigner by Greek cloak and shield, or scimitar and jacket; but the distinguishing mark of the Greek should be seen in virtue, and that of the foreigner in iniquity; clothing and food, marriage and manner of life they should regard as common to all, being blended into one by ties of blood and children.

Adapted from Frank Cole Babbitt (trans.), *Plutarch, Moralia*, vol. 4 (Cambridge, Mass., Harvard University Press, 1936).

Reading 5b. A Description of Alexandria

Alexandria was one of the ancient world's great cities, having been founded by Alexander the Great in 331 BC. It became the seat of the Ptolemaic rulers of Egypt, and remained important after the Roman conquest, being the Roman Empire's second largest city, eclipsed only by Rome in its size and wealth. Below, the Roman geographer Strabo describes it.

While reading the description, consider the following questions:

- What statement does the city make about the rule of the Ptolemies?
- What is Egyptian in the city and what Greek?

Strabo *Geography* 17. 1. 6-9

[6] Since Alexandria and its neighbourhood constitute the largest and most important part of this subject, I shall begin with them. The sea-coast, then, from Pelusium, as one sails towards the west, as far as the Canobic mouth, is about one thousand three hundred stadia — the "base" of the Delta, as I have called it; and thence to the island Pharos, one hundred and fifty stadia more. Pharos is an oblong isle, is very close to the mainland, and forms with it a harbour with two mouths; the shore of the mainland forms a bay, since it thrusts two promontories into the open sea, and between these is situated the island, which closes the bay, for it lies lengthwise parallel to the shore. Of the extremities of Pharos, the eastern one lies closer to the mainland and to the promontory opposite it (the promontory called Lochias), and thus makes the harbour narrow at the mouth; and in addition to the narrowness of the intervening passage there are also rocks, some under the water, and others projecting out of it, which at all hours roughen the waves that strike them from the open sea. And likewise the extremity of the isle is a rock, which is washed all round by the sea and has upon it a tower that is admirably constructed of white marble with many stories and bears the same name as the island. This was an offering made by Sostratus of Cnidus, a friend of the kings, for the safety of mariners, as the inscription says: for since the coast was harbourless and low on either side, and also had reefs and shallows, those who were sailing from the open sea thither needed some lofty and conspicuous sign to enable them to direct their course aright to the entrance of the harbour. And the western mouth is also not easy to enter, although it does not require so much caution as the other. And it likewise forms a second harbour, that of Eunostus, as it is called, which lies in front of the closed harbour which was dug by the hand of man. For the harbour which affords the entrance on the side of the above-mentioned tower of Pharos is the Great Harbour, whereas these two lie continuous with that harbour in their innermost recess, being separated from it only by the embankment called the Heptastadium. The embankment forms a bridge extending from the mainland to the western portion of the island, and leaves open only two passages into the harbour of Eunostus, which are bridged over. However, this work formed not only a bridge to the island but also an aqueduct, at least when Pharos was inhabited. But in these present times it has been laid waste by the deified Caesar in his war against the Alexandrians, since it had sided with the kings. A few seamen, however, live near the tower. As for the

Great Harbour, in addition to its being beautifully enclosed both by the embankment and by nature, it is not only so deep close to the shore that the largest ship can be moored at the steps, but also is cut up into several harbours. Now the earlier kings of the Aegyptians, being content with what they had and not wanting foreign imports at all, and being prejudiced against all who sailed the seas, and particularly against the Greeks (for owing to scarcity of land of their own the Greeks were ravagers and coveters of that of others), set a guard over this region and ordered it to keep away any who should approach; and they gave them as a place of abode Rhacotis, as it is called, which is now that part of the city of the Alexandrians which lies above the ship-houses, but was at that time a village; and they gave over the parts round about the village to herdsmen, who likewise were able to prevent the approach of outsiders. But when Alexander visited the place and saw the advantages of the site, he resolved to fortify the city on the harbour. Writers record, as a sign of the good fortune that has since attended the city, an incident which occurred at the time of tracing the lines of the foundation: When the architects were marking the lines of the enclosure with chalk, the supply of chalk gave out; and when the king arrived, his stewards furnished a part of the barley-meal which had been prepared for the workmen, and by means of this the streets also, to a larger number than before, were laid out. This occurrence, then, they are said to have interpreted as a good omen.

[7] The advantages of the city's site are various; for, first, the place is washed by two seas, on the north by the Aegyptian Sea, as it is called, and on the south by Lake Mareia, also called Mareotis. This is filled by many canals from the Nile, both from above and on the sides, and through these canals the imports are much larger than those from the sea, so that the harbour on the lake was in fact richer than that on the sea; and here the exports from Alexandria also are larger than the imports; and anyone might judge, if he were at either Alexandria or Dicaearchia and saw the merchant vessels both at their arrival and at their departure, how much heavier or lighter they sailed thither or therefrom. And in addition to the great value of the things brought down from both directions, both into the harbour on the sea and into that on the lake, the salubrity of the air is also worthy of remark. And this likewise results from the fact that the land is washed by water on both sides and because of the timeliness of the Nile's risings; for the other cities that are situated on lakes have heavy and stifling air in the heats of summer, because the lakes then become marshy along their edges because of the evaporation caused by the sun's rays, and, accordingly, when so much filth-laden moisture rises, the air inhaled is noisome and starts pestilential diseases, whereas at Alexandria, at the beginning of summer, the Nile, being full, fills the lake also, and leaves no marshy matter to corrupt the rising vapours. At that time, also, the Etesian winds blow from the north and from a vast sea, so that the Alexandrians pass their time most pleasantly in summer.

The shape of the area of the city is like a chlamys; the long sides of it are those that are washed by the two waters, having a diameter of about thirty stadia, and the short sides are the isthmuses, each being seven or eight stadia wide and pinched in on one side by the sea and on the other by the lake. The city as a whole is intersected by streets practicable for horse-riding and chariot-driving, and by two that are very broad, extending to more than a plethrum in breadth, which cut one another into two sections and at right angles. And the city contains most beautiful public precincts and also the royal palaces, which constitute one-fourth or even one-third of the whole circuit of the city; for just as each of the kings, from love of splendour, was wont to add some adornment to the public monuments, so also he would invest himself at his own expense with a residence, in addition to those already built, so that now, to quote the words of the poet, "there is building upon building." All, however, are connected with one another and the harbour, even those that lie outside the harbour. The Museum is also a part of the royal palaces; it has a public walk, an Exedra with seats, and a large house, in which is the common mess-hall of the men of learning who share the Museum. This group of men not only hold property in common, but also have a priest in charge of the Museum, who formerly was appointed by the kings, but is now appointed by Caesar. The Sema also, as it is called, is a part of the royal palaces. This was the enclosure which contained the burial-places of the kings and that of Alexander; for Ptolemy, the son of Lagus, forestalled Perdiccas by taking the body away from him when he was bringing it down from Babylon and was turning aside towards Aegypt, moved by greed and a desire to make that country his own. Furthermore, Perdiccas lost his life, having been slain by his soldiers at the time when Ptolemy attacked him and hemmed him up in a desert island. So Perdiccas was killed, having been transfixed by his soldiers' sarissae when they attacked him; but the kings who were with him, both Aridaeus and the children of Alexander, and also Rhoxanê, Alexander's wife, departed for Macedonia; and the body of Alexander was carried off by Ptolemy and given sepulture in Alexandria, where it still now lies — not, however, in the same sarcophagus as before, for the present one is made of glass, whereas the one wherein Ptolemy laid it was made of gold. The latter was plundered by the Ptolemy nicknamed "Cocces" and "Pareisactus," who came over from Syria but was immediately expelled, so that his plunder proved unprofitable to him.

[9] In the Great Harbour at the entrance, on the right hand, are the island and the tower Pharos, and on the other hand are the reefs and also the promontory Lochias, with a royal palace upon it; and on sailing into the harbour one comes, on the left, to the inner royal palaces, which are continuous with those on Lochias and have groves and numerous lodges painted in various colours. Below these lies the harbour that was dug by the hand of man and is hidden from view, the private property of the kings, as also Antirrhodos, an isle lying off the artificial harbour, which has both a royal palace and a small harbour. They so called it as being a rival of Rhodes. Above the artificial harbour lies the theatre; then the Poseidium — an elbow, as it were, projecting from the Emporium, as it is called, and containing a temple of Poseidon. To this elbow of land Antony added a mole projecting still farther, into the middle of a harbour, and on the extremity of it built a royal lodge which he called Timonium. This was his last act, when, forsaken by his friends, he sailed away to Alexandria after his misfortune at Actium, having chosen to live the life of a Timon the end of his days, which he intended to spend in solitude from all those friends. Then one comes to the Caesarium and the Emporium and the warehouses; and after these to the ship-houses, which extend as far as the Heptastadium. So much for the Great Harbour and its surroundings.

[10] Next, after the Heptastadium, one comes to the Harbour of Eunostus, and, above this, to the artificial harbour, which is also called Cibotus; it too has ship-houses. Farther in there is a navigable canal, which extends to Lake Mareotis. Now outside the canal there is still left only a small part of the city; and then one comes to the suburb Necropolis, in which are

many gardens and groves and halting-places fitted up for the embalming of corpses, and, inside the canal, both to the Sarapium and to other sacred precincts of ancient times, which are now almost abandoned on account of the construction of the new buildings at Nicopolis; for instance, there are an amphitheatre and a stadium at Nicopolis, and the quinquennial games are celebrated there; but the ancient buildings have fallen into neglect. In short, the city is full of public and sacred structures; but the most beautiful is the Gymnasium, which has porticoes more than a stadium in length. And in the middle are both the court of justice and the groves. Here, too, is the Paneium, a "height," as it were, which was made by the hand of man; it has the shape of a fir-cone, resembles a rocky hill, and is ascended by a spiral road; and from the summit one can see the whole of the city lying below it on all sides. The broad street that runs lengthwise extends from Necropolis past the Gymnasium to the Canobic Gate; and then one comes to the Hippodrome, as it is called, and to the other (streets?) that lie parallel, extending as far as the Canobic canal. Having passed through the Hippodrome, one comes to Nicopolis, which has a settlement on the sea no smaller than a city. It is thirty stadia distant from Alexandria. Augustus Caesar honoured this place because it was here that he conquered in battle those who came out against him with Antony; and when he had taken the city at the first onset, he forced Antony to put himself to death and Cleopatra to come into his power alive; but a little later she too put herself to death secretly, while in prison, by the bite of an asp or (for two accounts are given) by applying a poisonous ointment; and the result was that the empire of the sons of Lagus, which had endured for many years, was dissolved.

Adapted from W. Falconer, *The Geography of Strabo, Literally translated*, vol. 3 (London. George Bell & Sons. 1960).

Reading 5c. The Achaean League

In this passage, the Greek historian Polybius (264-146 BC) recounts the rise to power of the Achaean League. Polybius was himself a leading statesman of the League (of which he gives a highly celebratory account). In the Classical period, western and northern Greece, including Achaea in the north-west Peloponnese (and Aetolia, on the other side of the Gulf of Corinth), were political backwaters compared to Aegean Greece where the famous city-states had arisen (Athens in Attica, Thebes in Boeotia, Corinth and Argos in the north-east Peloponnese, Sparta in Laconia, as well as the cities of the islands and of Ionia on the other side of the Aegean sea). Areas like Achaea followed a different line of political development. Rather than seeing the formation of centralized, unitary city-states, in these areas 'leagues' (*koina* in Greek; singular, *koinon*) formed. These were loose coalitions of towns: alliances having some common political and religious institutions, rather than unitary states. The Achaean League that formed in the fifth century later fell apart, but was revived in the third century BC. In the Hellenistic period, however, while city-states like Athens and Sparta faded in political power, it was the leagues, especially the Achaean League and the Aetolian League, that became the major powers among the cities of Greece.

When reading Polybius' account, consider the relationship between the Greek cities and the Antigonid kingdom of Macedon. How might the rise of the successor kingdoms have promoted the rise of the leagues (simultaneous to the decline of the great Classical city-states)? Consider also what a league was—how it was constituted—and how it differed as a form of political organization from the polis.

Polybius, The Histories, 2.37-44

(37) But as regards the Achaean nation and the royal house of Macedon it will be proper to refer briefly to earlier events, since our times have seen, in the case of the latter, its complete destruction, and in the case of the Achaeans, as I said, a growth of power and a political union in the highest degree remarkable. For while many have attempted in the past to induce the Peloponnesians to adopt a common policy, no one ever succeeding, as each was working not in the cause of general liberty, but for his own aggrandizement, this object has been so much advanced, and so nearly attained, in my own time that not only have they formed an allied and friendly community, but they have the same laws, weights, measures and coinage, as well as the same magistrates, senate, and courts of justice, and the whole Peloponnese only falls short of being a single city in the fact of its inhabitants not being enclosed by one wall, all other things being, both as regards the whole and as regards each separate town, very nearly identical.

(38) In the first place it is of some service to learn how and by what means all the Peloponnesians came to be called Achaeans. For the people whose original and ancestral name this was are distinguished neither by the extent of their territory, nor by the number of their cities, nor by exceptional wealth or the exceptional valour of their citizens. Both the Arcadian and Laconian nations far exceed them, indeed, in population and the size of their countries,

and certainly neither of the two could ever bring themselves to yield to any Greek people the palm for military valour. How is it, then, that both these two peoples and the rest of the Peloponnesians have consented to change not only their political institutions for those of the Achaeans, but even their name? It is evident that we should not say it is the result of chance, for that is a poor explanation. We must rather seek for a cause, for every event whether probable or improbable must have some cause. The cause here, I believe to be more or less the following. One could not find a political system and principle so favourable to equality and freedom of speech, in a word so sincerely democratic, as that of the Achaean league. Owing to this, while some of the Peloponnesians chose to join it of their own free will, it won many others by persuasion and argument, and those whom it forced to adhere to it when the occasion presented itself suddenly underwent a change and became quite reconciled to their position. For by reserving no special privileges for original members, and putting all new adherents exactly on the same footing, it soon attained the aim it had set itself, being aided by two very powerful coadjutors, equality and humanity. We must therefore look upon this as the initiator and cause of that union that has established the present prosperity of the Peloponnese...

(39) Up to now, these principles of government had merely existed amongst them, but had resulted in no practical steps worthy of mention for the increase of the Achaean power, since the country seemed unable to produce a statesman worthy of those principles, anyone who showed a tendency to act so being thrown into the dark and hampered either by the Lacedaemonian power or still more by that of Macedon. (40) When, however, in due time, they found statesmen capable of enforcing them, their power at once became manifest, and the League achieved the splendid result of uniting all the Peloponnesian states. Aratus of Sicyon should be regarded as the initiator and conceiver of the project; it was Philopoemen of Megalopolis who promoted and finally realized it, while Lycortas and his party were those who assured the permanency, for a time at least, of this union. I will attempt to indicate how and at what date each of the three contributed to the result, without transgressing the limits I have set to this part of my work. Aratus' government, however, will be dealt with here and in future quite summarily, as he published a truthful and clearly written memoir of his own career; but the achievements of the two others will be narrated in greater detail and at more length. I think it will be easiest for myself to set forth the narrative and for my readers to follow it if I begin from the period when, after the dissolution of the Achaean League by the kings of Macedonia, the cities began again to approach each other with a view to its renewal. Henceforward the League continued to grow until it reached in my own time the state of completion I have just been describing.

(41) It was in the 124th Olympiad that Patrae and Dyme took the initiative, by entering into a league, just about the date of the deaths of Ptolemy son of Lagus, Lysimachus, Seleucus, and Ptolemy Ceraunus, which all occurred in this Olympiad. The condition of the Achaean nation before this date had been more or less as follows. Their first king was Tisamenus the son of Orestes, who, when expelled from Sparta on the return of the Heraclidae, occupied Achaea, and they continued to be ruled by kings of his house down to Ogygus. Being dissatisfied with the rule of Ogygus' sons, which was despotical and not constitutional, they changed their government to a democracy. After this, down to the reigns of Alexander and Philip, their fortunes varied according to circumstances, but they always endeavoured, as I said, to keep

their League a democracy. This consisted of twelve cities, which still all exist with the exception of Olenus and of Helice, which was engulfed by the sea a little before the battle of Leuctra. These cities are Patrae, Dyme, Pharae, Tritaea, Leontium, Aegium, Aegira, Pellene, Bura, and Caryneia. After the time of Alexander and previous to the above Olympiad they fell, chiefly thanks to the kings of Macedon, into such a state of discord and ill-feeling that all the cities separated from the League and began to act against each others' interests. The consequence was that some of them were garrisoned by Demetrius and Cassander and afterwards by Antigonus Gonatas, and some even had tyrants imposed on them by the latter, who planted more monarchs in Greece than any other king. But, as I said above, about the 124th Olympiad they began to repent and form fresh leagues. (This was about the date of Pyrrhus' crossing to Italy). The first cities to do so were Dyme, Patrae, Tritaea, and Pharae, and for this reason we do not even find any formal inscribed record of their adherence to the League. About five years afterwards the people of Aegium expelled their garrison and joined the League, and the Burians were the next to do so, after putting their tyrant to death. Caryneia joined almost at the same time, for Iseas, its tyrant, when he saw the garrison expelled from Aegium, and the monarch of Bura killed by Margus and the Achaeans, and war just about to be made on himself by all the towns round, abdicated and, on receiving an assurance from the Achaeans that his life would be spared, added his city to the League.

(42) Why, the reader will ask, do I go back to these times? It is, firstly, to show which of the original Achaean cities took the first steps to re-form the League and at what dates, and, secondly, that my assertion regarding their political principle may be confirmed by the actual evidence of facts. What I asserted was that the Achaeans always followed one single policy, ever attracting others by the offer of their own equality and liberty and ever making war on and crushing those who either themselves or through the kings attempted to enslave their native cities, and that, in this manner and pursuing this purpose, they accomplished their task in part unaided and in part with the help of allies. For the Achaean political principle must be credited also with the results furthering their end, to which their allies in subsequent years contributed. Though they took so much part in the enterprises of others, and especially in many of those of the Romans which resulted brilliantly, they never showed the least desire to gain any private profit from their success, but demanded, in exchange for the zealous aid they rendered their allies, nothing beyond the liberty of all states and the union of the Peloponnesians. This will be more clearly evident when we come to see the League in active operation.

(43) For twenty-five years, then, this league of cities continued, electing for a certain period a Secretary of State and two Generals. After this they decided to elect one General and entrust him with the general direction of their affairs, the first to be nominated to this honourable office being Margus of Caryneia. Four years later during Margus' term of office, Aratus of Sicyon, though only twenty years of age, freed his city from its tyrant by his enterprise and courage, and, having always been a passionate admirer of the Achaean polity, made his own city a member of the League. Eight years after this, during his second term of office as General, he laid a plot to rule the citadel of Corinth which was held by Antigonus, thus delivering the Peloponnesians from a great source of fear, and induced the city he had liberated to join the League. In the same term

of office he obtained the adhesion of Megara to the Achaeans by the same means. These events took place in the year before that defeat of the Carthaginians which forced them to evacuate Sicily and submit for the first time to pay tribute to Rome. Having in so short a space of time thus materially advanced his projects, he continued to govern the Achaean nation, all his schemes and action being directed to one object: the expulsion of the Macedonians from the Peloponnese, the suppression of the tyrants, and the re-establishment on a sure basis of the ancient freedom of every state. During the life of Antigonus Gonatas he continued to offer a most effectual opposition both to the meddlesomeness of this king and the lust for power of the Aetolians, although the two were so unscrupulous and venturesome that they entered into an arrangement for the purpose of dissolving the Achaean League. (44) But, on the death of Antigonus, the Achaeans even made an alliance with the Aetolians and supported them ungrudgingly in the war against Demetrius, so that, for the time at least, their estrangement and hostility ceased, and a more or less friendly and sociable feeling sprang up between them. Demetrius only reigned for ten years, his death taking place at the time the Romans first crossed to Illyria, and after this the tide of events seemed to flow for a time in favour of the Achaeans' constant purpose; for the Peloponnesian tyrants were much cast down by the death of Demetrius, who had been, so to speak, their furnisher and paymaster, and equally so by the threatening attitude of Aratus, who demanded that they should depose themselves, offering abundance of gifts and honours to those who consented to do so, and menacing those who turned a deaf ear to him with still more abundant chastisement on the part of the Achaeans. They therefore hurried to accede to his demand, laying down their tyrannies, setting their respective cities free, and joining the Achaean League. Lydiades of Megalopolis had even foreseen what was likely to happen, and with great wisdom and good sense had forestalled the death of Demetrius and of his own free will laid down his tyranny and adhered to the national government. Afterwards, Aristomachus, tyrant of Argos, Xenon, tyrant of Hermione, and Cleonymus, tyrant of Phlius, also resigned and joined the democratic Achaean League.

Adapted from W.R. Paton (trans.), *Polybius, The Histories*, vol. 6, Books 28-39 (Cambridge, Mass., Harvard University Press, 1927)

Reading 5d Lucian, *The Cynic*

Following the death of Socrates in 399 BC, his greatest pupil, Plato, founded the Academy, a philosophical school for men who withdrew from civic life to dedicate themselves to the life of ideas. Whereas Socrates had claimed that he knew only that he knew nothing, and limited his philosophy to questioning what we think we know in order to winnow down our beliefs to a fundamental core, Plato sought to build upon that core a positive, systematic philosophy, including a theory of ideas, a doctrine of the soul's immortality, and a political philosophy that theorized about the best form of government. After Plato, however, at the beginning of the Hellenistic period, the Academy returned to its Socratic roots, to questioning rather than building knowledge. It became a school for Skeptics: philosophers who believed that we can know nothing for certain. Another philosopher, Diogenes, the founder of the Cynic school of philosophy, emphasized another vein of Socrates' teaching: his rejection of social convention and worldly goods in favour of the true and sufficient goods of a virtuous life. Like another of the major Hellenistic philosophical schools, the Stoic school, the Cynics aimed at a secure life, a life in which happiness did not depend on external goods and was immune to external events. For the Cynics, this meant living a simple, natural life. The Cynics scandalized people by their trenchant criticisms of contemporary life and by their unconventional behaviour.

In the Classical period, the ideal of self-sufficiency had gone hand in-hand with the ideal of collective self-rule, through civic participation. While reading this dialogue, consider how the Cynics' conception of self-sufficiency, as involving the rejection of society and of worldly goods, might be seen as a reaction to the changed conditions of life in the Greek cities of the Hellenistic period.

The following dialogue was written by the satirist Lucian of Samosata (who lived in the second century after Christ). In it, he ('Lycinus') discusses the Cynic's way of life with a Cynic philosopher.

Scene: Lycinus asks a Cynic about his life

[1] **Lycinus:** Give an account of yourself, my man. You wear a beard and let your hair grow; you eschew shirts; you exhibit your skin; your feet are bare; you choose a wandering, outcast, beastly life; unlike other people, you make your own body the object of your severities; you go from place to place sleeping on the hard ground where chance finds you, with the result that your old cloak, neither light nor soft nor gay to begin with, has a plentiful load of filth to carry about with it. Why all this?

Cynic: It meets my needs. It was easy to come by, and it gives its owner no trouble. It is the cloak for me. [2] Pray tell me, do you not call extravagance a vice?

Lycinus: Oh, yes.

Cynic: And economy a virtue?

Lycinus: Yes, again.

Cynic: Then, if you find me living economically, and others extravagantly, why blame me instead of them?

Lycinus: I do not call your life more economical than other people's; I call it more destitute—destitution and want, that is what it is; you are no better than the poor who beg their daily bread.

[3] **Cynic:** That brings us to the questions, What is want, and what is sufficiency? Shall we try to find the answers?

Lycinus: If you like, yes.

Cynic: A man's sufficiency is that which meets his necessities; will that do?

Lycinus: I pass that.

Cynic: And want occurs when the supply falls short of necessity—does not meet the need?

Lycinus: Yes.

Cynic: Very well, then, I am not in want; nothing of mine fails to satisfy my need.

[4] **Lycinus:** How do you make that out?

Cynic: Well, consider the purpose of anything we require; the purpose of a house is protection?

Lycinus: Yes.

Cynic: Clothing—what is that for? protection too, I think.

Lycinus: Yes.

Cynic: But now, pray, what is the purpose of the protection, in turn? the better condition of the protected, I presume.

Lycinus: I agree.

Cynic: Then do you think my feet are in worse condition than yours?

Lycinus: I cannot say.

Cynic: Oh, yes; look at it this way: what have feet to do?

Lycinus: Walk.

Cynic: And do you think my feet walk worse than yours, or than the average man's?

Lycinus: No, not at all.

Cynic: Then they are not in worse condition, if they do their work as well.

Lycinus: That may be so.

Cynic: So it appears that, as far as feet go, I am in no worse condition than other people.

Lycinus: No, I do not think you are.

Cynic: Well, the rest of my body, then? If it is in worse condition, it must be weaker, strength being the virtue of the body. Is mine weaker?

Lycinus: Not that I see.

Cynic: Consequently, neither my feet nor the rest of my body need protection, it seems; if they did, they would be in bad condition; for want is always an evil, and deteriorates the thing concerned. But again, there is no sign, either, of my, body's being nourished the worse for its nourishments being of a common sort.

Lycinus: None whatever.

Cynic: It would not be healthy, if it were badly nourished; for bad food injures the body.

Lycinus: That is true.

[5] **Cynic:** If so, it is for you to explain why you blame me and depreciate my life and call it miserable.

Lycinus: Easily explained. Nature (which you honour) and the gods have given us the earth, and brought all sorts of good things out of it, providing us with abundance not merely for our necessities, but for our pleasures; and then you abstain from all or nearly all of it, and utilize these good things no more than the beasts. Your drink is water, just like theirs; you eat what you pick up, like a dog, and the dog's bed is as good as yours; straw is enough for either of you. Then your clothes are no more presentable than a beggar's. Now, if this sort of contentment is to pass for wisdom, God must have been all wrong in making sheep woolly, filling grapes with wine, and providing all our infinite variety of oil, honey, and the rest, that we might have food of every sort, pleasant drink, money, soft beds, fine houses, all the wonderful paraphernalia of civilization, in fact; for the productions of art are God's gifts to us too. To live without all these would be miserable enough even if one could not help it, as prisoners cannot, for instance; it is far more so if the abstention is forced upon a man by himself; it is then sheer madness.

[6] **Cynic:** You may be right. But take this case, now. A rich man, indulging genial kindly instincts, entertains at a banquet all sorts and conditions of men; some of them are sick, others sound, and the dishes provided are as various as the guests. There is one of these to whom nothing comes amiss; he has his finger in every dish, not only the ones within easy reach, but those some way off that were intended for the invalids; this though he is in rude health, has not more than one stomach, requires little to nourish him, and is likely to be upset by a surfeit. What is your opinion of this gentleman? is he a man of sense?

Lycinus: Why, no.

Cynic: Is he temperate?

Lycinus: No, nor that.

[7] **Cynic:** Well, then there is another guest at the same table; he seems unconscious of all that variety, fixes on some dish close by that suits his need, eats moderately of it and confines himself to it without a glance at the rest. You surely find him a more temperate and better man than the other?

Lycinus: Certainly.

Cynic: Do you see, or must I explain?

Lycinus: What?

Cynic: That the hospitable entertainer is God, who provides this variety of all kinds that each may have something to suit him; this is for the sound, that for the sick; this for the strong and that for the weak; it is not all for all of us; each is to take what is within reach, and of that only what he most needs.

[8] Now you others are like the greedy unrestrained person who lays hands on everything; local productions will not do for you, the world must be your storehouse; your native land and its seas are quite insufficient; you purchase your pleasures from the ends of the earth, prefer the exotic to the home-grown, the costly to the cheap, the rare to the common; in fact you would rather have troubles and complications than avoid them. Most of the precious instruments of happiness that you so pride yourselves upon are won only by vexation and worry. Give a moment's thought, if you will, to the gold you all pray for, to the silver, the costly houses, the elaborate

dresses, and do not forget their conditions precedent, the trouble and toil and danger they cost—nay, the blood and mortality and ruin; not only do numbers perish at sea on their account, or endure miseries in the acquisition or working of them; besides that, they have very likely to be fought for, or the desire of them makes friends plot against friends, children against parents, wives against husbands.

[9] And how purposeless it all is! Embroidered clothes have no more warmth in them than others, gilded houses keep out the rain no better, the drink is no sweeter out of a silver cup, or a gold one for that matter, an ivory bed makes sleep no softer; on the contrary, your fortunate man on his ivory bed between his delicate sheets constantly finds himself wooing sleep in vain. And as to the elaborate dressing of food, I need hardly say that instead of aiding nutrition it injures the body and breeds diseases in it.

[10] As superfluous to mention the abuse of the sexual instinct, so easily managed if indulgence were not made an object. And if madness and corruption were limited to that. But men must take nowadays to perverting the use of everything they have, turning it to unnatural purposes, like him who insists on making a carriage of a couch.

Lycinus: Is there such a person?

Cynic: Why, he is you; you for whom men are beasts of burden, you who make them shoulder your couch-carriages, and loll up there yourselves in luxury, driving your men like so many asses and bidding them turn this way and not that; this is one of the outward and visible signs of your happiness. [11] Again, when people use edible things not for food but to get dye out of—the murex-dyers, for instance—are they not abusing God's gifts?

Lycinus: Certainly not; the flesh of the murex can provide a pigment as well as food.

Cynic: Ah, but it was not made for that. So you can force a mixing-bowl to do the work of a saucepan; but that is not what it was made for. However, it is impossible to exhaust these people's wrong-headedness; it is endless. And because I will not join them, you reproach me. My life is that of the orderly man I described; I make merry on what comes to hand, use what is cheap, and have no yearning for the elaborate and exotic.

[12] Moreover, if you think that because I need and use but few things I live the life of a beast, that argument lands you in the conclusion that the gods are yet lower than the beasts; for they have no needs at all. But to clear your ideas on the comparative merits of great and small needs, you have only to reflect that children have more needs than adults, women than men, the sick than the well, and generally the inferior than the superior. Accordingly, the gods have no needs, and those men the fewest who are nearest gods.

[13] Take Heracles, the best man that ever lived, a divine man, and rightly reckoned a god; was it wrong-headedness that made him go about in nothing but a lion's skin, insensible to all the needs you feel? No, he was not wrong-headed, who righted other people's wrongs; he was not poor, who was lord of land and sea. Wherever he went, he was master; he never met his superior or his equal as long as he lived. Do you suppose he could not get sheets and shoes, and therefore went as he did? absurd! he

had self-control and fortitude; he wanted power, and not luxury.

[14] And Theseus his disciple—king of all the Athenians, son of Posidon, says the legend, and best of his generation—he too chose to go naked and unshod; it was his pleasure to let his hair and beard grow; and not his pleasure only, but all his contemporaries'; they were better men than you, and would no more have let you shave them than a lion would; soft smooth flesh was very well for women, they thought; as for them, they were men, and were content to look it; the beard was man's ornament, like the lion's, or the horse's mane; God had made certain beautiful and decorative additions to those creatures; and so he had to man, in the beard. Well, I admire those ancients and would fain be like them; I have not the smallest ' admiration for the present generation's wonderful felicity—tables! clothes! bodies artificially polished all over! not a hair to grow on any of the places where nature plants it!

[15] My prayer would be that my feet might be just hoofs, like Chiron's in the story, that I might need bedclothes no more than the lion, and costly food no more than the dog. Let my sufficient bed be the whole earth, my house this universe, and the food of my choice the easiest procurable. May I have no need, I nor any that I call friend, of gold and silver. For all human evils spring from the desire of these, seditions and wars, conspiracies and murders. The fountain of them all is the desire of more. Never be that desire mine; let me never wish for more than my share, but be content with less.

[16] Such are our aspirations—considerably different from other people's. It is no wonder that our get-up is peculiar, since the peculiarity of our underlying principle is so marked. I cannot make out why you allow a harpist his proper robe and get-up—and so the flute-player has his, and the tragic actor his—but will not be consistent and recognize any uniform for a good man; the good man must be like every one else, of course, regardless of the fact that every one else is all wrong. Well, if the good are to have a uniform of their own, there can be none better than that which the average sensual man will consider most improper, and reject with most decision for himself.

[17] Now my uniform consists of a rough hairy skin, a threadbare cloak, long hair, and bare feet, whereas yours is for all the world that of some minister to vice; there is not a pin to choose between you—the gay colours, the soft texture, the number of garments you are swathed in, the shoes, the sleeked hair, the very scent of you; for the more blessed you are, the more do you exhale perfumes like his. What value can one attach to a man whom one's nose would identify for one of those minions? The consequence is, you are equal to no more work than they are, and to quite as much pleasure. You feed like them, you sleep like them, you walk like them—except so far as you avoid walking by getting yourselves conveyed like parcels by porters or animals; as for me, my feet take me anywhere that I want to go. I can put up with cold and heat and be content with the works of God— such a miserable wretch am I—whereas you blessed ones are displeased with everything that happens and grumble without ceasing; what is is intolerable, what is not you pine for, in winter for summer, in summer for winter, in heat for cold, in cold for heat, as fastidious and peevish as so many invalids; only their reason is to be found in their illness, and yours in your characters.

[18] And then, because we occasionally make mistakes in practice, you recommend us to change our plan and correct our principles, the fact being that you in your own affairs go quite at random, never acting on deliberation or reason, but always on habit and appetite. You are no better than people washed about by a flood; they drift with the current, you with your appetites. There is a story of a man on a vicious horse that just gives your case. The horse ran away with him, and at the pace it was going at he could not get off. A man in the way asked him where he was off to; 'wherever this beast chooses,' was the reply. So if one asked you where you were bound for, if you cared to tell the truth you would say either generally, wherever your appetites chose, or in particular, where pleasure chose to-day, where fancy chose to-morrow, and where avarice chose another day; or sometimes it is rage, sometimes fear, sometimes any other such feeling, that takes you whither it will. You ride not one horse, but many at different times, all vicious, and all out of control. They are carrying you straight for pits and cliffs; but you do not realize that you are bound for a fall till the fall comes.

[19] The old cloak, the shaggy hair, the whole get-up that you ridicule, has this effect; it enables me to live a quiet life, doing as I will and keeping the company I want. No ignorant uneducated person will have anything to say to one dressed like this; and the soft livers turn the other way as soon as I am in sight. But the refined, the reasonable, the earnest, seek me out; they are the men who seek me, because they are the men I wish to see. At the doors of those whom the world counts happy I do not dance attendance; their gold crowns and their purple I call ostentation, and them I laugh to scorn.

[20] These externals that you pour contempt upon, you may learn that they are seemly enough not merely for good men, but for gods, if you will look at the gods' statues; do those resemble you, or me? Do not confine your attention to Greece; take a tour round the foreign temples too, and see whether the gods treat their hair and beards like me, or let the painters and sculptors shave them. Most of them, you will find, have no more shirt than I have, either. I hope you will not venture to describe again as mean an appearance that is accepted as godlike.

Adapted from H.W. Fowler and F.G. Fowler, *The Works of Lucian of Samosata* (Oxford: The Clarendon Press, 1905)

Chapter 6:
Roman Expansion

READING 6A. POLYBIUS: THE ROMAN CONSTITUTION

The Greek historian Polybius (c.200-c.118 B.C.) witnessed and documented the expansion of Rome into a great Mediterranean power. He lived at the time of several notable events, including the destruction of both Carthage and Corinth by Rome in 146 B.C., and he understood that he was witnessing the transition of power from the Greeks to the Romans. Polybius himself lived in Rome for sixteen years, one of a thousand Greek hostages brought to Rome in 170 B.C. to ensure good behaviour of the kingdoms and leagues of Greece. While he was there, however, he came to understand and appreciate Roman political and social institutions. He credited the might of Rome to the excellence of its citizens and to their political and social organization. In his work, The Histories, he outlines part of the history of Rome and explains its unusual organization.

In researching his history, Polybius consulted official documents and written memoirs and drew on his own first-hand accounts of some events as well as reports of others. His work provides us with valuable information on the political, social, religious, military and economic institutions of the Republic. But more than simply cataloguing facts, he sought to understand and explain the causes of events and to discover their interrelation. Polybius outlines the overall purpose of his work in his introduction: "Who," he inquires, "is so thoughtless and so irresponsible as not to wish to know by what means, and under what kind of construction, the Romans succeeded in subjugating nearly the whole inhabited world to their sole rule in not quite fifty-three years-an event unique in history?"

In The Histories, Polybius describes the nature and function of the Roman constitution as he understood it. Because of his Greek heritage and education, he perceived the Roman constitution in terms of Greek ideas and expectations. Nevertheless, his report provides the basis for our own understanding of the Roman political and social structure. Polybius saw that three features of government—monarchy, oligarchy and democracy—were all present in the Roman system, and that all functioned together within an elaborate system of checks and balances. Moreover, his extensive description of the nature of the Roman constitution has influenced generations of politicians and scholars for the last 2000 years, providing them with the tools to theorize about and formulate different political systems.

As you read, consider the following questions:

- Which features of the Roman constitution are monarchic, which oligarchic, and which democratic?
- How was authority over what areas divided among the different elements of government?
- In Polybius' view, what were the checks and balances that allowed the Romans to function?
- Were the different elements of the constitution—the monarchic, oligarchic, and democratic—really equal to one another? Explain why they are equal or why they are not.

Polybius, *Histories*, Book 6

I am aware that some will wonder why I have waited until this point before giving my account of the Roman constitution, since this obliges me to interrupt the run of my narrative. I have always regarded this account as one of the essential parts of my whole work, as I have surely made clear in many places and especially in the prefatory remarks dealing with the fundamental principles of my history, where I said that my highest hope is that readers of my work might gain a knowledge of how it happened, and by virtue of what specific political institutions, that in less than fifty-three years nearly the whole world was overcome and fell under the single dominion of Rome, something quite unique in human history.

Having decided to discuss the matter, I found no occasion more suitable than the present for turning my attention to Rome's constitution and testing the truth of what I am about to say on the subject. ...

On the Forms of States.

[3] In the past various Greek states have risen to greatness and then experienced a complete change of fortune. With these it is easy both to describe their past and to make predictions about their future. For it is easy to report the known facts, and it is not hard to predict the future by inference from the past. It is different with the Roman state, since it is difficult to explain the present situation, given the complicated character of its constitution. Nor is it easy to predict the future because of our ignorance of the specific features of public and private life at Rome in the past. Careful attention and study are therefore required if we want to gain a clear understanding of the distinctive qualities of their constitution.

Most of those who have attempted to offer a systematic analysis of such matters distinguish between three kinds of constitutions, which they call kingship, aristocracy, and democracy. In my opinion, however, we ought to ask them to enlighten us as to whether they assert that these three kinds are the only varieties or whether they regard them as the best variety. Either way, I think that they are wrong. For we must clearly regard as the best constitution one that combines all three of these varieties, as has been proved to us not only theoretically but by actual experience, since Lycurgus was the first to draw up a constitution — that of Sparta — on this principle. …

On the Roman Constitution at its Prime

[11] Now, I have already described in my history the growth of the Roman state. Here I will explain what its constitution was like at the time of their defeat at Cannae, when the Romans were brought face-to-face with disaster. … As for the Roman constitution, it shared all the three kinds of government that I mentioned above. Both the design of the constitution and its subsequent implementation demonstrated such fairness and propriety in its use of these three elements that it was impossible even for a native Roman to declare with certainty whether the whole system was aristocratic, democratic, or monarchical. This was only natural. For if one focussed one's attention on the power of the consuls, the constitution seemed completely monarchical and royal; if one looked at the power of the senate, it seemed to be aristocratic; and if one looked at the power of the masses, it seemed clearly to be a democracy. The parts of the state falling under the control of each element were and, with a few modifications still are, as follows.

[12] **The Consuls.** The consuls, before leading out the legions, stay in Rome and exercise authority over all public administration, since all the other magistrates except the tribunes are under them and take their orders. It is the consuls who introduce embassies to the senate. In addition to this, the consuls consult the senate on matters of importance, and they see to it that senatorial decrees are carried out. If there are any matters of state that require the authorization of the people, it is the consuls' duty to see to them: to summon the assemblies, to introduce proposals, and to oversee the implementation of the decisions. As for preparation for war and the general conduct of military operations, they have almost unlimited power; for they have the authority to decide what resources to demand from the allies, to appoint military tribunes, to recruit soldiers and select those who are fittest for service. They also have the authority to inflict, when on active service, punishment on anyone under their command. Finally, they are authorized to spend any sum from the public funds, being accompanied by a quaestor who faithfully executes their instructions.

So that if one looks at this part of the administration alone, one may reasonably describe the constitution as a pure monarchy or kingship. (I may remark that any changes in these matters or in others of which I am about to speak that may be made in present or future times do not in any way affect the truth of the views I here state.)

[13] **The Senate.** Let us now consider the senate. It has the control of the treasury, and all Rome's revenues and expenditures are regulated by it. For with the exception of payments made to the consuls, the quaestors are

not allowed to disburse money for anything without a decree of the senate. Even the outlay of money that the censors make every five years for construction and repairs of public building — an item of expenditure which is far greater and more important than any other — is under the control of the senate, which makes a grant to the censors for the purpose. Any crimes committed in Italy that require a public investigation, such as treason, conspiracy, poisoning, and assassination, are under the jurisdiction of the senate. In addition, if any private person or community in Italy requires arbitration or claims damages or requires aide or protection, the senate attends to all such matters. It also deals with the sending of embassies to countries outside of Italy, whether the purpose is to settle differences, offer friendly advice, impose demands, receive submission, or declare war. The senate also decides how and whether it should receive embassies arriving in Rome and what answers to give them. All these matters are in the control of the senate, and the people have nothing to do with them at all. So that again to one residing in Rome during the absence of the consuls the constitution appears to be entirely aristocratic; and this is the conviction of many Greek states and many kings, since the senate manages all business connected with them.

[14] **The People.** After this someone might naturally be inclined to ask what constitutional role is left for the people, considering that the senate has all the specific responsibilities that I mentioned, and, most importantly, manages all matters of revenue and expenditure, and considering that the consuls again have uncontrolled authority as regards armaments and operations in the field. But nevertheless there is a role left for the people, and a very important one. For it is the people that alone has the right to confer offices and inflict punishment, the only bonds by which kingdoms and states—indeed human society in general—are held together. …

The people are the only court that can impose a capital penalty, and it is before the people that offences punishable by a fine are tried if the accused has held high office. In capital trials they have a practice which is praiseworthy and should be mentioned. They allow those on trial for their lives when found guilty to leave the country openly, thus inflicting voluntary exile on themselves, provided that they do this before the last of the tribes that pronounce the verdict has voted. Such exiles enjoy safety in the territories of Naples, Praeneste, Tibur, and other cities that have treaties. In addition, it is the people who bestow office on the deserving, and this is the highest reward of virtue to be found in a state. The people also have the power to pass and repeal laws, and have the most important function of all: they deliberate on the question of war and peace. Finally, it is the people who ratify or reject alliances, terms of peace, and treaties. Consequently, here again one might plausibly say that the people's share in the government is the greatest, and that the constitution is a democratic one.

Checks and Balances

[15] Having demonstrated how political power is distributed among the different parts of the state, I will now explain how each of the three parts is able, if it chooses, to oppose or support the others.

When the consuls departs with his army, he is invested with the powers already mentioned, and he appears to have absolute authority in all matters necessary for carrying out his purpose. In fact, however, he requires the support of the people and the senate, and he is not able to bring his operations to a conclusion without them. For it is obvious that the legions require constant supplies, and the consent of the senate is needed to provide grain, clothing, or pay. As a result, a general's plans can be rendered useless if the senate chooses to be deliberately negligent or obstructive. The senate also decides whether or not a general can carry out his plans completely, since the senate has the authority either to replace him at the end of his year's term of office or to retain him in command. Again it is in the senate's power to add distinction and glory to the successes of a general or on the other hand to obscure and belittle them. For the Romans have parades that they call 'triumphs', in which the generals bring a visual demonstration of their achievements before the eyes of their fellow-citizens, but these cannot be celebrated with appropriate pomp — or sometimes celebrated at all — unless the senate consents and provides the necessary funds.

As for the people, it is highly necessary for the consuls to court their favour, no matter how far away from home they may be, since, as I said, the people approve or annul terms of peace and treaties. Still more importantly, on laying down office the consuls are obliged to account for their actions to the people.

As a result of this arrangement the consuls must continually seek the good will of both the senate and the people.

[16] In the same way the senate is also obliged to pay close attention to the people in public affairs and respect the wishes of the people, although it, too, has immense power. Without the authorization of the people, it cannot carry out inquiries into the most grave and important offences against the state, punishable by death, and correct them. The same is true in matters that directly affect the senate itself. For if anyone introduces a law meant to strip the senate of part of its traditional authority, or to abolish the precedence and other distinctions of senators, or even to interfere in their private business, it is the people alone that has the power to pass or reject such a measure. And, most importantly, if a single one of the tribunes interposes a veto, the senate is unable to make a final decision about any issue, and cannot even hold meetings, whether formal or informal. Here it is to be observed that the tribunes are always required to implement the decrees of the people and to pay close attention to their wishes. Therefore, for all these reasons, the senate is afraid of the masses and cannot ignore the popular will.

[17] Similarly, again, the people must submit to the senate and respect its members both in public and in private. Through the whole of Italy the censors give out a vast number of contracts, which it would not be easy to enumerate, for the construction and upkeep of public buildings. In addition to these are many state properties that are rented out, such as navigable rivers, harbours, gardens, mines, lands, in fact everything that forms part of Roman government. The people are employed in all these matters, and almost everyone is either a contractor or works for one. For some people purchase the contracts from the censors; others are their partners; others guarantee the contracts or pledge their own fortunes to the state for this purpose. In all these matters, however, the senate is supreme. It can grant extensions; it can relieve the contractor if any accident occurs; and if the work proves to be impossible to complete it can annul a contract. ... What is even more important is that in most civil trials of any magnitude the judges are appointed from the senate, whether

public or private. The result is that all citizens are at the mercy of the senate, and because they look forward with alarm to the uncertainty of litigation, they are very hesitant to obstruct or resist the senate's decisions. Similarly, everyone is reluctant to resist the wishes of the consuls, since practically everyone comes under their authority during military service.

[18] Because each element of the Roman state is able to hamper the others or co-operate with them, their union is sufficient to meet any emergency, and it is impossible to find a better political system than this. For whenever the menace of some common danger from abroad requires them to act in unison and to support each other, the strength of the state becomes so great that no necessary measure is neglected, since everyone competes in devising the best means of meeting the need of the hour, nor can any decision arrived at fail to be executed promptly, as all are co-operating both in public and in private to the accomplishment of the task that they have set themselves. Because of this, their constitution possesses an irresistible power of attaining every goal that it sets itself.

When they are freed from external threats, however, they reap the inevitable harvest of the good fortune and prosperity that comes from their success. This prosperity, however, brings with it a susceptibility to flattery, idleness, and insolent pride, as indeed happens often enough. It is at this moment, however, the constitution provides a remedy for the evil from which it suffers. For if one class becomes disproportionately influential and begins to aim at control and becomes too dominant, because (as we have seen) none of the three is absolute, the ambitions of one class can be opposed and thwarted by the others. For this reason no class will excessively outgrow the others or treat them with contempt, and everything remains in equilibrium because any aggressive impulse is sure to be checked from the outset by the fear of being interfered with by the others. ...

Adapted from Evelyn S. Shuckburgh, *Polybius, Histories* (London: Macmillan. 1889).

Reading 6b. Livy: The Case of Spurius Ligustinus

Rome's territorial expansion in the third and second centuries B.C. came at a great cost to poorer farmers. Traditionally, Rome had recruited its army from the farmers and small landholders of Italy, but almost continual military campaigning in the second century resulted in great loss of life and severe hardship. The soldiers who were drafted often found themselves fighting in foreign regions, such as Spain and North Africa, where campaigning was harsh. Armies often suffered from the lack of discipline and poor morale with the results that desertions and mutinies were threatened. The problem was exacerbated because many poor farmers had drifted away from their small land holdings and had settled in Rome. Some had lost their land when their families had been unable to maintain the farms while they were away on campaign. The result was a decline in the number of eligible men available for duty.

Some of these issues are echoed in the speech of Spurius Ligustinus as presented in the writing of the historian Livy. The speech was supposedly made in 171 B.C. during a debate over recruitment of veterans for the war against Macedonia. In this instance, a debate had arisen concerning the age at which a man should be exempt from military service, and whether a rank attained in one campaign should be maintained when that individual was levied for another battle. In his speech, Spurius Ligustinus, a veteran and former chief centurion, enumerates some of the problems that he faced.

Consider the following:

- What is Spurius Ligustinus' personal background and history of engagements? How long has he served in the army?
- What is Spurius Ligustinus' opinion about recruitment and the ranking of veterans?

Livy, Histories, 42. 32-35

32. [5] One of the consuls, P. Licinius, obtained Macedonia as his province, and C. Cassius, Italy. They then drew lots for the legions; the first and third were to be taken to Macedonia; the second and fourth to remain in Italy. [6] The consuls carried out the recuitment of troops for these legions much more carefully than at other times. Licinius called up the old soldiers and centurions, and many volunteers gave in their names because they saw that those who had served in the former Macedonian war or against Antiochus were rich men. [7] The military tribunes were choosing the centurions, not in order of precedence, but picking out the best men, and twenty-three centurions of the front rank appealed to the tribunes of the plebs. Two of the tribunes were in favour of referring the matter to the consuls, on the ground that the decision ought to rest with those to whom the recruitment had been entrusted. [8] The rest said they would go into the reasons of the appeal, and if an injustice had been done, they would come to the aid of their fellow-citizens.

33. The case was argued before the tribunes at their tribunal; M. Popilius and the con-

sul were present with the centurions. [2] The consul demanded that the matter should be heard before the assembly, and the assembly was accordingly convened. M. Popilius, who had been consul two years previously, spoke on behalf of the centurions. He reminded the assembly that these men had completed their term of military service, and were worn out by age and unceasing toil. [3] Still, they in no way objected to give their services to the state, only they protested against being assigned a position inferior to the one they held when on active service. [4] The consul P. Licinius ordered the resolutions passed by the senate to be read, first the one in which the senate decided upon war with Perseus, then the one in which it was determined that as many of the veteran centurions as possible should be called up for the war, and that there should be no exemption for any man who was not over fifty years of age. [5] He strongly deprecated any step being taken which would hamper the military tribunes in their task of recuiting troops for a fresh war, so close to Italy and against an extremely powerful monarch, or which would prevent the consul from assigning to each man the rank which, in the best interests of the republic, ought to be assigned to him. [6] If any doubt was still felt in the matter, let it be referred to the senate.

34. After the consul had said what he wanted to say, Spurius Ligustinus, one of those who were appealing to the tribunes, begged the consul and the tribunes to allow him to say a few words to the Assembly. [2] They all gave him permission, and he is recorded to have spoken to the following effect:

"My fellow citizens, I am Spurius Ligustinus, a Sabine by birth, a member of the Crustuminian tribe. My father left me a few acres of land and a small cottage in which I was born and bred, and I am living there today. [3] As soon as I came of age my father gave me his brother's daughter as a wife. She brought nothing with her but her personal freedom and her modesty, and together with these a fruitfulness which would have been enough even in a wealthy house. [4] We have six sons and two daughters. Four of our sons are adults, two are boys, and both the daughters are married. [5] I became a soldier in the consulship of P. Sulpicius and C. Aurelius [200 BC]. For two years I was a common soldier in the army, fighting against Philip in Macedonia; in the third year T. Quinctius Flamininus gave me in consideration of my courage the command of the tenth company of *hastati*. [6] After Philip and the Macedonians were defeated and we were brought back to Italy and disbanded, I at once volunteered to go with the consul M. Porcius to Spain. [7] Men who during a long service have had experience of him and of other generals know that of all living commanders not one has shown himself a keener observer or more accurate judge of military valour. It was this commander who thought me worthy of being appointed first centurion in the *hastati*. [8] Again I served, for the third time, as a volunteer in the army which was sent against Antiochus and the Aetolians. I was made first centurion of the vanguard by Manius Acilius. After Antiochus was driven out of Greece and the Aetolians were subjugated, we were brought back to Italy, where I served the two succeeding years in legions that were raised annually. [9] Then I served in Spain, once under Q. Fulvius Flaccus and again under Ti. Sempronius Gracchus. I was brought home by Flaccus amongst those whom, as a reward for their courage, he was bringing home to join his triumph. [10] I joined Tiberius Gracchus at his request. Four times, within a few years, have I been first centurion in the *triarii*; I have been rewarded for my courage by my commanders thirty-four times; I have received six civic crowns. [11] I have served for twenty-two years in the army and I am more than fifty years old. But suppose that I had not served my full time and my age did not give me exemption. I was still able to give you four soldiers for one (that is, myself), and so it would have been a right and proper thing that I should be discharged. [12] But I want you to take what I have said simply as a statement of my case. [13] So far as anyone who is raising troops judges me to be an efficient soldier, I am not going to plead excuses. [14] What rank the military tribunes think that I deserve is for them to decide; I will take care that no man shall surpass me in courage. I always have done so, as my commanders and fellow-campaigners can attest.

[15] And as for you, my fellow soldiers, you are only exercising your right of appeal. In your younger days you never did anything against the authority of the magistrates and the senate, and so now too it is only just and proper that you should place yourselves at the disposal of the senate and the consuls and count any position in which you are to defend your country as an honourable one."

35. When he had finished speaking, the consul commended him warmly and took him from the assembly to the senate. [2] There, too, he was thanked by the senate, and the military tribunes made him *primus pilus* in the first legion in recognition of his bravery. The other centurions abandoned their appeal and answered to the roll-call without hesitation.

Adapted from Rev. Canon Roberts, *Livy. History of Rome, an English Translation* (New York. E. P. Dutton and Co. 1912).

Chapter 7:

The Gracchi

READING 7A. PLUTARCH: TIBERIUS GRACCUS

By the mid-second century B.C., Rome was the undisputed master of the Mediterranean world. The territorial acquisitions and new found wealth that came with this new empire brought with them social, political and economic problems. The tribunate of Tiberius Gracchus in 133 B.C. marks a watershed moment in Republican history. It was the beginning of the end of the Roman Republic. Tiberius was a well-educated young aristocrat who sought to make changes. His primary goal was to institute land reforms. He believed that if the large tracts of land owned by the Roman state were subdivided and distributed to the urban poor, the number of unemployed men in Rome might be lessened. By restoring the farmers to the land, he would make them productive and they would once again be eligible to serve in the army. To this end, he instituted legislation in the assembly as Tribune of the Plebs. In doing this, however, he bypassed the Senate, which convention required be consulted before legislation was voted on by the people. Consequently, although his land reform bill was passed, the Senate felt that their authority was threatened and they sought to eliminate this danger. In the civil violence which followed, Tiberius was killed.

This reading is taken from Plutarch's Parallel Lives, which comprises a series of biographies on famous Greeks and Romans. Plutarch (A.D. c.50-c.127) was a Greek philosopher and biographer who lived almost two centuries after these events. He was educated in Athens and held political office in Greece. He produced many works, of which the Parallel Lives series is today the best known. Because he was also a philosopher, he pays particular attention in his biographies to the education and character of great men. He believed that great men shaped history and society and thus he sought to illuminate their personal virtues or vices, in order to understand better their contributions to history.

Consider the following:

- What was the problem with land ownership in the second century B.C.?
- What changes did Tiberius Gracchus try to institute?
- What was the reaction of the Senatorial class to this legislation? Why?
- Scholars often debate the political intentions of Tiberius. Do you believe that he was an idealistic social reformer, who sought to remedy social ills, or do you think he sought to use his office to gain political influence in an exceptional or even revolutionary manner?

Plutarch, LIfe of Tiberius Gracchus Plutarch.

8. The Romans had won much territory in their wars with their neighbours. Part of it they had sold, and part of it they made public land, and set it aside for poor and indigent citizens to occupy, on payment of a small rent into the public treasury. [2] And when the rich began to offer larger rents and drove out the poor, a law was enacted forbidding the holding by one person of more than five hundred acres of land. For a short time this enactment restrained the greed of the rich, and was of assistance to the poor, who remained in their places on the land which they had rented and occupied the allotment which each had held from the outset. [3] But later on the neighbouring rich men, by means of impersonation, transferred these rented lands to themselves, and in the end held most of the land openly in their own names. The poor, who had been ejected from their land, then ceased to be eager for military service, and neglected the bringing up of children, so that soon all Italy was conscious of a shortage of freemen, and was filled with gangs of foreign slaves, by whose aid the rich cultivated the estates that they they had expelled the free citizens from. [4] An attempt was therefore made to rectify this problem by Gaius Laelius the comrade of Scipio Aemilianus. Men of influence, however, opposed his proposal, and he desisted, fearing the disturbance which might ensue. Because of this, Laelius was given the surname of Wise or Prudent (for the Latin word 'sapiens' seems to have either meaning).

Tiberius Gracchus, however, on being elected tribune of the people, took the matter directly in hand. He was incited to this step, as most writers say, by Diophanes the rhetorician and Blossius the philosopher.... [5] Some, however, put part of the blame upon Cornelia the mother of Tiberius, who often reproached her sons because the Romans still referred to her as the mother-in-law of Scipio, rather than the mother of the Gracchi. [6] Still others again say that a certain Spurius Postumius was to blame. He was of the same age as Tiberius, and a rival of his in reputation as a speaker. When Tiberius came back from his campaign and found that his rival had far outstripped him in reputation and influence and was an object of public admiration, he seems to have decided to outdo him by engaging in a bold political measure that would arouse great expectations among the people. [7] But his brother Gaius, in a certain pamphlet, has written that as Tiberius was passing through Tuscany on his way to Numantia, and observed the lack of inhabitants in the country, and that those who tilled the soil or tended the flocks there were imported barbarian slaves, he then first conceived the public policy which was the cause of countless ills to the two brothers. The energy and ambition of Tiberius were especially kindled by the people themselves, who scribbled sayings on porticoes, house-walls, and monuments, calling upon him to recover for the poor the public land.

9. Tiberius, however, did not draw up his law by himself, but sought advice with the citizens who were foremost in virtue and reputation, among whom were Crassus, who was the pontifex maximus, Mucius Scaevola the jurist, who was consul in that year, and Appius Claudius, his father-in-law. [2] Many agree that no law dealing with injustice and rapacity so great was ever drawn up in milder and gentler terms than this one. For men who were occupying land that they had no legal claim to should have been punished for their occupation and should to have been forced to surrender it with a fine. These men, by contrast, were merely required to abandon what they had occupied illegally—after they had been compensated—and to allow the ownership to pass to citizens who needed

assistance. [3] Hence the correction of the wrong was exceedingly mild, and the people were satisfied to let bygones be bygones, provided that they could be secure from such wrong in the future. The men of wealth and substance, however, were led by their greed to oppose the law, and because of their anger and obstinacy to hate the lawgiver. They therefore tried to persuade the people to oppose the law by alleging that Tiberius was proposing to redistribute land in order to divide the body politic, and was intending to stir up a general revolution.

[4] But these men accomplished nothing; for Tiberius, striving to support a measure which was honourable and just with an eloquence that would have adorned even a lesser cause. In crowded public meetings his influence over the people was formidable and invincible. He took his stand there and pleaded for the poor. 'All the wild beasts that roam over Italy,' he would say, 'have a cave or lair to lurk in; [5] but the men who fight and die for Italy enjoy the air and light that we all share, but nothing else; without houses and homes they roam about with their wives and children. And it is with lying lips that their generals exhort the soldiers in their battles to defend the graves of their ancestors and shrines of their gods from the enemy. For none of these men has an hereditary altar; not one of them has an ancestral tomb. But they fight and die to support others in wealth and luxury. Although they could be described as conquerors of the world, they have not a single clod of earth that is their own.'

10. Such words as these were the product of a lofty spirit and genuine feeling; they were heard in the ears of a people profoundly moved and fully aroused to the support the speaker. No adversary of Tiberius could successfully withstand them. Instead of marshalling counter-arguments, therefore, they desided to approach a certain Marcus Octavius, one of the popular tribunes. He was a young man of sober character, discreet, and a close friend of Tiberius. [2] Because of this friendship, Octavius at first tried to stay neutral, out of regard for Tiberius. He was eventually forced from his position, however, by the requests and supplications of many influential men, with the result that he began to oppose Tiberius and prevented the passage of the law. Now, in the Roman system any tribune who interposes his veto has the decisive power; for the wishes of the majority have no impact if a single tribune is opposed. [3] Angered at this procedure, Tiberius withdrew his conciliatory law, and introduced in its place one that was more agreeable to the multitude and more severe against the wrongdoers, since it simply ordered them to vacate the land which they had acquired in violation of the earlier laws without any compensation.

[4] Almost every day, therefore, there were passionate arguments between Tiberius and Octavius. In these, as we are told, the two struggled with one another with the greatest degree of earnestness and rivalry, but neither uttered a word of abuse or uttered a single unseemly word about the other. For in the exercise of rivalry and wrath, a noble nature and a sound training restrain and regulate the mind. [5] Moreover, when Tiberius learned that Octavius himself was a large holder of the public land and therefore affected by the law, he begged him to give up his opposition and promised to pay him the value of the land out of his own wealth, although this was quite modest. But Octavius would not agree to this, and therefore Tiberius issued an edict forbidding all the other magistrates to transact any public business until such time as the vote could be taken either for or against his law. [6] He also sealed the temple of Saturn, in order that the quaestors might not take any money from its treasury or pay any into it, and he made proclamation that a penalty would be imposed upon such praetors as

disobeyed, so that all magistrates grew fearful and ceased performing their several functions. [7] Thereupon the men of property put on the garb of mourning and went about the forum in pitiful and lowly guise; but in secret they plotted against the life of Tiberius and tried to raise a band of assassins to kill him, so that Tiberius on his part—and everybody knew it—wore a concealed short-sword such as bandits use.

11. When the appointed day was come and Tiberius was summoning the people to the vote, the voting urns were stolen away by the faction of the rich, and great confusion arose. The supporters of Tiberius, however, were numerous enough to force the issue, and were mustering themselves together for this purpose, when Manlius and Fulvius, men of consular dignity, fell down before Tiberius, clasped his hands, and with tears begged him to stop. [2] Tiberius, sensing that the situation was now becoming dangerous, and moved by respect for these men, asked them what they wanted him to do. They replied that they were not competent to advise in so serious a crisis, and fervently asked him to submit the case to the senate. To this Tiberius agreed.

But the senate in its session accomplished nothing, given the prevailing influence of the wealthy class in it, and therefore Tiberius resorted to a measure which was illegal and unseemly, the ejection of Octavius from his office; but he was unable in any other way to bring this law to the vote. [3] In the first place, however, he addressed Octavius in public with friendly words, clasping his hands and begging him to give in and accomodate the people's wish, who demanded only their just rights. Without a change, the common people would receive only a trifling return for great toils and perils. But Octavius rejected the request. Tiberius and Octavius were colleagues in office with equal powers but differing on an important matter of policy. Because of that Tiberius now decided that it was impossible for the two of them to complete their term of office without open conflict. There only one remedy for this, he said, and that was for one or the other of them to resign his office. [4] Indeed, he urged Octavius to put to the people a vote on his own case first, promising to retire at once to private life if this would be the will of the citizens. But Octavius was unwilling, and therefore Tiberius declared that he would propose the removal of Octavius if he did not take heart and change his mind.

12. With this understanding, he dissolved the assembly for that day; but on the following day, after the people had come together, he ascended onto the speaker's podium and once more attempted to persuade Octavius. When, however, Octavius was not to be persuaded, Tiberius introduced a law depriving him of his tribuneship, and summoned the citizens to vote on it without delay. [2] Now, the Roman plebs vote in thirty-five tribes. After seventeen of them had voted to expel Octavius, and the addition of one more vote would have expelled Octavius from office, Tiberius called a halt in the voting, and again entreated Octavius, embracing and kissing him in the sight of the people, and fervently begging him not to allow himself to be dishonoured, and not to attach to a friend responsibility for a measure so grievous and severe.

[3] On hearing these entreaties, we are told, Octavius was not altogether untouched or unmoved; his eyes filled with tears and he stood silent for a long time. But when he turned and saw the men of wealth and substance standing there together, his awe of them, as it would seem, and his fear of ill-repute among them, led him to take risk everything; he instructed Tiberius do what he wanted. [4] And so the law was passed, and Tiberius ordered one of his freedmen to drag Octavius from the rostra; for Tiberius used his freedmen as officers, and this

made the sight of Octavius being ignominiously dragged from the podium a more pitiful one. [5] Moreover, the people rushed toward him, and although the men of wealth ran in a group to his assistance and spread out their hands against the crowd, it was with difficulty that Octavius was safely rescued from the crowd. ...

13. Under the agrarian law, three men were to be appointed for the survey and distribution of the public land. These were Tiberius himself, Appius Claudius his father-in-law, and Gaius Gracchus his brother, who was not at Rome, but was serving under Scipio in the expedition against Numantia in Spain. [2] Tiberius successfully carried out these measures quietly and without opposition. He also arranged the election of a tribune in the place of Octavius. The new tribune was not a man of rank or note, but a certain Mucius, a dependent of Tiberius. The propertied classes, however, who were troubled by these proceedings and feared the growing power of Tiberius, began to attack and oppose him in the senate. When he asked for the customary tent at public expense, for his use when dividing up the public land, they would not allocate it, [3] although other men had often obtained one or less important purposes; and they fixed his daily allowance for expenses at a trivial sum. These things were done on motion of Publius Nasica, who was completely overwhelmed by his personal hatred of Tiberius. For he was a very large holder of public land, and bitterly resented his being forced to give it up.

[4] But the people became all the more angry. When a friend of Tiberius died suddenly and his body broke out all over with evil spots, they ran in throngs to the man's funeral, shouting that he had been poisoned to death, and they carried the bier themselves, and stood by at the last ceremonies. ... [5] On hearing of this, Tiberius tried to stir up the multitude even more by putting on mourning clothes and bringing his children before the assembly where he begged the people to care for them and their mother, saying that he feared for his own life.

14. And now the king of Pergamum, Attalus Philomator, died, and the king's last will and testament was brought to Rome. When it was opened, it was found that he had made the Roman people his heir. At once Tiberius courted popular favour by proposing a law which provided that the money of King Attalus, when brought to Rome, would be given to the citizens who received a parcel of the public land, to aid them in stocking and equipping their farms. [2] The kingdom of Attalus also included many cities. Tiberius argued that it was not the senate's right to decide about them, but he himself would submit a proposal to the people about them. With this proposal he gave even more offence than ever to the senate; and Pompeius, rising to speak there, said that he was a neighbour of Tiberius, and therefore knew that Eudemus of Pergamum had presented Tiberius with a royal diadem and purple robe, believing that he was going to be king in Rome. [3] ... Titus Annius, too, challenged Tiberius to a judicial wager. He contended that by deposing Octavius Tiberius had acted with contempt against his colleague, who by law was sacred and inviolable. As many senators applauded this speech, Tiberius dashed out of the senate-house, called the people together, and ordered Annius to be brought before them, with the intention of denouncing him. [5] Annius was far inferior to Tiberius both in eloquence and in reputation, but he resorted to his unrivalled skill in cross-examination and called upon Tiberius to answer a few questions before the speeches began. Once Tiberius agreed and the multitude was silenced, Annius asked: 'Tiberius, if you wish to heap insult upon me and degrade me, and if I invoke the aid of one of your fellow tribunes, and if he ascends the podium to speak

in my defence, will you fly into a passion and deprive that tribune of his office, too?' [6] At this question, we are told, Tiberius was so shaken that, although he was one of the most eloquent men of his time as well as one of the most fearless, he held his peace.

15. Consequently, he temporarily dissolved the assembly; but he perceived that his actions with regard to Octavius had become displeasing not only to the propertied classes, but also to the multitude. For the Romans considered that the high and honourable dignity of the tribunate should be carefully guarded, which it had been up to that time, but his actions were seen to have had been insulted and degraded it. Therefore he soon delivered a lengthy speech before the people on this theme, and I consider it important to lay out a few of his arguments before you, so that you can get a conception of the man's subtlety and persuasiveness. [2] A tribune, he said, was sacred and inviolable, because he was consecrated to the people and was a champion of the people. 'If, then,' said Tiberius, 'a tribune should turn around, wrong the people, harm its power, and rob it of the privilege of voting, he has by his own acts deprived himself of his honourable office by not fulfilling the conditions on which he received it; [3] for otherwise there would be no interference with a tribune even though he should try to demolish the Capitol or set the naval arsenal on fire. If a tribune does these things, he is a bad tribune; but if he annuls the power of the people, he is no tribune at all. Is it not, then, a monstrous thing that a tribune should have power to drag a consul to prison, while the people cannot deprive a tribune of his power when he employs it against the very ones who bestowed it? For consul and tribune alike are elected by the people. [4] And surely the kingly office, besides comprehending in itself every civil function, is also consecrated to the Deity by the performance of the most solemn religious rites; and yet the king Tarquinius was expelled by the city for his wrong-doing, and because of one man's insolence the power which had founded Rome and descended from father to son was overthrown. Again, what institution at Rome is so holy and venerable as that of the vestal virgins, who tend and watch the eternal flame? And yet if one of these breaks her vows, she is punished by being buried alive; for when the vestals sin against the gods, they do not preserve that inviolable character which is given them for their service to the gods. [5] Therefore it is not right that a tribune who wrongs the people should retain the inviolable character that was given him to serve the people, since he is destroying the very power which is the source of his own power. And surely, if it is right for him to be made tribune by a majority of the votes of the tribes, it must be even more right for him to be deprived of his tribuneship by a unanimous vote. [6] And again, nothing is as sacred and inviolate as objects consecrated to the gods; and yet no one has ever prevented the people from using such objects, or moving them, or changing their position in such manner as may be desired. It therefore must be permissible for the people to transfer the tribunate also, as a consecrated thing, from one man to another. And that the office is not inviolable or irremovable is plain from the fact that many times men holding it resign it under oath of disability, and of their own accord ask to be relieved of it.'

16. These were the chief points that Tiberius made to justify his actions. And now his friends, observing the threats and the hostile combination against him, thought that he ought to be re-elected tribune again for the following year. Once more, therefore, Tiberius sought to win the favour of the multitude by introducing new laws, reducing the time of military service, granting appeal to the people from the verdicts of the jurors, adding to the jurors, who at that time were composed of senators only, an equal

number from the equestrian order. [2] These changes were wholly designed to diminish the power of the senate, and the motivation was more from anger and vengeance rather than from calculations of justice or the public good. And when the voting began, the friends of Tiberius sensed that their opponents were getting the better of them, since all the people were not present. They then began to denounce his fellow tribunes so as to delay the proceedings; then, they dismissed the assembly, and ordered that it should reconvene on the following day. [3] Then Tiberius, going down into the forum, at first appealed to the citizens in a humble manner and with tears in his eyes; next, he declared he was afraid that his enemies would break into his house by night and kill him. In this way he so upset his hearers that great numbers of them took up their station around his house and spent the night there on guard.

......

17. [5] At the same time also many of his friends on the Capitol came running to Tiberius with urgent appeals to hasten thither, since matters there were going well. And in fact things turned out splendidly for Tiberius at first; as soon as he came into view the crowd raised a friendly shout, and as he came up the hill they gave him a cordial welcome and ranged themselves about him, that no stranger might approach.

18. But after Mucius began once more to summon the tribes to the vote, none of the customary forms could be observed because of the disturbance that arose on the outskirts of the throng, where there was jostling back and forth between the friends of Tiberius and their opponents, who were striving to force their way in and mingle with the rest. Moreover, at this juncture Fulvius Flaccus, a senator, posted himself in a conspicuous place, and since it was impossible to make his voice heard from such a distance, indicated with his hand that he wished to tell Tiberius something meant for his ear alone. [2] Tiberius ordered the crowd to part for Flavius, who struggled to make his way up to him. He then told him that at a session of the senate a group of wealthy senators were making plans to kill Tiberius themselves since they could not persuade the consul to do so, and were arming a multitude of their friends and slaves for this purpose.

19. Tiberius, accordingly, reported this to those who stood around him, who immediately girded up their togas, and began breaking into pieces the staffs with which the officers were keeping the crowd in order; they then distributed the fragments among themselves so that they might defend themselves against the coming onslaught. Those who were farther off, however, wondered at what was going on and asked what it meant. [2] Because of this Tiberius put his hand to his head, making this visible sign that his life was in danger, since the questioners could not hear his voice. But his opponents, on seeing this, ran to the senate and told that body that Tiberius was asking for a crown; and that his putting his hand to his head was a sign that meant this. [3] The senators, of course, were all greatly disturbed, and Nasica demanded that the consul should come to the rescue of the state and put down the aspiring tyrant. The consul replied with mildness that he would resort to no violence and would put no citizen to death without a trial; if, however, the people, under persuasion or compulsion from Tiberius, should vote anything that was unlawful, he would not regard this vote as binding. Thereupon Nasica lept to his feet and said: 'Since, then, the chief magistrate betrays the state, those of you who wish to protect its laws must follow me.' [4] With these words he covered his head with the skirt of his toga and set out for the Capitol. All the senators who followed him wrapped their togas about their

left arms and pushed aside those who stood in their path. No one stood in their way because of their high rank, and everyone fled before them, trampling over one another.

[5] The attendants of the senators carried clubs and rods which they had brought from home; but the senators themselves seized the fragments and legs of the benches that were shattered by the crowd in its flight. They then attacked Tiberius, at the same time striking those who were trying to protect him. Some of these were routed; others, killed. Just as Tiberius himself turned to flee, someone managed to grab his toga. [6] So he let his toga go and fled in his tunic. But he stumbled and fell to the ground among some bodies that lay in front of him. As he was trying to rise to his feet, he received his first blow, as everybody admits, from Publius Satyreius, one of his colleagues, who struck him on the head with the leg of a bench. … Some three hundred of Tiberius' supporters were killed by blows from sticks and stones, but not one by the sword.

20. This is said to have been the first time at Rome since the expulsion of the kings that civil strife had ended in bloodshed and the death of citizens. All other disputes had been settled by concessions and compromise, even though they were serious disputes about serious matters. Nonetheless, the nobles yielded from fear of the multitude, and the people out of respect for the senate. And it was thought that even on this occasion Tiberius would have given way without difficulty, if greater attempts had been made to persuade him [2] and that he would have yielded still more easily if his assailants had not resorted to violence and bloodshed; for Tiberius' supporters numbered not more than three thousand. But the forces united against him would seem to have arisen from the hatred and anger of the rich rather than from the pretexts which they alleged; and there is strong proof

of this in their lawless and savage treatment of his dead body. For they would not listen to his brother's request that he might take up the body and bury it by night, but threw it into the river along with the other dead. [3] Nor was this all; they banished some of his friends without a trial and others they arrested and put to death. … Blossius of Cumae was brought before the consuls, and when he was asked about what had passed, he admitted that he had done everything that Tiberius had asked. [4] When Nasica asked of him, 'What, then, if Tiberius had ordered them to set fire to the Capitol?' Blossius at first replied that Tiberius would not have given such an order; but when the same question was asked of him repeatedly by many others, he said: 'If such a man as Tiberius had ordered such a thing, it would also have been right for me to do it; for Tiberius would not have given such an order if it had not been for the interest of the people.' Blossius was ultimately acquitted, and later went to Asia where he joined Aristonicus' revolt, and after Aristonicus was defeated, he committed suicide.

21. But the senate, trying to conciliate the people now that matters had gone so far, no longer opposed the distribution of the public land, and proposed that the people should elect a commissioner in place of Tiberius. So they took a ballot and elected Publius Crassus, who was a relative of Gracchus; for his daughter Licinia was the wife of Gaius Gracchus. [2] … Moreover, since the people felt bitterly over the death of Tiberius and were clearly awaiting an opportunity for revenge, and since Nasica was already threatened with prosecutions, the senate, fearing for his safety, voted to send him to Asia, although it had no need of him there. [3] For when people met Nasica, they did not try to hide their hatred of him, but grew savage and cried out upon him wherever he chanced to be, calling him an accursed man and a tyrant, who had defiled with the murder of an inviolable

and sacred person the holiest and most awe-inspiring of the city's sanctuaries. And so Nasica left Italy secretly, although he was bound there by the most important and sacred functions; for he was pontifex maximus. He roamed and wandered about in foreign lands ignominiously, and after a short time died at Pergamum.

Adapted from Bernadotte Perrin, *Plutarch. Plutarch's Lives with an English Translation.* (London. William Heinemann Ltd. 1926.)

Reading 7b. Plutarch: Gaius Graccus

Gaius Gracchus was ten years younger than Tiberius and soon followed in his brother's footsteps. He was elected Tribune of the Plebs in 123 B.C., ten years after his brother's assassination. Using this office he introduced a programme of legislation aimed at solving much broader problems within Roman society. His reforms were popular with the people and he was easily re-elected Tribune in 122 B.C. Opposition from the Senate, however, grew during his second year in office. The senate was able to turn public opinion against him, and when he sought a third term in office, he was not re-elected. The Senators, still fearing his power, passed a resolution (*senatus consultum ultimum*) declaring that the state was in danger from Gaius and his supporters. Then in a situation similar to that of his brother, Gaius and some 3,000 of his supporters were murdered.

The death of Gaius effectively revealed the depth of the problems and tensions within the Roman state. The far-reaching nature and haste of Gaius' reforms truly frightened the Senatorial class, since they believed that he sought to reduce their power and authority. Again misunderstandings on both sides eventually led to violence. Following this event there seemed little hope that Rome would ever be able to solve any political or social crisis through democratic or constitutional means.

Ultimately the Gracchi did bring about changes to Roman society. The office of the Tribune, which originally was instituted to protect ordinary citizens from aristocratic magistrates, was used to bring forth legislation and change. The urbàn populace also realized that through the assemblies they could wield more power. This was not always a positive development, however, as the people became the pawns of ambitious politicians, who could sway the assemblies through their charisma, oratory and bribery. Roman politics became more divided as aristocratic leaders chose to champion either popular or senatorial policies. Thus, the senatorial ruling class came to be divided into two ideological groups now referred to as the Optimates (pro-senators) and the Populares (pro-plebeian).

Like his brother, Gaius Gracchus was well-educated, resourceful and eloquent young statesman. His programme of legislation was well constructed and encompassed far more solutions than his brother's. In general, he sought to continue Tiberius' land reforms, but also to relieve the suffering of the urban poor, to increase the status and authority of the Italian allies, and to improve the army. The following reading is also taken from Plutarch's Parallel Lives series. Plutarch provides a pro-Gracchan summary of the events surrounding the Tribunate of Gaius, but it must be remembered that his main concern was the character and moral actions of Gaius Gracchus.

Consider the following:

- What were some of the specific reforms that Gaius Gracchus sought to institute?
- Why was the senatorial class opposed to these changes?
- What was the ultimate outcome of the Gracchan reforms?

Plutarch, LIfe of Gaius Gracchus

1. Gaius Gracchus, at first, either because he feared his enemies, or because he wished to bring hatred on them, withdrew from the forum and lived quietly by himself, like one who was humbled for the present and for the future intended to live the same inactive life.... [2] And he was also quite young, for he was nine years younger than his brother, and Tiberius was not yet thirty when he died. But as time went on he gradually showed a more mature disposition, with no inclination towards idleness, effeminacy, drinking, or money-making. He worked hard and refining his oratorical skills which were to raise him to great influence in public life, he made it clear that he was not going to remain quiet. [3] He defended Vettius, a friend of his who was under prosecution, with a speech inspired the people about him with sympathetic delight, and made the other speakers appear to be no better than children. Once more, therefore, the nobles began to be alarmed, and there was much talk among them about preventing Gaius from being made tribune.

[4] By accident, however, it happened that the lot fell on him to go to Sardinia as quaestor for Orestes the consul. This gave pleasure to his enemies, but did not displease Gaius. For he was fond of war, and quite as well trained for military service as for pleading in the courts.

......

2. After reaching Sardinia, then, Gaius proved himself to be excellent in every way and far surpassed all the other young men in engagements with the enemy, in just dealings with the subject peoples, and in the good will and respect which he showed towards his commander.

......

In Rome, however, the senate passed a decree that fresh troops should be sent to relieve the soldiers in Sardinia, but that Orestes should remain, assuming that Gaius also would remain with him by virtue of his office. [4] When Gaius heard this, however, he immediately sailed to Rome. His unexpected appearance in Rome was criticized by his enemies, and made many think it that it was strange that he, quaestor as he was, had left his post before his commander. When he was denounced before the censors, however, he asked permission to speak, and was so successful in changing the opinions of his hearers that he left the court with the reputation of having been most unfairly wronged. [5] For he said that he had served in the army twelve years, although other men were required to serve for only ten, and that he had continued to serve as quaestor under his commander for more than two years, although the law permitted him to come back after one year. He was the only man in the army, he said, who had entered the campaign with a full purse and left it with an empty one; the rest had drunk up the wine which they took into Sardinia, and had come back to Rome with their wine-jars full of gold and silver. …

3. After he cleared himself of all suspicion and had proven his entire innocence, he immediately began to campaign for election to the tribuneship. All the men of note, without exception, were opposed to him, but so great a throng poured into the city from the country and took part in the elections that many could not be housed, and since the Campus Martius could not accommodate the multitude, they gave in their voices from the roof-tops. [2] The nobility, however, did prevail somewhat against the people and disappoint the hopes of Gaius, since he was not elected with the most votes, as he expected, but with the fourth most votes. After entering his office he quickly became the most influential of the tribunes, since he had an incomparable power in oratory, and the loss of his brother gave him great boldness of speech in bewailing his brother's fate. [3] For to this subject he would gather the people together on every pretext and remind them of what had happened to Tiberius… 'Before your eyes,' he would say, 'these men beat Tiberius to death with clubs, and his dead body was dragged from the Capitol through the midst of the city to be thrown into the river Tiber; moreover, those of his friends who were caught were put to death without trial. …

4. After he stirred up the people with such words as these (and he had a very loud voice, and was spoke extremely vigorously), he proposed two laws. The first provided that if the people had deprived any magistrate of his office, that man would not be allowed to hold any other office subsequently. Another law provided that if any magistrate had banished a citizen without trial, he would be liable to public prosecution. [2] The first law had the direct effect of branding Marcus Octavius, who had been deposed from the tribunate by Tiberius, with infamy. The other law affected Popillius, for as praetor he had banished the friends of Tiberius. Popillius, indeed, chose not to appear for his trial, but fled from Italy before it was held.…

5. In order to gratify the people and overthrow the senate he proposed several other laws. One was an agrarian law, which divided the public land among the poor citizens. Another law concerned the military. It established that clothing would be furnished to the soldiers at the public expense, so that nothing would be deducted from their pay to meet this cost, and that no one under seventeen could be enrolled as a soldier. Another law concerned the allies, which gave the Italians equal voting rights with Roman citizens; [2] still another related to the supplies of grain, and lowered the market price to the poor. Another law, which dealt with the appointment of jurors, radically curtailed the power of the senate. For up to this time only senators could serve as jurors in criminal cases, and this privilege made them formidable both with regards to the common people and to the equestrian order. Gaius' law added to the membership of the senate, which was three hundred, three hundred men from the equestrian order, and made service as juror a prerogative of the whole six hundred. [3] In his efforts to carry this law Gaius is said to have shown remarkable earnestness in many ways,

and especially in this: previously all popular orators had turned their faces towards the senate when speaking; Gaius now set a new example by turning towards the other part of the forum as he addressed the people, and continued to do this from that time on. By this slight change of posture and departure from accepted practice, Gaius raised an important question and in effect shifted the Roman practice from an aristocratic to a democratic basis. For the implication was that speakers ought to address themselves to the people, and not to the senate.

6. The people not only approved this law, but also entrusted to its author the selection of the jurors who were to come from the equestrian order, so that he found himself invested with something like monarchical power, and even the senate consented to follow his advice. But when he advised them, it was always in support of measures that were a credit to that body; [2] as, for instance, the very equitable and honourable decree concerning the grain which Fabius the governor sent to Rome from Spain. Gaius persuaded the Senate to sell the grain and send the money back to the cities of Spain, and further, to censure Fabius for making his government of the province intolerably burdensome to its inhabitants. This decree brought Gaius great reputation as well as popularity in the provinces.

[3] He also introduced bills for sending out colonies, for constructing roads, and for establishing public granaries. He acted himself as director and supervisor of all these projects, and apparently never grew weary in the execution of all these different and great enterprises. Quite the contrary, he in fact carried out all of them with an astonishing speed and efficiency, as if this were the only thing that he had to do. Because of this, even those who greatly hated and feared him were struck with amazement at the powers of achievement and accomplishment which marked all that he did. [4] In all this the common people were astonished when they saw him closely attended by a throng of contractors, craftsmen, ambassadors, magistrates, soldiers, and men of letters. He dealt with all of them with a courteous ease; he could show kindness to everyone and give to each man the courtesy due him without compromising his dignity. In doing this he made those who accused him of being threatening or arrogant appear to be nothing but violent malignant slanderers. Thus he was a more skilful popular leader in his private dealings with men and in his business transactions than in his speeches from the speaker's podium.

……

8. [2] When the consular elections were approaching and everyone was eagerly anticipating the contest, Gaius was seen leading Gaius Fannius down into the Campus Martius and joining in the campaigning for him along with his friends. This turned the tide strongly in favour of Fannius, with the result that he was elected consul. What is more, Gaius was elected tribune for the second time, even though he was not officially a candidate and had not campaigned for the office. This happened because the people were so eager to have it so.

[3] However, Gaius soon realized that the senate was completely hostile to him, and that the good will of Fannius towards him had lost its edge, and therefore again began to court the favour of the multitude to himself by proposing other laws. He propose to send colonies to Tarentum and Capua, and to grant to the Latins participation in the votes in Rome. The senate, however, began to fear that Gracchus would become completely unstoppable, and made a new and unusual attempt to divert the people from him. They decided to compete with him in courting the favour of the peo-

ple, and began to grant their wishes contrary to the best interests of the state. [4] For one of the colleagues of Gaius in the tribunate was Livius Drusus, a man who was not inferior to any Roman either in birth or rearing, while in character, eloquence, and wealth he could compete with those who were most honoured and influential in consequence of these advantages. The nobles turned, then, to this man and asked him to attack Gaius and become their ally against him, not by resorting to violence or attacking the masses, but by administering his office in such a way as to please them and by making concessions where it would have been honourable to incur their hatred.

9. With these aims, then, Livius put his influence as tribune at the service of the senate and began to draw up laws which aimed at what was neither honourable nor advantageous. Quite the contrary, his keen ambition aimed at achieving one thing—surpassing Gaius in pleasing and flattering the people. In this way the senate revealed most plainly that it was not displeased with Gaius' policy proposals, but instead wanted by any means to humiliate and destroy the man himself. [2] For when Gaius proposed to found two colonies, and these composed of the most respectable citizens, they accused him of pandering to the people. When Livius proposed to found twelve colonies, however, and to send out to each of them three thousand of Rome's most needy citizens, they supported him. When Gaius distributed public land to the poor, but required them all to pay rent for these properties into the public treasury, they were angry, alleging that his aim was to win over the gratitude of the multitude; but Livius met with their approval when he proposed to relieve these tenants even from this rent. [3] And further, when Gaius proposed to bestow upon the Latins equal voting rights, the senate objected; but when Livius brought in a bill forbidding that any Latin could be punished with beatings even during military service, he had the senate's support. And indeed Livius himself, in his public speeches, always said that he introduced these measures on the authority of the senate, which desired to help the common people. [4] This in fact was the only positive thing that came from his political measures, for the people became more positively disposed towards the senate. Before this they had suspected and hated the nobles. Now, however, Livius softened their memories of past grievances and their bitter feelings by assuring them that it was the nobles themselves who had induced him to begin to conciliate the people and gratify the wishes of the many.

10. But the best evidence that Livius was well disposed towards the people and honest, lay in the fact that he never appeared to propose anything for himself or in his own personal interests. For he moved to send out other men as managers of his colonies, and would play no role in the expenditure of moneys. Gaius, by contrast, had assigned to himself most of such functions and the most important of them. [2] And now Rubrius, one of his colleagues in the tribuneship, brought in a bill for the founding of a colony on the site of Carthage, which had been destroyed by Scipio, and Gaius, upon whom the lot fell, sailed off to Africa to supervise its foundation. In his absence, therefore, Livius made all the more headway against him, winning his way into popular favuor and attaching the people to himself.

11. In Africa, moreover, Gaius was busy with the planting a colony on the site of Carthage, which he gave the name Junonia. There were reports, however, that this colony was now associated with many unfavorable omens from the gods. ... [2] Notwithstanding this, Gaius managed to arrange everything necessary in a mere seventy days, and then returned to Rome, because he learned that Fulvius was being hard

pressed by Drusus, and because matters there required his presence. For Lucius Opimius, a man of oligarchical principles with great influence in the senate, ran for office. He had earlier failed in his attempt to be elected to the consulship when Gaius had brought forward Fannius and supported his candidacy for the office. Now, however, Opimius had the aid and assistance of many, [3] and it was expected that he would in fact be elected consul. It was also expected that as consul he would oppose Gaius, whose influence was already somewhat on the decline, both because the people had had their fill of his policies and because many other leaders were now courting their favour and the senate readily yielded to them.

12. On returning to Rome from Africa, the first thing Gaius did was change his residence from the Palatine hill to the region adjoining the forum, which he thought more democratic, since most of the poor and lowly had come to live there. Next, he introduced the rest of his laws, intending to get the people to vote for them.

......

13. The enemies of Gaius, however, were successful in getting Opimius elected as consul, and then proceeded to revoke many of the laws which Gaius had managed to get passed and to meddle with the organization of the colony at Carthage. This was was done to irritate Gaius, so that his reaction might provide grounds for criticism, and so he might be finally put in his place. At first Gaius endured all this patiently, but finally, under the instigations of his friends, and especially of Fulvius, he set out to gather a fresh body of partisans to oppose the consul.
...

[3] On the day when Opimius and his supporters were going to attempt to annul Gaius' laws, the Capitol had been occupied by both factions since earliest morning. After the consul had offered sacrifice, one of his servants, Quintus Antyllius, as he was carrying from one place to another the entrails of the victims, said to the partisans of Fulvius: 'Make way for honest citizens, you scoundrels!' Some say, too, that along with this speech Antyllius bared his arm and waved it with an insulting gesture. [4] At any rate he was killed at once and on the spot, stabbed with long writing styluses, which some say were made for just this purpose. The murder threw the multitude into a complete state of confusion. In addition it produced directly opposite reactions in the leaders of the two factions. Gaius was deeply distressed and reproached his followers for having given their enemies the grounds for accusing them that they had long been looking for. Opimius, however, was elated as though he had got something that he was waiting for and urged his followers to take vengeance.

14. A shower of rain fell just then, and the assembly was dissolved; but early next morning the consul called the senate together indoors and proceeded to transact business, while others placed the body of Antyllius without covering upon a bier, and carried it, as they had agreed to do, through the forum and past the senate-house, with wailings and lamentations. Opimius knew what was going on, but pretended to be surprised, so that even the senators went out into the forum. [2] After the bier had been set down in the midst of the throng, the senators began to denounce what they called a heinous and monstrous crime. The common people, however, were moved to hatred and abuse of the oligarchs. In their view the oligarchs had not only murdered Tiberius Gracchus on the Capitol with their own hands, although he was a tribune, but had also thrown away his dead body. [3] Antyllius, by contrast, was a mere servant. Granted, he had perhaps suffered more than he deserved, but was himself chiefly to blame for it and now was being

laid out in the forum, and was surrounded by the Roman senate, which shed tears and shared in the praises of an unimportant person in order that they might do away with the sole remaining champion of the people. Then the senators went back into the senate-house, where they formally instructed the consul Opimius to save the city as best he could, and to overthrow the tyrants.

[4] The consul therefore ordered the senators to take up arms, and every member of the equestrian order was instructed to come the next morning with two fully armed servants; Fulvius, on the other hand, made counter preparations and got together a mob, but Gaius, as he left the forum, stopped in front of his father's statue, gazed at it for a long time without uttering a word, then burst into tears, and with a deep sigh departed. [5] Many of those who saw this were moved to pity Gaius; they reproached themselves for abandoning and betraying him, and went to his house, and spent the night at his door.…

15. When day came, his partisans had a difficult time waking Fulvius from his drunken sleep. They then armed themselves and with much threatening and shouting went to seize the Aventine hill. Gaius, on the other hand, was unwilling to arm himself, but went forth in his toga, as though on his way to the forum, with only a short dagger on his person. …

16. When the people had assembled together, Fulvius, at Gaius' suggestion, sent his youngest son with a herald's wand into the forum. The young man was a handsome youth, and now, with all due respect and modesty, and with tears in his eyes, he spoke conciliatory words to the consul and the senate. [2] Most of those who heard himwere ready to accept his terms of peace. Opimius, however, declared that the petitioners ought not to try to persuade the senate through messenger; they should rather approach the senate and surrender themselves for trial, like citizens subservient to the laws, begging for mercy. He also told the young man bluntly that he was to come back again on these terms or not at all. [3] Gaius, accordingly, as we are told, was willing to come and try to persuade the senate; but no one else agreed with him, and so Fulvius sent his son again to plead in their behalf as before. Opimius, however, who was eager to attack, at once seized the youth and put him under guard, and then advanced on Fulvius' men with numerous men-at-arms and Cretan archers. [4] And it was the archers who, by discharging their arrows and wounding their opponents, were most instrumental in throwing them into confusion. After the rout had taken place, Fulvius fled for refuge into an unused bath, where he was shortly discovered and slain together with his elder son. Gaius, however, was not seen to take any part in the battle, but in great displeasure at what was happening he withdrew into the temple of Diana. There he intended to kill himself, but was prevented by his companions, Pomponius and Licinius; for they were right there, and took away his sword, and urged him to take flight. [5] Then, indeed, as we are told, he sank upon his knees, and with hands outstretched towards the goddess prayed that the Roman people, as payment for their great ingratitude and treachery, might never cease to be in servitude; for most of them were clearly changing sides, now that a proclamation of amnesty had been made.

17. So then, as Gaius fled, his foes pursued him and began to overtake him at the wooden bridge over the Tiber. His two friends sent him ahead, while they themselves turned to confont his pursuers. They fought there at the head of the bridge and would allow no man to pass, until finally they were themselves killed. [2] Gaius had with him in his flight a single slave

by name Philocrates. Gaius barely succeeded in escaping into a sacred grove, and there was killed by the hand of Philocrates, who then killed himself over his dead master. [3] According to some writers, however, both were taken alive by the enemy, but because the slave had thrown his arms about his master, no one was able to strike the master until the slave had first been killed by many blows. Someone cut off the head of Gaius, we are told, and was carrying it along, but was robbed of it by a friend of Opimius Septimuleius; for at the beginning of the battle there had been a proclamation that the men who brought the head of Gaius or Fulvius would be paid its weight in gold. [4] So Septimuleius stuck the head of Gaius on a spear and brought it to Opimius, and when it was placed in a balance it weighed seventeen and two-thirds pounds. In this case, however, Septimuleius had shown himself to be both a villain and a cheat, for he had taken out the brain and filled the cavity with molten lead in its place. Those who brought the head of Fulvius, however, were nobodies and therefore got nothing. [5] The bodies of Gaius and Fulvius and of the other slain were thrown into the Tiber. In total they numbered three thousand; their property was sold and the proceeds paid into the public treasury. In addition, their wives were forbidden to go into mourning, and Licinia, the wife of Gaius, was also deprived of her dowry. Most cruel of all, however, was the treatment of the younger son of Fulvius, who had neither lifted a hand against the nobles nor been present at the fighting, but had come to seek a truce before the battle and had been arrested. After the battle he was executed. [6] However, what especially offended the people more than this or anything else was the erection of a temple of Concord by Opimius; for it was felt that he was exulting and boasting in the manner of celebrating a triumph owing to all this slaughter of citizens. Therefore at night, beneath the inscription on the temple, somebody carved this verse:— 'A work of mad discord produces a temple of Concord.'

18. This Opimius was the first consul to act like a dictator. He put to death three thousand citizens without trial, including Gaius Gracchus and Fulvius Flaccus, one of whom had been consul and had celebrated a triumph, while the other was the foremost man of his generation in virtue and reputation. Opimius, however, could not keep his hands from fraud, but when he was sent as ambassador to Jugurtha the Numidian was bribed by him, and after being convicted most shamefully of corruption, he spent his old age in infamy, hated and insulted by the people. [2] The people were humiliated and cowed at the time when the Gracchi were killed, but soon afterwards showed how much it missed them and longed for them. For it had statues of the brothers made and set up in a conspicuous place, consecrated the places where they were slain, and brought to those places offerings as though they were visiting the shrines of gods....

19. And further, his mother Cornelia is reported to have borne all her misfortunes in a noble and magnanimous spirit, and to have said of the sacred places where her sons had been slain that they were tombs worthy of the dead which occupied them. She resided on the promontory called Misenum, and made no change in her customary way of living. [2] She had many friends, and kept a good table that she might show hospitality, for she always had Greeks and other literary men about her, and all the reigning kings exchanged gifts with her. She was indeed very agreeable to her visitors and associates when she discussed with them about the life and habits of her father Africanus, but most admirable when she spoke of her sons without grief or tears, and narrated their achievements and their fate to anyone who

asked as if she were speaking of men of the early days of Rome. [3] Some therefore suspected that old age or the greatness of her sorrows had impaired her mind and made her incapable of suffering. In fact, however, such persons themselves fail to understand how much help in banishing grief a noble nature and an honourable birth and rearing can bring. They also forget that although fate can often overcome virtue when it tries to ward off misfortune, it cannot deprive us of the power to endure those evils with calm assurance.

Adapted from Bernadotte Perrin (1847-1920), *Plutarch's Lives with an English Translation*. (London: William Heinemann Ltd., 1926)

Chapter 8:
The Augustan Reorganization

READING 8A. VERGIL, AENEID

The peace and prosperity of the Augustan age produced a flowering of Latin literature. Of the several notable poets of this age, Vergil (70-19 B.C.) is perhaps the most famous. His final work, composed at the suggestion of Augustus, was the Aeneid. It is an epic poem written in Latin, narrating the travels and adventures of the hero Aeneas, a Trojan prince who survives the great Trojan War. After enduring many hardships, Aeneas settles in Italy and founds a new civilization composed of Trojans and native Italians. It is their descendants who eventually become the Romans.

In the Aeneid Vergil imitates Homeric style. The themes and experiences of the characters follow the patterns set in the Iliad and the Odyssey. Human actions are shaped by fate and divine forces, as Aeneas, for example, wanders the Mediterranean at the mercy of the gods, as had Odysseus in the Odyssey. The poem at once emulates Homer and sets itself up as a rival to Homer: the definitive Latin epic to rival the definitive epics of the Greeks. The central theme of the poem is the destiny of Aeneas to become the founder of the Roman race.

Vergil composed the Aeneid in the last eleven years of his life, and when he died in 19 B.C. it was still not quite complete. In his will, therefore, he urged that the manuscript should be burned, but this wish was countermanded by Augustus. The poem, by its allusions and the echoes between its account of this first foundation of the Roman race and Augustus' re-foundation of the Roman order, seems to celebrate Augustus and his restoration of Rome after the civil wars. The poem may be read as presenting Augustus' Rome as the fulfillment of Rome's destiny of greatness, fulfilling the plan of the gods that had begun with Aeneas, who as well as founder of the Roman race was the ancestor of the Julian line. Certainly the poem was quickly and proudly embraced by the Romans as their national epic. At the same time, however, many modern scholars see dark, ironic, and subversive strains in the poem, which, it is argued, undercut this surface reading of the poem.

The following excerpts from the Aeneid are taken from books I and VI. The extract from Book I introduces the main theme of the poem: the destiny of Aeneas, as predetermined by Jupiter, to found a line of illustrious men. The second excerpt, from Book VI, takes place in the underworld, where Aeneas journeyed to see his dead father once more. While he is there his father introduces him to the future leaders and heroes of Rome. This parade of illustrious men convinces Aeneas of the necessity of following his destiny.

Consider the following:
- How is Aeneas characterized as a figure? What does he represent?
- Look-up at least of the five of the great men that Aeneas sees in the underworld: for what were they famed?
- Does this poem read as nationalist jingoism and Augustan propaganda?

Virgil, Aeneid Book 1

1. 1-11 Invocation to the Muse

I sing of arms and of the man who was exiled by fate, and first arrived from the coast of Troy in Italy on Lavinian shores. He had been much buffeted on land and sea, by the will of the gods and by the unforgetting anger of cruel Juno. [5] He suffered much also in war, until he finally founded a new city and brought to Latium his gods. From him the Latin people descended, the forefathers of Alba Longa, the walls of lofty Rome.

Tell me, Muse, the cause: what so offended her in her divinity? How was the Queen of Heaven angered so as to drive a man, noted for his virtue, to endure such trials, to face so many dangers? Can the gods possess such terrible anger?

1. 12-49 The origins of Juno's anger

An ancient city, Carthage, was occupied by exiles from Tyre. It lay across the sea from Italy and the distant mouths of the river Tiber. Its wealth was great, as was its energetic pursuit of war. They say that Juno loved this one land more than all others, [15] even more than Samos: her weapons were here, as was her chariot. Even then did the goddess keenly strive, if the fates should allow, that it should have supremacy over the nations. But she had heard prophecy about another race, descended from Trojan blood, that would some day topple the Tyrian citadel: [20] that from that stock a proud and warlike people would come, ruling widely and bringing ruin to Libya: thus the fates had decreed.

Juno feared this, because she remembered the ancient war she had fought at Troy, for her beloved Argos, which had caused anger and bitter sorrows that had not yet faded from her memory. [25] The judgement of Paris, though long ago, lingered in her heart with its insult to her scorned beauty, as did her hatred of the race and the kidnapping of Ganymede. Provoked by these grievances, the daughter of Saturn drove the Trojans through the seas,[30] although they had survived the Greeks and pitiless Achilles, preventing them from reaching Latium. They have now wandered for many years, driven by the fates across the deep. Such a great task was it to found the Roman race.

The Trojans had just left Sicily and were hardly out of its sight in deep water, [30] joyfully spreading sail and ploughing the brine with bronze keel, when Juno, nursing in her breast her unending grievance, spoke to herself: 'Shall I abandon my initial purpose, defeated, and fail to turn the Trojan king away from Italy? ... [42] I, the queen of the gods, wife and sister of Jove, have been waging war on this whole race for so many years. If I fail, will anyone ever worship my power from now on, or place offerings, humbly, on my altars?'

1. 50-80 Juno seeks help from Aeolus

[50] So she argued with herself. But now with her heart inflamed, the goddess flew to Aeolia, to the land of storms, the country of wild winds. This is where King Aeolus lives in a vast cave, where he keeps swirling winds and roaring gusts, curbing them with locks and chains. They growl angrily behind his doors, with a mountain's vast echoes. Aeolus sits there in his vast stronghold, wielding his sceptre, soothing their passions and restraining their rage: otherwise they would surely escape and carry away both sea and land and the vault of heaven in a whirlwind, sweeping them through the sky.

[60] But fearing this, the omnipotent Father hid them in deep caves, and buried them under a high mountain range. He also gave them a king who would understand when to order a tightening or slackening of the reins.

Juno now approached him humbly and spoke these words to him:

'My dear Aeolus, it was the Father of gods and king of men, my husband, who gave you the power both to quell and to stir the waves with the winds. I hate a people who are now sailing the Tyrrhenian Sea, carrying the conquered gods of Troy to Italy. Sink their wretched boats for me by stirring up the power of the winds, or tear their ships apart and scatter their bodies over the sea. I have fourteen nymphs of outstanding beauty. If you do what I ask, I'll give you Deiopea, the loveliest of them, to be joined to you in eternal marriage, and to have for ever. Thus in return for this favor I ask, she'll spend her whole life with you and make you the father of beautiful children.'

Aeolus replied: 'It is your place, O queen, to decide what you want; it is my place to fulfil your commands. You created this entire kingdom of mine; my sceptre was Jupiter's gift; you gave me a place among the gods at their feasts; and you made me master of storm and tempest.'

1. 81-123 Aeolus releases a great storm

[81] He spoke these words. Then lowering his spear, he struck the side of his hollow mountain. The winds lined up like soldiers in formation, rushed out the door that his spear had made, and set out whirling across the earth. [85] The East and West wind pressed down on the sea, as did the wind from Africa. Squalls were everywhere, stirring the whole sea up from its furthest deeps and creating vast waves that rolled towards shore. Now came the shouts of men and the groaning of the ships' cables. In a moment the clouds took away the sky, and then day disappeared from the Trojans' sight as the dark night descended to the sea. [90] The thunder crashed, and the air flashed with lightening, and everything threatened sudden death for all.

Aeneas now groans, his limbs aching with cold: he stretches both hands upwards towards the heavens, and cries out: [95] 'Those who died before their father's eyes under Troy's high walls were three or four times luckier than me! Diomedes, son of Tydeus, was bravest of Greeks! Why could I not have fallen at *his* hand in the fields of Ilium? Why could I have had my blood spilled where warlike Hector and brave Sarpedon fell beneath Achilles' spear? [100] Why couldn't I have fallen where the river Simois flows, sweeping away with its waves so many men's shields, helmets, and brave bodies?'

As he shouts these words, a howling gust from the north strikes the sail full on, and the seas are sent heavenward. The oars break; the prow swings backwards and turns the ship broadside to the waves: [105] a great mountain of water crashes in a mass. These ships pause on top of the wave's crest. From them can be seen the exposed shoals between the waves, and the water is full of sand. Three ships are caught by the south wind, which tosses them onto hidden rocks. (The Italians call these rocks 'the Altars', a vast reef near the surface in the middle the sea.) [110] Then the east wind drives three more from the deep and into the shallows (a pitiful sight), throws them against the sea bottom, and covers them with a mound of sand.

Right in front of Aeneas' very eyes, one ship, which carries trusty Orontes and the Lycians, is toppled by a huge wave after being struck on its side. [115] Its steersman is thrown overboard and hurled headlong while the sea turns the ship three times, spinning it around right there, and the rushing vortex sucks it into the deep. In this vast waste there are scattered men swimming, together with weapons, planking, and Trojan treasure, all floating among the waves. [120] Now the storm crushes Iloneus' strong ship, now that of Achates, now the one that carried Abas, and then old Aletes'. With timbers weakened, the ships let in the invading flood and are split open at the seams.

1. 124-156 Neptune intervenes

Neptune, meanwhile, becomes greatly troubled when he notices the sea being stirred up with great crashes, [125] and that a storm has been released so that the still waters are stirred up from the depths. So he calmly raises his face from the waves and gazes across the sea. Now he sees the fleet of Aeneas scattered across the ocean, and the Trojans being crushed by waves and the plummeting sky. [130] He recognizes his sister Juno's anger, and her stratagems, and senses them here. He summons the East and West winds before him and addresses them saying: 'Are you so confident in your birth? Winds, do you dare to mix earth with sky without my permission and to create such mischief? [135] I should take you and…. But never mind. First, these raging waves must be calmed! You'll pay for this misdeed later, with a different punishment. Hurry, rush back to your king and say this to him: that it was allotted not to him, but to me, to control the sea; to me, too, was allotted the fierce trident. He owns the wild rocks, your home: [145] let Aeolus rule in his palace, and be king of the locked-up prison of the winds.'

As soon as he speaks these words, he calms the raging sea and scatters the darkened clouds, and coaxes back the sun. Cymothoë and Triton work together to push the ships away from the jagged rocks, [145] while Neptune uses his trident to help. The sand-banks open, the flood is calmed, and Neptune himself skims over the waves on his chariot. It is like when a revolution breaks out in a great nation, and the lower classes rage with anger and begin throwing stones and burning torches. [150] Madness supplies their weapons. But often if they then see a man of great authority, and of weighty stature, they fall silent before him and listen there attentively. His words soothe their passions and calms their anger. That is what it was like when the raging seas fell silent as soon as the old god, [150] surveying the vast waters while being carried through the open sky, turned his horses and gave them reign, while flying behind them in his chariot.

1. 157-222 Refuge on the coast

Aeneas' weary men did their best to set a course for the nearest land, and made their way towards the Libyan coast. There is a place there with a deep inlet with a harbour formed by an island mass. On it every wave of the sea breaks and disperses into harmless ripples. … [170] Aeneas limped into this harbour with his seven surviving ships and the Trojans, with a passionate longing for dry land, threw themselves onto it, embracing the sands they longed for and stretching their salt-encrusted bodies on the shore.…

[180] Meanwhile, Aeneas climbed a crag, and scannned the whole horizon of the sea far and wide, looking if he could see anything of the Phrygian ships of Antheus or Capys, or whether he could spot Caicus' ship, blazoned with his coat of arms. No ship was visible, but he did see three stags down on the shore, [185] behind which were great herds of deer grazing in the valley. He stood still, slowly took his bow in hand and the swift arrows that faithful Achates handed to him. First he shot the herd's leaders with their heads held high with their lofty antlers; [190] then he shot arrows into the herd, which dissolved into confusion. The hero continued until he'd felled seven huge stags, one for each of his ships. Then he returned to the harbour and distributed them to his friends.

[195] Then Aeneas took and distributed the wine that noble Acestes had stored in casks while on the Trinacrian coast and had given them on their departure. Aeneas addressed his men and soothed their saddened hearts: 'My friends, we were already well-acquainted with trouble before this. You all have endured worse, and the gods will bring an end to these troubles, too. [200] Remember wild Scylla? You faced her and her deep-echoing cliffs! You also experienced the rocks of the Cyclopes! Remember the courage you had? Now drive out any lingering fears. Someday you'll take pride in remembering these misfortunes. Through all these troubles, these dangerous moments, [205] we are heading for Latium, where the fates have promised to us a new life of peace. Troy's kingdom will rise again there. Hold fast, then and keep yourselves safe for happier times.' These are his words, and although he was sick with heavy worries, he manufactured a hopeful look, and hid his pain deep in his chest.…

1. 223-256 Venus appeals to Jupiter

It was at this moment that Jupiter, from high in the heavens, looked down on the earth and saw the sea with its sailing ships, and the wide lands around its coasts, and the nations spread far and wide. [225] He paused there, high up in the heavens, and fixed his gaze on the kingdom of Libya. And while he considered the great troubles that he carried in his heart, Venus approached him with her eyes brimming with tears and said: 'You are the one who rules over all matters human and divine with eternal laws. [230] You are the one who terrifies all with your bolts of lightning. What could my son Aeneas have done to you that's so loathsome? What sin have the Trojans committed that has caused them to suffer so many calamities? It seems that because of Italy the whole world is closed to them. But why? [235]

At some point, as the years roll by, the Romans will surely rise from them, rulers to be restored from the Trojans' blood. They are fated to hold power over the sea and the whole world. What has changed your mind, Father? This is what comforted me while Troy had its fall and its sad ruin. I was able to weigh one fate against opposing fates. But now the same misfortunes are following the men who have been harassed by great disasters. [240] How, my lord, will you bring their trials to an end? … [250] But although I am your child and you've given me a heavenly home, our ships have been lost! This is shameful! And because of the anger of a single goddess, we are kept far from Italy's shores. Is this the reward for virtue? Is this how you restore us to power?'

1. 257-296 Jupiter's prophecy about Rome

But the father of men and gods smiled at her and gave her that look that he uses to clear the sky of storms. He kissed her and then said this: 'Fear not, Venus. Your child's fate is unchanged. You will see his city of Lavinium with its walls, just as I promised you. [260] You will raise magnanimous Aeneas skywards into the starry heavens. My mind has not at all changed. Since I have this concern now in my heart, I'll speak about this son of yours and reveal the secrets of his destiny. He will wage a great war in Italy and destroy proud peoples. He will establish laws for his men and build city walls [265] while three summers see his reign in Latium, and three winters will pass after the Rutulians are beaten. Then his son Ascanius will rule. His name is Iulus now, and previously he was called Ilus while the Ilian kingdom stood strong. He will rule thirty series of the turning months. [270] He will transfer his throne from its site at Lavinium, and ruling firmly he will build the walls of Alba Longa. Here the kings of Hector's race will rule for three hundred full years, until a royal priestess, Ilia, pregnant by Mars, shall give birth to twins. [275] Then Romulus will extend the race. … He will lay out new walls for Mars and call his people Romans, named after himself. Their possessions will have no fixed boundaries or limits: to them I have allotted empire without end. [280] Granted, fierce Juno now torments land and sea and sky with terror. But she will arrive at better judgement and will finally join me in favouring the Romans—the masters of the world, the people of the toga. This is what is decreed. And so the time will come, as the years slide by, when the Trojan house of Assaracus will reduce Phthia to slavery, and be lords of defeated Argos. [285] From this glorious line will be born a Trojan Caesar. He will expand Rome's empire as far as the Ocean and extend his fame to the stars. He will be Augustus, a Julius, his name derived from the great Iulus. You, your fears long banished, will someday receive him in heaven, carrying his Eastern spoils: [290] he himself will be invoked in prayer. At that time wars will have ceased, and the ages will have grown mild. Ancient good-faith, and Vesta, Romulus with his brother Remus will make the laws. The savage gates of War will be locked with iron bolts while sinful rage roars inside with its terrifying blood-stained mouth, seated on its weapons, [295] hands bound by a hundred knots behind its back.'

(Aeneas then takes refuge in Africa and has a famous affair with Dido, queen of Carthage, whom he finally abandons when his destiny calls him to sail to Italy. After he lands safely in Italy, he is guided into the underworld by the Sibyl at Cumae. While in the underworld he speaks with the spirit of his father and is offered a prophetic vision of the destiny of Rome.)

Aeneid Book 6

6. 1-12 Arrival in Italy

Aeneas directed his fleet forward and led them at last to the shores of Euboean Cumae. They turned the beaks of their ships toward the sea and cast off the ships' anchors, which secure the ships in a line along the beach. [5] The eager band of young warriors leapt to shore and to work: some began to build fire with a flint, others hunted in the woods for game, pointing out streams they found. Pious Aeneas, however, sought out the heights where Apollo rules. [10] Nearby he found the great cave, the hidden lair of the terrifying Sibyl, whom the god of Delos inspires with greatness of mind and spirit, and to whom he reveals the future. …

[33] Achetes now arrived with the Sibyl, Deiophobe, Glaucus' daughter, the priestess of Phoebus and Diana. She spoke to the leader: 'This is not the time for sightseeing: what is needed now is for you to sacrifice seven bullocks from an unbroken herd, and the same number of choice two-year old sheep.'

Once she said these things to Aeneas, his men immediately made the sacrifice that they had been ordered. Then the priestess summoned the Trojans to her shrine. The great face of the cliff here was pitted with caves, each of which had a hundred wide tunnels with a hundred mouths from which as many voices pour: the voices of Sibyl's prophecies. [45] When they reached the threshold, the prophetess cried out: 'It is time to question the fates! Behold! the god! the god!' As she shouted this before the doors, her face and colour suddenly changed! Her hair became unbound and her chest heaved as her heart pounded with wild frenzy! [50] She appeared taller and sounded unhuman, for now the power of the god came closer. 'Why are you slow with your vows and prayers, Aeneas of Troy?' she shouted. 'Without them, the great mouth of the House of Inspiration will not open!' She said this and then fell silent. …

6. 106-155 Aeneas Asks Entry to Hades

Then Aeneas, the Hero, began again to speak: 'One thing I ask. They say the gate to the King of Darkness is near here, and here is found the shadowy marsh and Acheron's overflow. I desire to see again my dear father's face: show me the way and open wide the sacred doorways. [110] I saved him and rescued him from the thick of the battle, carrying him on my shoulders through the flames and a thousand spears. He was my companion on our journey; he endured all the seas with me, and shared all the threats of sky and ocean, despite being weak, overwhelmed, and beyond his allotted span of old age. [115] He gave me a firm order to seek you out and approach humbly your doorway. I ask you, dear one, take pity on both father and son. You are all powerful, and it was for this purpose that Hecate set you to govern the groves of Avernus. [120] Others have made that journey, and my ancestry, too, descends from lofty Jupiter.'

With these words he made his request and laid hold of the altar. The priestess gave this answer: [125] 'Trojan son of Anchises, you are descended from the blood of the gods. Know this: the path to hell is easy, for the door of black Dis is open day and night. But to retrace your steps and return to the upper air, that is a difficult task! … [135] If such a desire has entered your mind, listen to what you must first do. A golden bough lies hidden in a dark tree; it has golden leaves and a flexible stem. It is sacred to Persephone, the underworld's Juno, hidden amidst all the groves and enclosed within the shadows of secret valleys. [140] Only someone who has plucked a gold-leaved fruit from the tree is allowed to enter the hidden places of the earth. For lovely Proserpine has ordered this to be brought to her as tribute: another fruit of gold always appears in place of one that is picked, and the branches sprout leaves of the same metal. So search for it up high, and when you've spotted it, grasp it directly in your hand. If the Fates have chosen you, the fruit will be plucked easily, freely of its own accord: otherwise you won't overcome it by any force, or cut it with even the sharpest blade.

(Aeneas finds the golden bough and returns with it. The Sybil makes a sacrifice to Hecate and leads Aeneas into the underworld. After being ferried across the river Styx, Aeneas encounters dead companions and Dido, who had killed herself after Aeneas had abandoned her. The Sybil describes to Aeneas the horrible punishments in Tartarus.)

6. 633-678 The Fields of Elysium

So, side by side, they hurry along the dark path. Once they cross the intervening ground and approached the doors. [635] Aeneas enters first, sprinkling fresh water over his body, and hangs the golden bough on the threshold before him. Now that this at last had been done and the goddess' task fulfilled, they reached happy places, the delightful green meadow of the Fortunate Groves, and the homes of the blessed. [640] Here the air is freer, and a radiant light fills the plain. These places have their own sun and their own stars. Some of its inhabitants exercise their bodies in a playing-field, competing in sports and wrestling on the golden sand. Others make the steps of a dance and sing songs. … [651]

6. 679-702 Aeneas finds his father Anchises

In a deep green valley Aeneas' father Anchises stood thinking while his eyes surveyed the spirits kept there, destined for the upper world. As it happened, he was right then considering the number of his descendants, his precious grandsons, and the fate and fortunes of men, and their characters and works.

[685] Then he saw Aeneas moving towards him across the grass. With hands outstretched and his face full of tears, these words came from his lips: 'Have you finally come, my son? and has your piety (which your father expected of you) finally overcome its harsh road? Now at last am I allowed to see your face, my son, and hear your voice and speak to you?' … [699] So speaking, Aeneas' face was drenched in a flood of tears. Three times he tried to throw his arms around his father; three times, he reached forth in vain and the ghostly apparition slipped though his hands like the wind or a fleeting dream.

6. 703-723 Aeneas is shown souls soon to be reborn

And now Aeneas saw a grove secluded in a hidden valley. In it were rustling thickets, [705] with the river Lethe flowing slowly past peaceful meadows. Vast tribes and countless peoples waited beside. It was just like when the bees settle on the many flowers of a meadow on a sunny day of summer, and hover round white lilies, and all the fields hum with their buzzing. [710] This sight thrilled Aeneas. Not knowing what it meant he asked what river this was in the distance, who were the men crowding along banks in such numbers.

His father Anchises answered him: 'These are the spirits who are owed a second body by destiny. They come to the water of Lethe's stream and drink its happy liquid and a final forgetting. [716] Indeed, for a long time I've wanted to tell you about them, and to show them to you personally. By enumerating my children's descendants in this way, you might with me rejoice more at coming to Italy.'…

6. 752-807 The Future Generations

Anchises had spoken, and he then led the Sibyl and his son into the middle of the murmuring throng. He chose a small hill from which he could survey the entire long row that lined up opposite, and see their faces as they walked by.

[756] 'Come, I will now set forth what glory will follow the children of Dardanus, what offspring awaits you from Italian stock. While these illustrious spirits pass by us, I will teach you about your destiny.

'Do you see that boy who leans on a headless spear? He has been granted the place nearest the light. He will be the first of Italian blood to arrive in the upper world. He is Silvius (which is an Alban name) and will be the youngest of your sons born to your wife Lavinia; he will come late in your old age and will be born in the forest. He will be both king and the father of kings, and through him our race will rule in Alba Longa.

[766] 'Next to him is Procas, pride of the Trojans, and then Capys and Numitor. Next is the one who will revive your name, Silvius Aeneas; he will have your virtue and martial skill, if he might at last gain the Alban throne.…

[778] 'And look! There is Romulus! His mother Ilia will bear him into Assaracus's line. Do you see how Mars' twin plumes stand on his crest? and how his father uses his own emblem to mark him out for the world above? Under his command glorious Rome will bring together the power of the earth and the will of heaven. With a single wall he will encircle seven hills, happy in her race of men.…

[788] 'And look over here! Gaze at this people, your own Romans! Here is Caesar, and all the descendents of Iulus who are fated to live under the vault of heaven. Here is the man! This is he! This is the one you so often heard promised! Augustus Caesar, son of the Deified one! He will bring a Golden Age again to the fields where Saturn once reigned. He will extend Rome's empire beyond Libya and India, [795] to a land beyond the path of the stars, beyond the annual journey of the sun, to where Atlas turns the sphere on his shoulders, inset with gleaming stars. Even now the Caspian kingdoms and Maeotian lands tremble at the prophecies of his coming, and the restless mouths of the seven-branched Nile quake.…

[808] 'Who is that man, over there, crowned with olive branches and carrying sacred vessels? I know the hair and that white-beard. They belong to a king of Rome, Numa, called to the highest office from the poor soil of tiny Cures. He will be the first to set our first city under the rule of law. Tullus will com after him. He will shake up the country's rest and call its troops to arms, men now unaccustomed to triumphs. [815] Behind him is boastful Ancus, too pleased even now with his popularity. Do you also see the dynasty of Tarquinius? and the brave spirit of Brutus the avenger, who will reclaim the fasces? He will be the first to hold a consul's powers and the severe axes. [820] When his sons stir up a new civil war, their father will take them to task for the sake of freedom. He is to be pitied, regardless of how later generations praise his actions: but love of country prevails, and great desire for glory.

[824] 'Look, too, over there! See the Decii and Drusi, and Torquatus with his cruel axe, and Camillus bringing back the standards. But those others that you can see, standing together in matching armour, their souls are in harmony now, while they are standing in

darkness. Alas, if they reach the light of the living, what civil war, what battle and slaughter, they'll start! The father-in-law, Julius Caesar, descending from Alpine ramparts, from the fort of Monoecus; [830] his son-in-law, Pompey, opposing him with Eastern forces. You two! My sons! Never allow your spirits even to consider such wars! Never turn your homeland's powerful forces on itself! You who derive your race from heaven, you must be the first to halt, the first to hurl weapons from your hands, you who are my descendants!

[836] 'And look, there's Mummius. He will triumph over Corinth and drive his chariot in victory to the high Capitol, famed for the Greeks he will have slaughtered. Next is Aemilius Paulus, avenger of his Trojan ancestors and of Minerva's desecrated shrine. He will destroy Agamemnon's Mycenae, and Argos, and defeat Perseus, the Aeacid, descendant of warlike Achilles.

[841] Who could leave you unmentioned, great Cato? or you Cossus? or the clan of Gracchus? or the two Scipios, the lightning bolts of war and the destroyers of Libya? or you Fabricius, poor but great? or you, Serranus, sowing your fields with seed when called to greatness? Fabii, where do you hurry my weary steps? [845] You, Fabius Maximus, are the one who saved our state by delaying.

'What is the point? Others nations, I believe, will fashion bronze more artistically than we Romans, or shape living features from marble; others will argue their cases better and trace the movement of the heavens with instruments, [850] predicting the movement of the stars. But remember, Roman, that it is for you to govern the nations with empire. This will be your skill: to impose the ways of peace, to spare the conquered, and subdue the proud.' …

6. 886-901 The Gates of Sleep

Onwards they wander here and there and over the wide plain, and gaze at everything in these broad lands. Anchises now leads his son through each place and sets his spirit ablaze with love of future glory; [890] he tells him now of the wars that must soon be fought and tells him about the Laurentine peoples and the city of Latinus. He instructs him which trials to avoid and which to face.

At the edge of the plain stand two gates of Sleep. One of them is said to be of horn, and through it true dreams find easy passage. [895] The other is perfectly polished ivory and gleams white. Through it, however, the dead send false dreams into the upper world.

After his words, Anchises accompanies his son to that place and sends him back through the ivory gate, together with the Sibyl. Aeneas makes his way back to the ships where he rejoins his friends, and they set sail straight to Caieta's harbour along the shore.

Adapted from John Conington, *The Works of Vergil translated into English Prose* (Philadelphia: David McKay, 1893).

Reading 8b. The Achievements of the Divine Augustus

The murder of Julius Caesar led to the outbreak of a new civil war. After a tumultuous decade, Octavian, the adoptive son of Caesar, was left as the preeminent ruler of the Roman world. He consolidated his position by instituting numerous political, social, and economic changes. The most significant of these changes were made in the year 27 BC. At this time he officially changed his name to Augustus and established his authority as the ***princeps*** (first citizen). The new system of government which he refined was later termed the "Principate" by historians, but Augustus himself called it "a restoration of the Republic." The changes Augustus made introduced a new age of internal peace and prosperity for Rome and the Empire. His reorganization of the Empire initiated a system which saw lasting peace for almost one hundred years. Suetonius, who wrote biographies of Rome's first emperors, records the intentions of Augustus as outlined in an official edict:

> May I be privileged to build firm and lasting foundations for the government of the state. May I also achieve the reward to which I aspire: that of being known as the author of the best possible Constitution, and of carrying with me, when I die, the hope that these foundations, which I have established for the state, will abide secure.

There are several ancient writers who detail events and changes in the age of Augustus, but we are fortunate to have a work written by Augustus himself. When Augustus died in AD 14, he left behind a document which catalogued the most significant achievements of his career. This document, termed the *Res Gestae Divi Augusti* (*The Achievements of the Divine Augustus*), was inscribed on bronze tablets and set up in front of his great mausoleum in Rome. Other copies still exist, inscribed on a temple of Rome and Augustus in the city of Ankara in Turkey.

The *Res Gestae* was addressed to the people of the city Rome, and most of the detailed information contained in it are of special interest to the inhabitants of that city. Augustus wrote it just before his death in AD 14, and it offers details about the achievements that Augustus was particularly proud of. It emphasizes his generosity, the honours he was awarded, his military victories, and the expenditures he made as the leading citizen of Rome. All of these virtues are offered to justify his position as *princeps*.

The documentation of these underscores his supreme authority and personal glory, and as such it fits into a long traditional of funeral orations and honorific inscriptions employed by great men of the late Republic. For this reason it is not a complete summation of his Principate, since it reveals little about his administrative changes, his legislation, or even his foreign policy. Instead it stands as an example of the Augustus' skill in self-promotion by clearly detailing the great achievements which Augustus preferred were remembered.

Consider the following:

- Did Augustus really 'restore the Republic' in 27 BC?
- What is the overall significance of the titles assumed by Augustus?
- List some examples of expenditures by Augustus. On what does he spend his money?

Augustus' account of his own reign

1. Appended is a record of the deeds of the Deified Augustus, through which he reduced the whole world to the rule of the Roman people, and of the sums which he spent on the Roman state and the Roman people. They were engraved upon two bronze columns which have been set up in Rome.

When I was nineteen I collected an army on my own initiative and at my own expense that I used to restore freedom to the state, which had been enslaved by the tyranny of a faction. For these services, the senate, in complimentary decrees, added my name to the roll of their House in the consulship of Gaius Pansa and Aulus Hirtius (43 BC), granting to me at the same time the right to vote amongst the ex-consuls as well as a formal command. The senate ordered me as a propraetor 'to see along with the consuls that the republic suffered no damage.' Moreover, in the same year, when both consuls had died, the people elected me consul and a triumvir for restoring the constitution.

2. I drove those who killed my father into exile, punishing their crime according to the law, and afterwards when these same men rose in arms against the state I conquered them twice in battle.

3. I undertook wars by land and sea, civil and foreign, all over the world, and when victorious I spared surviving citizens. I preferred to preserve rather than exterminate those foreign nations that could safely be pardoned. Some 500,000 Roman citizens took the military oath to me. Of these I settled considerably more than 300,000 in colonies or sent back to their own towns, after their terms of service were over. I assigned to them all lands that I had purchased by myself, or some I gave money in lieu of lands. I captured 600 ships, not counting those below the rating of warship.

4. I twice celebrated an ovation, three times curule triumphs, and was twenty-one times saluted as *imperator*. Though the senate afterwards voted me several triumphs I declined them. I frequently also deposited laurels in the Capitol after performing the vows which I had taken in each war. For successful operations by land and sea performed by myself or by subordinates acting under my auspices, the senate fifty-three times decreed official thanks-givings to the immortal gods. The number of days during which, in accordance with a decree of the senate, thanksgivings were offered amounted to 890. Nine kings or sons of kings were led before my chariot in my triumphs. At the time that I wrote this, I had been consul thirteen times, and am now in the middle of the thirty-seventh year of my tribunician power (AD 13-14).

5. During the consulship of Marcus Marcellus and Lucius Arruntius (BC 22) a dictatorship was offered me by the senate and people, but I declined to accept it. A commissionership of corn supply I did not refuse to undertake at a time of great scarcity of corn, and I administered it in such a way that within a few days the entire population was freed from fear and danger. I was then offered a consulship to be held each year for the rest of my life but I declined it.

6. In the consulship of M. Vinicius and Q. Lucretius (19 BC), of P. and Cn. Lentulus (18 BC), and of Paullus Fabius Maximus and Q. Tubero (11 BC), when the senate and people of Rome unanimously agreed that I should be elected overseer of the laws and morals, with unlimited powers and without a colleague, I refused any office offered me that was contrary to the

customs of our ancestors. But what the senate at that time wanted me to oversee, I carried out in virtue of my tribunician power, and in this office I received at my own request a colleague from the senate five times.

7. I was a triumvir for the restoration of the constitution for ten consecutive years. As I write this I have been 'First man of the senate' for forty years. I am Pontifex Maximus, Augur, one of the fifteen commissioners for religion, one of the seven for sacred feasts, an Arval brother, a sodalis Titius, and a fetial priest.

8. In my fifth consulship (29 BC), on an instruction from the people, I increased the number of the patricians. On three occasions I revised the roll of the senate, and in my sixth consulship (28 BC) I conducted a census of the Roman people with M. Agrippa as my colleague. After an interval of forty-one years, I completed the census in which the number of Roman citizens entered on the census roll was 4,063,000. Conferred with consular power, I took the census by myself a second time in the consulship of Gaius Censorinus and Gaius Asinius (8 BC), in which the number of Roman citizens enrolled was 4,223,000. I took a third census with consular power with my son Tiberius Caesar acting as my colleague in the consulship of Sextus Pompeius and Sextus Appuleius (AD 14); in it the number of Roman citizens entered on the census roll was 4,937,000. By passing new laws I restored numerous traditions of our ancestors that were falling into disuse, and in many areas I myself set precedents for future generations to imitate.

9. The senate decreed that every fifth year the consuls and priests should make vows for my health. In fulfilment of these vows games have been celebrated many times, often by the four chief colleges of priests or the consuls. In addition the people at large both individually and in their towns always offered prayers at all the temples for my health.

10. By a decree of the senate my name was included in the hymn of the Salii, and it was ordained by a law that my life should be sacred and that I should have the tribunician power for the term of my natural life. I declined to become Pontifex Maximus in the place of my colleague while he was still alive, though the people offered me that sacred office, which was formerly held by my father. Some years later I accepted that sacred office following the death of the man who had used the civil war to secure it; in the consulship of P. Sulpicius and C. Valgius (12 BC), a great multitude flocked to my election of this priesthood from all parts of Italy; the crowd was larger than ever recorded to have come to Rome before.

......

13. Our ancestors ordered the temple of Janus to be closed whenever peace came to the whole empire of the Roman people by land and sea through victory. From the time of our city's foundation down to the time of my bith it is recorded to have been shut only twice. During my principate, the senate ordered its closure three times.

14. As a compliment to me, the senate and Roman people awarded the office of consul to my sons Gaius and Lucius Caesar, whom fortune stole from me in their early manhood. This was done in their fifteenth year with the proviso that they should enter on that office after an interval of five years. From the day that they assumed the toga of manhood, the senate decreed that they should take part in public business. Moreover, the Roman knights as a collective gave each of them the title of *princeps iuventutis* ('leader of the youth') and presented each with a silver shield and spear.

15. To the Roman plebs I paid 300 sesterces per head in virtue of my father's final will and testament; and in my own name I gave 400 apiece in my fifth consulship (29 BC) from the sale of the spoils of war; and a second time in my tenth consulship (24 BC) out of my own private property I gave a gift of 400 sesterces per man, and in my eleventh consulship (23 BC) I measured out twelve distributions of corn, having purchased it from my own resources. In the twelfth year of my tribunician power (11 BC), I gave a bounty of 400 sesterces a head for the third time. These largesses of mine were never given to fewer than 50,200 persons. In the eighteenth year of my tribunician power and my twelfth consulship (5 BC) I gave 320,000 of the urban plebs sixty denarii a head....

16. I paid municipalities for the lands that I distributed to soldiers in my fourth consulship (30 BC) and again in the consulship of M. Crassus and Cn. Lentulus the augur (14 BC). The amount was about 600,000,000 sesterces for lands in Italy, and about 260,000,000 for lands in the provinces.

Of all the generals who settled soldiers and established colonies in Italy and the provinces, I was the first and only figure within the memory of my own generation to pay for land. And afterwards in the consulship of Tib. Nero and Cn. Piso (7 BC), and again in the consulship of C. Antistius and D. Laelius (6 BC), and of C. Calvisius and L. Pasienus (4 BC), and of L. Lentulus and M. Messalla (3 BC), and of L. Caninius and Q. Fabricius (2 BC), I paid retirement allowances in cash to soldiers, and I sent them back to their own towns after their terms of service. This act of kindness cost 400,000,000 sesterces.

17. I subsidised the public treasury from my own money four times; the sums which I paid over to the commissioners of the treasury amounted to 150,000,000 sesterces. And in the consulship of M. Lepidus and L. Arruntius (AD 6), I contributed from my own estate 170,000,000 sesterces to the military treasury which was established on my initiative to pay retirement allowances for soldiers who had served twenty years or more....

19. I built the senate house and the Chalcidicum adjoining it, and the temples of Apollo on the Palatine with its colonnades, the temple of the Deified Julius, the Lupercal, the colonnade at the Flaminian circus, which I allowed to be called the Portico of Octavius after the name of the builder of the earlier one on the same site, the state box at the Circus Maximus, the temples of Jupiter Feretrius and of Jupiter Tonans on the Capitol, the temple of Quirinus, the temples of Minerva and of Juno the Queen, and of Jupiter Liberalis on the Aventine, the temple of the Lares at the head of the *via Sacra*, the temple of the divine Penates in the Velia, the temple of Youth, the temple of the Mater Magna on the Palatine.

20. The Capitolium and the Pompeian theatre — both very costly works — I restored without adding any inscription of my own name. In many places where aquaducts were decaying from age, I repaired them; and I doubled the size of the aqueduct called the Aqua Marcia by turning a new spring into its channel.

I completed the Forum Iulium and the Basilica, which was between the temple of Castor and the temple of Saturn, works begun and almost completed by my father. When the same basilica was destroyed by fire, I began its reconstruction on an enlarged site, to be inscribed with the names of my sons, and in case I do not live to complete it I have ordered it to be completed by my heirs.

In my sixth consulship (28 BC), I repaired eighty-two temples of the gods in the city in accordance with a decree of the senate, passing over none that at that time stood in need of repair. In my seventh consulship (27 BC) I constructed the Flaminian road from the city to Ariminum, and all the bridges except the Mulvian and Minucian.

21. On ground belonging to myself I built a temple to Mars the Avenger and the Forum Augustum, with money arising from sale of the spoils of war. I built a theatre next to the temple of Apollo, on ground for the most part purchased from private owners, which was named after my son-in-law Marcus Marcellus. Offerings from money raised by sale of war-spoils I consecrated in the temple of Apollo, and in the temple of Vesta, and in the temple of Mars Ultor, which cost me about 100,000,000 sesterces. In my fifth consulship (29 BC), I refunded thirty-five thousand pounds of gold, which was the crown money contributed by the municipalities and colonies of Italy for my triumphs; subsequently, as often as I was saluted as Imperator, I again refused to receive crown money, although the municipalities and colonies had decreed it with the same enthusiasm as before.

22. I gave gladiatorial shows in my own name three times, and five times in the name of my sons and grandsons; some 10,000 men fought in them. I twice gave the people a show of athletes collected from all parts of the world in my own name, and a third time in the name of my grandson. I gave games in my own name four times, and in place of other magistrates twenty-three times. On behalf of the quindecimviri, and as master of the college, with M. Agrippa as colleague, I gave the Secular games in the consulship of C. Furnius and C. Silanus (17 BC). In my thirteenth consulship (2 BC), I gave for the first time the games of Mars which, since that time, the consuls have given in subsequent years. I gave the people wild-beast hunts, of African animals, in my own name and that of my sons and grandsons, in the circus and forum, and the amphitheatres twenty-six times, in which about 3,500 animals were killed.

23. In order to entertain the masses I staged a naval battle on the other side of the Tiber, in the spot where the grove of the Caesars is now, after having created a basin that was 1,800 feet long and 1,200 feet wide. In it a mock-battle took place with thirty beaked warships and a still larger number of smaller vessels. Some three thousand men fought these fleets, not counting the rowers.

25. I cleared the sea of pirates, and in doing so I captured some 30,000 slaves who had run away from their masters and had taken up arms against the state. I then handed them back to their owners to be punished.

In the war in which I won the victory off Actium, the whole of Italy took the oath to me spontaneously, and demanded that I should be its leader. The provinces of the Gauls, the Spains, Africa, Sicily, Sardinia, took the same oath. Among those who fought under my standards were more than seven hundred senators, eighty-three of whom had been, or have since been, consuls; 170 of them were or have since been members of the sacred colleges.

26. I extended the frontiers of all the provinces of the Roman people, which were bordered by tribes that had not submitted to our Empire. The provinces of the Gauls, and Spains and Germany, bounded by the Ocean from Gades to the mouth of the river Elbe, I reduced to a peaceful state. ... By my command and under my auspices, two armies were marched into Ethiopia and Arabia Felix, nearly simultaneously, and large hostile forces of both of these nations were cut to pieces in battle, and a large number of towns were captured. ...

27. I added Egypt to the Empire of the Roman people. When I might have made the Greater Armenia a province after the assassination of its king Artaxes, I preferred, on the precedent of our ancestors, to hand over that kingdom to Tigranes, son of King Artavasdes, grandson of King Tigranes, by the hands of Tiberius Nero, who was then my stepson....

28. I settled colonies of soldiers in Africa, Sicily, Macedonia, both the Spains, Achaia, Asia, Syria, Gallia Narbonensis, and Pisidia. Italy has twenty-eight colonies established under my auspices, which have in my lifetime become very densely inhabited and places of great resort.

29. Following victories in Spain, Gaul, and Dalmatia, I recovered a large number of military standards, which had been lost under other commanders. I also compelled the Parthians to restore the spoils and standards of three Roman armies, and to seek as suppliants the friendship of the Roman people. These standards I deposited in the inner shrine belonging to the temple of Mars Ultor. ...

34. In my sixth and seventh consulships (28 and 27 BC), after I had extinguished the flames of civil war, and while I possessed full control of the state, I transferred the state from my power to the control of the senate and people of Rome. For this service of mine I was given the name of Augustus by a decree of the senate, and the door-posts of my house were covered with laurels in the name of the state, and a civic crown was fixed up over my door, and a golden shield was placed in the Curia Iulia, which it was declared by its inscription the senate and people of Rome gave me in recognition of valour, clemency, justice, and piety. After that time I took precedence of all in rank, but of power I had nothing beyond what was held by those who were my colleagues in the various magistracies.

35. While I was administering my thirteenth consulship (2 BC), the senate and equestrian order and the Roman people with unanimous consent greeted me as Father of my Country, and decreed that this tile should be inscribed on the vestibule of my house, and on the senate house, and in the Forum Augustum, and under the chariot which was there placed in my honour in accordance with a senatorial decree.

When I wrote this I was in my seventy-sixth year (AD 13-14).

Adapted from Frederick William Shipley (1871-1945), *The Res Gestae of Augustus* (London, Heinemann, 1924).

Reading 8c. Tacitus on Augustus' Reign

One of the greatest Roman historians was Cornelius Tacitus (A.D. c.56-c.118), whose various works cover the history of Rome from the death of Augustus to the death of the emperor Domitian in A.D. 96. Like many Roman historians, he was interested in moral lessons, believing that decline and disaster resulted from vice and moral decay. As a result his writing is full of sardonic commentary on the underlying psychological motives of the emperors and their families, whom he sees as corrupt and flawed.

His own experiences and observations during the autocratic regime of the Emperor Domitian (A.D. 81-96) affected his view of the Principate established by Augustus. He believed that the Republican period, when Rome was ruled by senatorial oligarchy, was preferable to that of his own day. He idealized the old republican period as a time of opportunity and liberty, a view which reflected his upper class, senatorial values.

Tacitus is the best literary source for events of the first century A.D. He is noted for his ability to collect and evaluate evidence, constructing a carefully structured narrative. Like Sallust and Livy, Tacitus' goal was to draw moral lessons from the past, but while Livy's subject matter was the romantic and glorious achievements of the early republic, Tacitus' subject matter was the recent past under the rule of Rome's emperors. He states in the *Annals*, "It seems to me a historian's foremost duty to ensure that merit is recorded, and to confront evil words and deeds with the fear of posterity's denunciations." To that end he pursued the moral lessons which he believed history could provide posterity.

In the introduction to the Annales, Tacitus briefly discusses the Principate of Augustus in order to introduce the reign of Tiberius, who succeeded Augustus. He offers competing interpretations of Augustus' reign.

Tacitus, Annals, 1. 1-10

1. ROME in the beginning was ruled by kings. Freedom and the consulship were established by Lucius Brutus. Occasionally dictatorships were needed, but only for a temporary crisis. The power of the decemvirs did not last beyond two years, nor was the consular jurisdiction of the military tribunes of long duration. The despotisms of Cinna and Sulla were brief; the power of Pompeius and of Crassus soon yielded to Caesar, and the arms of Lepidus and Antonius yielded to Augustus. It was Augustus who, when the world was wearied by civil strife, subjected it to his power under the title of *princeps*.

The successes and reverses of the ancient Romans have been recorded by famous historians; and there was no lack of impressive intellects available to describe the times of Augustus, until growing sycophancy scared them away. But while Tiberius, Gaius, Claudius, and Nero were in power, the histories of their reigns were falsified through fear, and after their death historical accounts were written under the irritation of recent hatred. Hence my purpose is to describe the reign of Tiberius and all events following, but first I must relate a few facts about Augustus, especially his final acts. My account of this period is written without either bitterness or partiality and I have no motive for either.

2. After the destruction of Brutus and Cassius there were no longer any Republican forces. Pompeius was crushed in Sicily. Once Lepidus was pushed aside and then Antonius slain, even the Julian faction had only Caesar left to lead it. Then Augustus dropped the title of triumvir. From that point on he presented himself first as Consul and then claimed that he was satisfied with a tribune's authority for the protection of the people. While doing this he won over the soldiers with gifts, the populace with cheap corn, and everyone with the sweet gift of peace. In this way his power grew greater by slow steps, while he concentrated in himself the functions of the senate, the magistrates, and the laws. He was completely unopposed, for the boldest spirits had fallen in battle or had been murdered during the proscriptions. The remaining nobles were ready to give up their freedom because they were elevated through wealth and promotion. The result was that, aggrandised by revolution, they preferred the safety of the present to the dangerous past. Nor were the provinces dissatisfied with the new arrangement, for they distrusted the government of the senate and the people. They had been left vulnerable to the various rivalries between the leading men and the rapacity of their officials, and existing laws had offered them no protection. As a result they were continually victimized by violence, intrigue, and finally by corruption.

3. Augustus meanwhile began to build safeguards to his power. He promoted Claudius Marcellus, his sister's son to a pontificate and curule aedileship, even though he was a mere boy. He gave Marcus Agrippa two consecutive consulships, despite his humble birth, because he was a good soldier and someone who had shared his victories. When Marcellus died soon afterwards, he also made Agrippa his own son-in-law.

He honoured Tiberius Nero and Claudius Drusus, his stepsons, with imperial titles, although his own family was as yet undiminished. For he had admitted Gaius and Lucius, the sons of Agrippa, into the house of the Caesars. Before these boys had yet laid aside the dress of boyhood he had most fervently desired that they should have the titles "princes of the youth" and be consuls-elect, although he had pretended to be reluctant. Agrippa died, however, as did Lucius and Gaius: Lucius, on his way to our armies in Spain, and Gaius while returning from Armenia, where he had been wounded in battle. Both were prematurely cut off by destiny, unless it was by their step-mother Livia's treachery. Of Augustus' stepsons, Drusus had long been dead and only Tiberius Nero remained, and towards him all eyes were beginning to turn. He was adopted as a son, as a colleague in empire and a partner in the tribunitian power. He was paraded through all the armies, no longer through his mother's secret intrigues, but at her open suggestion. For she had gained such a hold on the aged Augustus that he sent his only grandson, Agrippa Postumus, as an exile to the island of Planasia. Postumus, though devoid of worthy qualities, and having only the brute courage of physical strength, had not been convicted of any serious offence. And yet Augustus had appointed Germanicus, the son of Drusus, to the command of eight legions on the Rhine, and required Tiberius to adopt him, although Tiberius already had a grown son in his house. Augustus did this in order that he might have several safeguards to rest on. Augustus had no ongoing war now except the one against the

Germans, and this was more to remove the disgrace of the loss of Quintilius Varus and his legions than out of an ambition to extend the empire. At home all was tranquil, and government was being handled by the regular magistrates. There was now a younger generation taking over, who had grown up since the victory of Actium, and even many of the older men had only been born during the civil wars. How few were left who had seen the Republic!

4. Thus the state had been fundamentally changed, and there was not a vestige left of the old sound morality. Stripped of equality, everyone looked confidently to the commands of a sovereign. This confidence lasted while Augustus was alive and could maintain his own position, as well as the position of his house and the general state of peace and stability.

As Augustus began to advance towards old age, and became worn out by an increasingly sickly body, his end was growing near and new attitudes began to appear in the people. A few even spoke in vain of the blessings of freedom. Most dreaded war, while others longed for it. The popular gossip of the large majority fastened itself variously on their future masters. "Agrippa was savage, and had been exasperated by insult, and neither from age nor experience in affairs was equal to so great a burden. Tiberius Nero was of mature years, and had established his fame in war, but he had the old arrogance inbred in the Claudian family, and many symptoms of a cruel temper, though they had been repressed, occasionally broke out. He had also from earliest infancy been reared in an imperial house; consulships and triumphs had been heaped on him in his younger days; even in the years that, on the pretext of seclusion, Tiberius spent in exile at Rhodes, he had only thought about wrath, hypocrisy, and secret perversions. There was his mother, too, with her capricious character. Now it seemed inevitable that control would fall to a woman and two young men, who for a while would burden the state and some day destroy it."

5. While these and like topics were discussed, Augustus grew increasingly frail. Some even suspected treachery on his wife's part. For a rumour had surfaced that a few months before his death Augustus had secretly sailed to Planasia to visit Agrippa, with one companion, Fabius Maximus. Only a few of his closest friends knew of this. Many tears were said to have shed on both sides, with expressions of affection, and that thus there was a hope of the young man being restored to the home of his grandfather. This, it was said, Maximus had divulged to his wife Marcia, and she in turn reported it to Livia. All this became known to Tiberius. Maximus died soon afterwards. Some thought the death was self-inflicted since at his funeral there were reports that his wife Marcia reproached herself there for having been the cause of her husband's destruction.

Whatever the facts of this were, news that Augustus was dying reached Tiberius just as he was entering Illyria. He was summoned home by an urgent letter from his mother. Tiberius found Augustus at the city of Nola, though it is unclear whether he was still living or had already died. For Livia had surrounded the house and its approaches with a strict watch, and favourable bulletins were being published from time to time. This continued until provision had been made for the demands of the crisis, and then a bulletin was released that told everyone that Augustus was dead and that Tiberius Nero was master of the state.

6. The first crime of the new reign was the murder of Postumus Agrippa. Though he was taken by surprise and was unarmed, one of the most battle-hardened centurions was able to kill him only with difficulty. Tiberius gave

no explanation of the matter to the senate; he pretended that there were directions from his father ordering the tribune in charge of the prisoner not to delay the slaughter of Agrippa, once Augustus himself had taken his last breath. Without doubt, Augustus had often complained of the young man's character, and had thus succeeded in obtaining a decree of the senate sanctioning the young man's banishment. But he never was hard-hearted enough to destroy any other member of his family, nor was it believable that he would sentence a grandson to death in order that his stepson might feel secure. It was more probable that Tiberius and Livia, the one from fear, the other from a stepmother's hate, hastened the destruction of a youth whom they suspected and hated. When the centurion reported, according to military custom, that he had carried out his orders, Tiberius replied that he had not given the command, and that the act must be justified to the senate. This terrified Sallustius Crispus, who shared in the secret (he had, in fact, sent the written order to the tribune). For he feared that responsibility would now be shifted on himself. Seeing that his peril was the same whether he told fiction or truth, he advised Livia not to divulge the secrets of her house or the counsels of friends, or any services performed by the soldiers, nor to let Tiberius weaken the strength of imperial power by referring everything to the senate. "The secret," he said, "of keeping power is that the accounts cannot be balanced unless they are rendered to one person."

7. Meanwhile at Rome, everyone plunged into slavery, especially the consuls, senators, and knights. The higher a man's rank, the keener was his hypocrisy and the more careful was his exertnal reaction. He must be careful neither to show joy at the decease of one emperor nor to sorrow at the accession of another, thus requiring a careful mix of joy, lamentation, and flattery. Sextus Pompeius and Sextus Apuleius, the consuls, were the first to swear allegiance to Tiberius Caesar, and in their presence the oath was taken by Seius Strabo and Gaius Turranius, respectively the commander of the praetorian cohorts and the superintendent of the corn supplies. Then the senate, the soldiers and the people did the same. For Tiberius would inaugurate everything with the consuls, as though the ancient constitution remained, and he hesitated about being emperor. Even the proclamation by which he summoned the senators to their chamber, he issued merely with the title of Tribune, which he had received under Augustus. The wording of the proclamation was brief, and in a very modest tone. "He would," it said, "provide for the honours due to his father, and not leave the lifeless body, and this was the only public duty he now claimed."

As soon as Augustus was dead, however, Tiberius had given the watchword to the praetorian cohorts, as commander-in-chief. He had the guard under arms, with all the other trappings of a court; soldiers attended him to the forum; soldiers went with him to the senate House. He sent letters to the different armies, as though supreme power was now his, and showed hesitation only when he spoke in the senate. His chief motive was fear that Germanicus, who had at his disposal so many legions, such vast auxiliary forces of the allies, and such amazing popularity, might prefer being ruler to the expectation of later rule. Tiberius also was considering public opinion. He wanted to get credit for having been called and elected by the state rather than of having crept into power through the adoption of a senile old man under the influence of a scheming wife. It was subsequently understood that Tiberius also pretended hesitance in order to test the temper of the nobles. For he would twist a word or a look into a crime and store it up in his memory for later use.

8. On the first day of the senate he allowed nothing to be discussed but the funeral of Augustus, whose will, which was brought in by the Vestal Virgins, named as his heirs Tiberius and Livia. The latter was to be admitted into the Julian family with the name of Augusta; next in expectation were the grand and great-grandchildren. In the third place, he had named the chief men of the state, most of whom he hated, simply out of ostentation and to win credit with posterity. His legacies were not beyond the scale of a private citizen, except a bequest of 43,500,000 sesterces "to the people and populace of Rome", of one 1000 to every praetorian soldier, and of 300 to every man in the legionary cohorts composed of Roman citizens. Next followed a deliberation about funeral honours. Of these the most imposing were thought fitting. The procession was to be conducted through "the gate of triumph," on the motion of Gallus Asinius. Lucius Arruntius proposed that the titles of the laws he passed and the names of the nations he conquered were to be borne in front of this procession. Messala Valerius further proposed proposed that the oath of allegiance to Tiberius should be yearly renewed, and when Tiberius asked him whether it was at his bidding that he had brought forward this motion, he replied that he had proposed it spontaneously, and that in whatever concerned the state he would use only his own discretion, even at the risk of giving offence. This was the only style of adulation that yet remained. The senators unanimously exclaimed that the body ought to be borne on their shoulders to the funeral pyre. The emperor, with disdainful moderation, excused them from that burden. He then issued an edict admonishing the common peope not to indulge in that tumultuous enthusiasm which had disturbed the funeral of the Divine Julius, nor carry out a wish that Augustus should be cremated in the Forum instead of in his appointed resting-place in the Campus Martius. On the day of the funeral, there was a detachment of soldiers standing guard, a fact heavily criticized by those who had witnessed Julius Caesar's funeral themselves or who had heard about it from their parents. Then, of course, slavery was still something new, and freedom had been resought in vain, and the assassination of Caesar, the Dictator, seemed to some the vilest, to others, the most glorious of deeds. "Now," they said, "an aged sovereign, whose power had lasted long, who had provided his heirs with abundant means to coerce the state, surely requires the defence of soldiers that his burial may be undisturbed."

9. Then followed much talk about Augustus himself, and many were struck by the remarkable coincidence that the same day marked the beginning of his assumption of empire and the end of his life, and, again, that he had ended his days at Nola in the same house and room as his father Octavius. People extolled, too, the number of his consulships, in which he had equalled Valerius Corvus and Gaius Marius combined; the continuance for thirty-seven years of the tribunitian power; the title of Imperator earned twenty-one times; and his other honours which had either frequently repeated or were wholly new.

Sensible men, however, spoke variously of his life with praise and censure. On the one hand, some observed he was driven to civil war by his sense of duty towards his father and by the needs of a republic in which laws had come to be meaningless. This was a situation that could neither be planned nor undertaken with any moral principles. He had often compromised with Antonius, while he was taking vengeance on his father's murderers, often also with Lepidus. When the latter sank into feeble dotage and the former had been ruined by his profligacy, the only remedy for his long-suffering country was the rule of a single man. Yet the republic had been organized under the name neither of a kingdom nor a dictatorship, but under that of a *princeps*. The ocean and remote rivers were the boundaries of the empire; the legions, provinces, fleets, all things were linked together; there was law for the citizens; there was respect shown to the allies. The capital had been embellished on a grand scale; only in a few instances had he resorted to force, but only when it was necessary to secure general peace.

10. On the other hand some complained that filial duty and state necessity were assumed as a pretext. It was really lust for power that led him to stir up his father's veterans by bribery. It was also lust for power that led him to raise an army, although a young man and a private citizen, and to tamper with the consul's legions, and pretend sympathy for the faction of Pompeius. Then he usurped the high functions and authority of Praetor by a decree of the senate. When Hirtius and Pansa were killed—whether they were destroyed by the enemy, or Pansa by poison infused into a wound and Hirtius by his own soldiers and Octavian's treacherous machinations—he at once took control of both their armies, wrested the consulate from a reluctant senate, and turned against the state the arms with which he had been entrusted to lead against Antonius. Citizens were proscribed and their lands divided. These acts that were condemned by everyone, even those who benefited from them. One might allow that the deaths of Cassius and of the Bruti were sacrifices to an enmity that he inherited (though duty requires us to waive private feuds for the sake of the public welfare). Nevertheless he tricked Pompeius by the phantom of peace, and Lepidus by the mask of friendship. Subsequently, he entrapped Antonius through the treaties of Tarentum and Brundisium and by a marriage to the sister, and Antonius paid by his death the penalty of a treacherous alliance. No doubt, there was peace after all this, but it was a peace stained with blood; there were the disasters of Lollius and Varus, the murders at Rome of Varro, Egnatius, and Jullus. Nor was domestic life of Augustus spared. "Nero's wife had been taken from him, and there had been the farce of consulting the pontiffs, whether, with a child conceived and not yet born, she could legitimately marry. There were the excesses of Quintus Tedius and Vedius Pollio; last of all, there was Livia, terrible to the republic as a mother, terrible to the house of the Caesars as a stepmother. No honour was left for the gods when Augustus allowed himself to be worshipped with temples and statues, like those of the deities, and with his own priests. He had not even adopted Tiberius as his successor out of affection or any regard to the state, but, having thoroughly seen his arrogant and savage temper, he had sought glory for himself by a contrast of extreme wickedness." For, in fact, Augustus, a few years before, when he was a second time asking from the senate the tribunitian power for Tiberius, though his speech was complimentary, had thrown out certain hints as to his manners, style, and habits of life, which he meant as criticisms, while he seemed to excuse them. However, when his obsequies had been duly performed, a temple with a religious ritual was decreed him.

Adapted from A.J. Church and W.J. Brodribb, *Annals of Tacitus* (London: Macmillan and Co., 1876)

Chapter 9:

The Julio-Claudians

Reading 9a. Tacitus: The Trial of Piso

The following excerpt is taken from the Annales of Tacitus. This selection contains a description of the events surrounding the death of Germanicus in Syria and the subsequent treason trial of Piso, early in the reign of Tiberius.

Germanicus was by birth the nephew of Tiberius, but had been adopted as his son late in the reign of Augustus. He married Agrippina, a grand-daughter of Augustus, and was extremely popular in Rome, having led Rome's armies in successful campaigns in Germany.

In A.D. 18, however, he was sent to Rome's eastern frontier to deal with diplomatic troubles there. Soon he and Gnaeus Piso, whom Tiberius sent to Syria as governor, began to quarrel. Finally, Germanicus expelled Piso from the province, but soon fell ill and died. Some thought he was poisoned. When Piso heard about Germanicus' death he tried unsuccessfully to force his way back into the province. When he returned to Rome, he was tried for murder and treason.

Some questions:

- What do you think Piso was guilty of?
- Who was more at fault in these quarrels: Piso or Germanicus?

Tacitus, Annals, Book II

[41] In the consulship of C. Caelius and L. Pomponius (AD 17), on the 26th day of May, Germanicus Caesar celebrated his triumph over the Cherusci, Chatti, and Angrivarii, and the other German tribes as far as the Elbe. The spoils, prisoners-of-war, and pictures of mountains, rivers, and battles were carried in the triumphal procession. The war was presented as having been finished, even though Germanicus had been forbidden to finish it. The admiration of the onlookers was heightened by the striking good looks of the general and the grandeur of

the chariot that bore his five children. Still, there was an underlying sense dread when people remembered what little good popular favour had done in the case of Drusus, his father. They also noted how popular his uncle Marcellus had been, only to be stolen from them while still a youth. The Roman people's favorites seemed all to be short-lived and ill-starred.

[42] Tiberius meanwhile gave every member of the city populace three hundred sesterces in the name of Germanicus, and nominated him to serve as his own colleague in the consulship. This failed to win him any credit for sincere affection towards his nephew, so he decided to get the young prince out of the way, pretending to be conferring a great distinction on him. To do this he had to invent reasons, or eagerly seize any reasons that opportunity presented.

King Archelaus had been ruler of Cappadocia for fifty years, and Tiberius hated him because he had not shown him any mark of respect while he was at Rhodes. … Archelaus, however, died, though it is unclear whether it was by his own act or by natural causes. Archelaus' kingdom was then reduced to a province, and Caesar declared that, with its revenues, the one per cent tax could be lowered for the future to one-half percent. … At about the same time, news arrived that Antiochus and Philopator had died, kings respectively of the Commageni and Cilicians, and that their nations were in turmoil. Most of their subjects wanted direct Roman rule; others, however, preferred to be ruled by their kings. Also, the provinces of Syria and Judaea, exhausted by their burdens, were begging for a reduction of tribute.

[43] Tiberius accordingly brought these matters before the Senate, as well as the state of affairs in Armenia. "The commotions in the East," he said, "can be quieted only by the wisdom, of Germanicus." He also noted that his own life was on the decline and that his son Drusus was not yet mature enough. And so, by a decree of the Senate, the provinces beyond sea were entrusted to Germanicus, with greater powers wherever he went than were given to those who obtained their provinces by lot or by the emperor's appointment. …

Tiberius also reassigned the sitting govenor of Syria Creticus Silanus, who was connected by a close tie with Germanicus, his daughter being betrothed to Nero, the eldest of Germanicus' children. In his place he appointed Gnaeus Piso, a man of violent temper, completely independent, with a natural arrogance…. To further inflame his ambition there was the noble rank and wealth of his wife Plancina. Piso could barely recognize himself as the inferior of Tiberius; as for Tiberius' children, he looked down on them as completely beneath him. He thought it clear that he had been chosen to govern Syria in order to thwart the aspirations of Germanicus. Some believed that he had even received secret instructions from Tiberius, and it was clear that Plancina was being advised by Livia Augusta, who was motivated by feminine jealousy to persecute Agrippina. For there was division and discord in the imperial family. Some were secretly loyal towards Drusus; others to Germanicus. Tiberius obviously favoured Drusus, since he was his son and born of his own blood. As for Germanicus, his uncle's animosity had increased the affection that everyone else felt for him, and there was the fact too that he had an advantage in the illustrious rank of his mother's family, among whom he could point to his grandfather Marcus Antonius and to his great-uncle Augustus….

[53] In the following year (AD 18) Tiberius held his third consulship and Germanicus his second. Germanicus, however, entered on the office at Nicopolis, a city of Achaea, where he had arrived along the coast of Illyricum, after having

seen his brother Drusus, who was then serving in Dalmatia, and having endured a stormy voyage through the Adriatic and afterwards the Ionian Sea. He accordingly spent a few days refitting his fleet, and, at the same time, in remembrance of his ancestors, he visited the bay that the victory of Actium had made famous. He saw the spoils consecrated by Augustus there, and the camp of Antonius. For, as I have said, Augustus was his great-uncle, Antonius his grandfather, and vivid images of disaster and success rose before him in that place. From there he went to Athens where, as a concession to our treaty with an allied and ancient city, he was accompanied only by a single lictor. The Greeks welcomed him with elaborate honours and boasted about all the ancient achievements and sayings of their countrymen in order to give additional dignity to their flattery.

[54] Then he sailed on to Euboea and then crossed to Lesbos, where Agrippina gave birth to their youngest child, Julia. He then reached the remoter parts of the province of Asia and visited the Thracian cities, Perinthus and Byzantium. From there he continued to the narrow strait of the Propontis and the entrance of the Pontus. His chief concern was to become acquainted with those ancient and celebrated localities.... He visited Ilium and surveyed a scene famous both as an example of the vicissitudes of fortune and as the birthplace of the Roman people. Then he coasted back along Asia, touching at Colophon to consult the oracle of Clarian Apollo. The oracle is is not a woman, as at Delphi, but a priest chosen from certain families, generally from Miletus, who ascertains simply the number and the names of the applicants. Then he descends into a cave and drinks a draught from a secret spring. Despite the fact that he is commonly ignorant of letters and of poetry, he then utters a response in verse answering to the unexpressed thoughts of the inquirer. It was said that he prophesied an early doom for Germanicus, though in coded language, as oracles usually do.

[55] Meanwhile Gnaeus Piso, rushing eastwards to carry out his assignment, terrified the citizens of Athens by entering the city precipitously and then attacking them in an antagonistic speech, making oblique criticisms of Germanicus, who, he said, had compromised the honour of the Roman name by having treated the Athenians with too much courtesy. They were not, he emphasized, the true people of Athens, who had been exterminated by repeated disasters. Rather, they were a miserable medley of tribes. As for the people standing before him? They had been allies of Mithridates against Sulla, and allies of Antonius against the Divine Augustus. He also mocked them with the past: with their failures against the Macedonians and the violence that they had committed against their own countrymen. In fact he had his own special grudge against Athens: because they refused his request that they pardon a certain Theophilus, whom their highest court had found guilty of forgery.

Then, by sailing rapidly and by the shortest route through the Cyclades, Piso overtook Germanicus at the island of Rhodes. Germanicus was not unaware of the insults that Piso had hurled against him. Germanicus' generous spirit was such that when a storm drove Piso's ship on the rocks, and his enemy's destruction could have been left to chance, he nevertheless sent some warships, and rescued him from danger. But this did not soften Piso's hatred. Scarcely allowing a day's interval, he left Germanicus and hastened on ahead. When he reached Syria and the legions, he began, by bribery and favoritism, to pander to even the humblest private, removing the old centurions and the strict tribunes and giving their positions to his supporters or to men of the worst character. He also allowed idleness in the camp, licentiousness in the towns, and the soldiers to roam through the country and take their pleasure. He was so successful in corrupting them that among themselves they called him 'the father of the legions'.

Nor was Plancina able to keep her behaviour within the proper limits of a woman's behaviour. She attended cavalry exercises and the maneuvers of the cohorts and would make snide remarks at the expense of Agrippina and Germanicus. Even some good soldiers began to fall under their corrupt influences, especially after a rumour began to gain ground that the emperor himself was sympathetic to their actions. Germanicus was aware of all of this, but his most pressing worry was to reach Armenia as quickly as possible.

[56] In ancient times, Armenia had been an unstable country. This was partly because of the character of its people and partly because of its geographical position, since it borders on our provinces and stretching far away to Media. Thus it lies between the world's two greatest empires, and has very often been at war with them, hating Rome and jealous of Parthia. It had at this time no king, having expelled Vonones. The nation inclined towards Zeno, son of Polemon, king of Pontus, who from his earliest infancy had imitated Armenian manners and customs, loving hunting, banqueting, and all the popular pastimes of barbarians, and who had in this way ingratiated himself to both its leaders and its people. Germanicus accordingly crowned him king in their capitol city of Artaxata in the presence of a vast multitude, with the approval of their nobility. All paid him homage and saluted him as King Artaxias, naming him after the city....

[57] This settlement was a great success and protected the interests of our allies, but it gave Germanicus little joy because of the arrogance of Piso, who had been ordered to lead some of the legions into Armenia under his own or his son's command. Piso had neglected to do either. When the two finally met at Cyrrhus, the winter-quarters of the tenth legion, they were both careful to control their appearance. Piso concealed his fears, Germanicus avoided any appearance of menace. He was indeed, as I have said, a kind-hearted man. His friends knew only too well, however, how to inflame this quarrel, and they began to exaggerate what was true and add lies in addition, alleging various charges against Piso, Plancina, and their sons.

At last, in the presence of a few close friends, Germanicus spoke to Piso. His words revealed his hidden resentment, and Piso replied with insincere apologies and arrogance. They now parted open enemies. After this Piso seldom appeared at Caesar's tribunal, and if he ever sat by him, it was with a frown and undisguised animosity. Once at a banquet given by the king of Nabataea, some golden crowns of great weight were presented to Caesar and Agrippina and light ones to Piso and the others. In response to this Piso declared that the reception was supposed to honour the son of a Roman emperor, not of a Parthian king. Then he threw his crown on the ground and began a long speech denouncing luxury. Although this angered Germanicus greatly, he still patiently endured it....

[59] In the consulship of Marcus Silanus and Lucius Norbanus (AD 19), Germanicus set out for Egypt to study its antiquities. His pretended motive, however, was to care for the province. Once there he lowered the price of grain by opening the granaries, and adopted many practices pleasing to the multitude. He would go about without soldiers, with sandaled feet, and dressed after the Greek fashion, in imitation of Publius Scipio, who, it is said, habitually did the same in Sicily, even when the war with Carthage was still raging. Tiberius expressed gentle disapproval of Germanicus' dress and manners. He also, however, pronounced a very sharp criticism of

his visit to Alexandria without the emperor's permission, since this was against the rules. For Augustus had forbidden senators and Roman knights of the higher rank to enter Egypt except with permission—this was one of his secrets of imperial policy—and he had specially isolated the country, fearing that any one who held a province containing the key of the land and of the sea, with ever so small a force against the mightiest army, might subject Italy to famine.

[60] Germanicus, however, had not yet learnt how much he was being criticized for his expedition, and so sailed up the Nile from the city of Canopus as his starting-point. ... Next he visited the vast ruins of ancient Thebes. ... [61] But Germanicus also paid attention to other wonders. One of these was the stone image of Memnon, which, when struck by the sun's rays, gives out the sound of a human voice. He also saw the pyramids, rising up like mountains amid almost impassable wastes of shifting sand, erected by the competitive nature and vast wealth of kings. He saw the great lake hollowed out of the earth to receive the Nile's floods, and elsewhere the river's narrow channel and profound depth which no explorer can plumb. He finally reached Elephantine and Syene, which was then the limit of the Roman Empire, which now extends to the Red Sea. ...

[69] On his return to Syria from Egypt, Germanicus found that all his orders to the legions and to the various cities had been repealed or reversed. This led to an angry outburst at Piso, who in turn savagely responded to Germanicus. Piso then decided to leave Syria. His departure, however, was delayed by the failing health of Germanicus. Learning of his recovery, however, and hearing that people who had made vows for his safety were now paying them, he took his lictors and drove away the victims placed by the altars with all the preparations for sacrifice, as well as the festal gathering of the populace of Antioch. Then he left for Seleucia and waited for news about the sickness, which had again beset Germanicus. The effect of the illness on Germanicus was made much worse by Germanicus' belief that Piso had poisoned him. A discovery made all this worse. For hidden in the floor and in the walls were found the disinterred remains of human bodies, incantations and spells, and the name of Germanicus inscribed on leaden tablets, half-burnt cinders smeared with blood, and other horrors by which the superstitious believe souls are devoted to the gods of the underworld. Piso, too, was accused of sending spies to report on every unfavorable symptom of the illness.

[70] Germanicus heard of all this with a combination of anger and fear. "If my doors," he said, "are to be besieged, and if I must gasp out my last breath while my enemies watch, what will then be the lot of my wretched wife? or of my infant children? Poison apparently is too slow; he is in a great hurry to gain sole control of the province and the legions. But Germanicus is not out of it yet! Nor will the murderer be able to keep the rewards of his monstrous act for long."

Germanicus then wrote a letter to Piso in which he renounced his friendship, and (according to many reports) ordered him to leave the province. Without further delay Piso now set sail, though slowly, so that his return journey would not have to be long if Germanicus' death leave Syria open to him.

[71] For a short time the prince's hopes rose; then his frame became exhausted, and, as his end drew near, he spoke as follows to the friends who were by his side:

"If I were succumbing to nature, I would be justified to complain even against the gods for tearing me away as a young man from parents, children, country by an untimely death. As it is, I'm being cut off by the wickedness of Piso and

Plancina, and so I leave to your hearts my last entreaties. Report to my father and brother how I was harmed by treachery and beset by treason, and how I have ended the most miserable of lives with the worst of deaths. If anyone was ever inspired by my bright prospects, by the stature of my relatives, or even by some envy held towards me while I lived, he will surely weep that the once prosperous survivor of so many wars has killed by a woman's treachery. You will have the opportunity to make our case before the Senate and appeal to Rome's laws. The most important duty of a friend, however, is not to bestow useless laments on a fallen friend, but to remember his wishes and to fulfill his instructions. Even strangers will shed tears for Germanicus. Vengeance can only come from you, if you loved the man more than his luck. Point out to the people of Rome the woman who as my wife—she is the granddaughter of the Divine Augustus! Bring my six children into their sight. Sympathy will be on your side if you bring this accusation, and if they try to protect themselves by alleging wicked orders, they will be disbelieved and unforgiven." His friends clasped the dying man's right hand, and swore that they would sooner lose their lives than the opportunity to avenge him.

[72] Germanicus then turned to his wife and begged her by the memory of her husband and by their shared children to lay aside her pride and to submit herself to the cruel blows of fortune. She must not, when she returned to Rome, enrage those who were stronger than her by competing for power. This was said openly; other words were whispered, which may suggest according to some that Tiberius was seen as a possible threat. Soon afterwards Germanicus died, to the intense sorrow of the province and of the region. Foreign nations and kings grieved over him, so great had been his courtesy to allies and his humanity to enemies. He inspired reverence both by his appearance and by his words, and while he maintained the greatness and dignity of the highest rank, he had escaped the hatred that typically follows arrogance.

[73] His funeral, though it lacked the customary statues of his family and procession, was honoured by eulogies and a commemoration of his virtues. There were some who, as they thought of his beauty, his age, and the manner of his death, as well as the region of the world where he died, likened his end to that of Alexander the Great. Both were handsome and of noble birth; neither was much older than thirty years of age, and both fell by the treachery of their own people in foreign lands. Germanicus had been gracious to his friends, moderate in his pleasures, the husband of one wife, and all his children had been born in wedlock. He was no less a warrior, though he lacked Alexander's recklessness, and although he had beaten Germany by his many victories, he was kept from completing their subjection. If he had had the sole power, or if had he possessed the full power and title of a king, he would have matched Alexander's military glory as easily as he had outstripped him in clemency, in self-restraint, and in all other virtues....

[74] Then the generals and other senators in Syria met to discuss the appointment of a new governor to Syria. No one was interested except Vibius Marsus and Gnaeus Sentius, who had had a long rivalry. In the end Marsus yielded to Sentius as an older and keener competitor. Vitellius and Veranius and others, who were preparing the accusation and the indictment as if a prosecution had already been commenced, demanded that Sentius immediately send to Rome a woman named Martina. She was notorious for poisonings in the province and a special favorite of Plancina.

[75] Meanwhile, although Agrippina was worn out with sorrow and bodily weakness, was

nonetheless impatient of everything which might delay her vengeance. She therefore embarked with the ashes of Germanicus and with her children, to universal expressions of sympathy. Here indeed was a woman of the highest nobility. Until just recently she was always seen amid an admiring and sympathizing crowd because of her splendid marriage. Now here she was clutching the ashes of her dead husband to her bosom. Her hope of revenge was uncertain, however, and her fears for herself very real: because of the ill-starred fruitfulness of her marriage, she had multiple hostages to fortune.

When news reached Piso that Germanicus was dead, he was at the island of Cos. He received the news with extravagant joy. He made sacrifices to the gods, visited the temples, with no moderation in his conduct. And Plancina's insolence increased even more. Indeed, she then for the first time ceased mourning for her lost sister and began wearing cheerful clothes.

Centurions kept approaching Piso, hinting to him that he had the sympathy of the legions at his command. "Go back," they said, "to the province that was wrongly taken from you, for it is still vacant." While he was considering what he should do, his son, Marcus Piso, urged him to return as quickly as possible to Rome. "So far," he said, "you have not done anything that can't be forgiven, and you need not fear feeble suspicions or vague rumours. Your strife with Germanicus may have won people's hatred, perhaps, but not guaranteed punishment. The fact that you have been deprived of the province will fully satisfy your enemies. But if you return to Syria and Sentius resist you? That is civil war, and you will not keep the centurions and soldiers on your side, who are powerfully swayed by the yet recent memory of their general and by a deep-rooted affection for the Caesars."

[77] Against this view Domitius Celer, one of Piso's closest friends, argued that he ought to take advantage of the opportunity. "It was Piso, not Sentius, who had been appointed to govern Syria. It was to Piso that the symbols of power and a praetor's jurisdiction and the legions had been allotted. If hostilities should break out, who would more rightfully confront them militarily than the man who had received the authority and special commission of a governor? And as for rumours, it is best to leave time in which they may die away. Often the innocent cannot stand against the first burst of unpopularity. But if Piso gets control of the army, and increases his resources, much that cannot be predicted will probably turn out in his favour. Are we hastening to reach Italy along with the ashes of Germanicus, that, unheard and undefended, you may be hurried to ruin by the wailings of Agrippina and the unpredictable reactions of an ignorant mob to wild rumour? You have on your side the complicity of Augusta and the emperor's favour, though in secret. Mark my words: no one will make a bigger show of mourning the death of Germanicus than those who most rejoice at it."

[78] Piso, who was always ready for violence, was persuaded by this view without much difficulty. He sent a letter to Tiberius accusing Germanicus of luxury and arrogance. He also asserted that, although he had been driven away to make room for a revolution, he had now resumed the command of the army in the same loyal spirit in which he had held it before. At the same time he put Domitius on board a warship, with an order to avoid the coast and to push on to Syria through the open sea away from the islands. He formed into regular companies the deserters who flocked to him, armed the camp-followers, crossed to the mainland with his ships, intercepted a detachment of new levies on their way to Syria, and sent instructions to the minor kings of Cilicia that they were to help him with

auxiliaries. In all the business of war, Piso's son actively helped him, even though he had advised against it.

[79] And so they sailed along the coast of Lycia and Pamphylia, and on meeting the fleet that was carrying Agrippina, both sides in hot anger at first armed for battle, and then in mutual fear confined themselves to insults. Marsus Vibius shouted to Piso that he should go to Rome to defend himself. Piso mockingly replied that he would be there as soon as the praetor who had to try poisoning cases had fixed a trial date for the accused and his prosecutors.

Meanwhile Domitius landed at Laodicea in Syria. He was on his way to the winter-quarters of the sixth legion, which he believed was especially susceptible to revolution. Its commander, however, Pacuvius anticipated this and prevented it. Sentius then informed Piso in a letter of these events and warned him not to disturb the armies through agents of corruption and not to disturb the province by war. Sentius further pointed out that he had gathered round him all whom he knew to cherish the memory of Germanicus, and to be opposed to his enemies, dwelling at length on Germanicus' greatness. Hinting that the State was being threatened with an armed attack, he said that he had put himself at the head of a strong force and was prepared for battle.

[80] Piso made sure to take precautions under present circumstances, and so occupied a very strongly fortified position in Cilicia, named, Celenderis. He took the Cilician auxiliaries that the minor kings had sent and added to them some deserters, some recently intercepted recruits, and his own and Plancina's slaves. By doing this he brought his force up to the strength of a legion. He also protested that he, though Caesar's legate, was kept out of the province which Caesar had given him, not by the legions (for he had come at their invitation) but by Sentius, who was disguising private animosity under false accusation. "All we have to do," he said, "is stand in battle formation. The soldiers will not fight when they see the Piso whom they themselves recently called 'father'. They know that he has the stronger case if it comes to arguments of justice; and if it comes to arms, he is far from powerless."

He then deployed his troops before the lines of the fortress on a high and precipitous hill, with the sea surrounding him on every side. Against him were the veteran troops drawn up in ranks and with reserves. Thus on one side was a formidable soldiery and a formidable position on the other. But his men had neither heart nor hope, and only rustic weapons, improvised for the moment. When they came to fighting, the result was doubtful only while the Roman cohorts were struggling up to level ground; then, the Cilicians turned their backs and shut themselves up within the fortress.

[81] Meanwhile Piso attempted an attack on the fleet, but it kept its distance and the attempt had little affect. He then returned to his fort. Standing before the walls, he tried to stir up a mutiny: beating his chest, calling on individual soldiers by name, and trying to entice them with rewards. He was partly successul—a standard bearer of the sixth legion went over to him with his standard. But then Sentius ordered the horns and trumpets to be sounded, the rampart to be assaulted, the scaling ladders to be raised, all the bravest men to mount on them, while others were to discharge from the engines spears, stones, and brands. Finally Piso's stubborness was overcome. He requested that he might surrender his arms and remain in the fortress while the emperor was consulted about the appointment of a governor to Syria. These proposals were refused. The only thing granted to him were some ships and a safe return to Rome.

[82] In Rome, meanwhile, when the illness of Germanicus became widely known, there was grief and indignation. All the news was coming from a distance, and this tended to exaggerate the danger. A storm of complaints burst out. "This was obviously the intention," they said, "behind banishing Germanicus to the ends of the earth, and assigning this province to Piso; this was the point of Augusta's secret interviews with Plancina. It was true, then, what old men said of Drusus the Elder: that rulers disliked a democratic tendencies in their sons. Apparently both young princes had been put out of the way because they were considered restoring freedom to the Roman people under equal laws."

The arrival of the news that Germanicus had died further inflamed popular gossip, with the result that there was a voluntary suspension of public business even before the magistrate's proclamation or the Senate's resolution: of their own accord, the public courts were deserted, and private houses closed. Everywhere there was a silence, broken only by groans; nothing was arranged for mere effect. And though they did not at all refrain from the ordinary signs of mourning, they carried an even deeper sorrow in their hearts.

It happened that some merchants, who had left Syria while Germanicus was still alive, brought happier news about his health. This news was instantly believed. It spread widely, since everyone passed the report on to others whom he met, ill-authenticated as it was, and they again to many more, with joyous exaggeration. … But when the truth was learned, the people grieved the more bitterly as though Germanicus was again lost to them.

Tacitus, Annals, Book III

[1] Without pausing in her winter voyage, Agrippina arrived at the island of Corcyra, facing the shores of Calabria. There she spent a few days to compose herself, for her grief was overwhelming and she did not know how to endure. Meanwhile, at the news of her arrival, the crowds eagerly rushed to Brundisium, which was the nearest and safest landing place for her. All her close friends were present, and many officers who had served under Germanicus; many strangers, too, came from the neighbouring towns, some thinking it respectful to the emperor, and still others who following their example.

As soon as the fleet was seen on the horizon, the whole harbour was filled with crowds of mourners. So, too, were the adjacent shores, the city walls, the roofs and any place commanding a good view of the horizon. People kept asking one another whether they should greet her arrival in respectful silence or with some audible expression of emotion. There was no consensus about what was appropriate as the flotilla approached little by little. Its crews were all wearing expressions of grief, with none of joy usual for a return home. When Agrippina disembarked from the vessel with her two children, clasping the funeral urn, with her eyes riveted to the earth, a single groan arose from the multitude. From their reactions it would be impossible to distinguish family from strangers, or the laments of men from those of women. These new mourners, fresh in their grief, now met the attendants of Agrippina, worn out as they were by their long sorrow.

[2] The emperor had dispatched two praetorian cohorts with instructions that the magistrates of Calabria, Apulia, and Campania were to pay the last honours to his son's memory. Accordingly tribunes and centurions bore Germanicus' ashes

on their shoulders. They were preceded by the standards unadorned and facing backwards. As they passed colony after colony, the populace was dressed in black and the local magistrates in their state robes; they burned garments and perfumes and performed other usual funeral rites in keeping with what their wealth could afford. Even those whose towns were not on the procession's route journeyed to meet the mourners, offered victims and built altars to the dead, thus proving their grief with tears and wailings. Drusus went as far as Tarracina with Claudius, Germanicus' brother, and the children who had been at Rome. Marcus Valerius and Caius Aurelius, the consuls, who had already entered office, and a great number of the people filled the road in scattered groups, every one weeping uncontrollably. None of this was flattery, since everyone knew that Tiberius could scarcely conceal his joy at the death of Germanicus.

[3] Tiberius and Augusta refrained from appearing in public. Apparently they considered it beneath their dignity to shed tears in public, or perhaps they feared that, if all eyes scrutinized their faces, their hypocrisy would be revealed. I do not find in any historian's account, or in the daily register, whether Antonia, Germanicus' mother, performed any conspicuous honour to the deceased, though in addition to Agrippina, Drusus, and Claudius, all his other family members are mentioned by name. It may be either that she was hindered by illness, or perhaps her spirit was so overpowered by grief that she did not have the heart to endure the sight of so great an affliction. But it is easier to believe that Tiberius and Augusta, who did not leave the palace, kept her there too, so that their sorrow might seem equal to hers, and that the grandmother and uncle might be thought to follow the mother's example in staying at home.

[4] The day on which the remains were consigned to the tomb of Augustus was alternately desolate in its silence and a turmoil of lamentation. The streets of the city were crowded, and torches were blazing throughout the Campus Martius. The soldiers under arms, the magistrates without their symbols of office, the people in the tribes, were all gathered there. Everyone was saying that the commonwealth was ruined and that no hope remained. So boldly and openly did they say this that it was clear that they had forgotten who their rulers were. But nothing affected Tiberius more deeply than the enthusiasm kindled in favor of Agrippina, whom men spoke of as the glory of the country, the sole surviving descendant of Augustus, the only surviving example of the old times. While they said such things, they would look up to heaven and the gods, praying for the safety of her children and that they might outlive their oppressors....

[6] Tiberius knew all this, and to silence the rumours he reminded the people in a proclamation that many eminent Romans had died for their country and that none of them had been honoured with such passionate regret. This regret was a compliment highly valued both by himself and by everyone, provided that moderation is observed; for what was acceptable in humble homes and communities were not necessarily appropriate to the leaders of the state and an imperial people. Tears and the solace found in mourning were suitable enough for the first burst of grief; but now they must brace their hearts to endurance, as happened in the past when the Divine Julius lost his only daughter, or when the Divine Augustus lost his grandchildren. They had had to set a limit on their sorrow. There was no need of examples from the past, showing how often the Roman people had patiently endured the defeats of armies, the destruction of generals, the total extinction of noble families. Princes were mortal; the state was everlasting. People should therefore return to their everyday pursuits, and, since the shows

of the festival of the Great Goddess were at hand, even resume their amusements.

[7] The suspension of business then came to an end, and people went back to their occupations. Drusus was sent to the armies of Illyricum. In the general populace, however, there was a widespread eagerness to exact vengeance on Piso. Many complained that he had spent the intervening time roaming through the more pleasant parts of Asia and Achaea, with the purpose of weakening any arguments of his guilt by an insolent and artful procrastination. It was indeed widely rumoured that the notorious poisoner Martina, who, as I have related, had been dispatched to Rome by Gnaeus Sentius, had died suddenly at Brundisium; that poison was concealed in a knot of her hair, and that no symptoms of suicide were discovered on her person.

[8] Meanwhile Piso sent his son on to Rome with a message intended to pacify the emperor. Piso himself made his way to Drusus, who would, he hoped, be not so much angered at his brother's death as thankful towards Piso because of a rival's removal. Tiberius, to show his impartiality, received the young man courteously, and enriched him with the gifts that he usually bestowed on the sons of noble families. Drusus replied to Piso that if certain accusations were true, his anger would be revealed, but he preferred to believe that they were false and groundless, and that Germanicus' death need be the ruin of no one. This he said openly, avoiding anything like secrecy. Most were convinced, however, that Drusus' answer had been given to him by Tiberius, inasmuch as he was someone who generally displayed all the simplicity and candour of youth, but now was using what seemed to be the artifices of old age.

[9] Piso, after crossing the Dalmatian sea and leaving his ships at Ancona, journeyed through Picenum and along the Flaminian road, where he overtook a legion that was marching from Pannonia to Rome and was about to be sent to reinforce Africa. Many people noted unfavorably how he had repeatedly displayed himself to the soldiers on the road during the march. From Narnia, to avoid suspicion or perhaps because fear makes men uncertain, he sailed down the Nar river, then down the Tiber, bringing his vessel to shore at the tomb of the Caesars. This only increased the fury of the populace. In broad daylight, when the river-bank was full of people, he himself went forwards with a large following of dependents, and Plancina with a retinue of women, all with joy on their faces. Among other things that provoked the public's anger was that his house towering above the forum was decorated with festal decorations, and that he threw banquets and feasts. Because the place was so public such behaviour could not be kept secret.

[10] On the next day, Fulcinius Trio asked the consul's permission to prosecute Piso. He was opposed by Vitellius and Veranius and the others who had been Germanicus' companions. Trio, they argued, had no standing in the case, and that they themselves meant to report their instructions from Germanicus, not as accusers, but as witnesses to facts. Trio, abandoning the prosecution on this charge, obtained leave to prosecute Piso for his earlier career. Then the emperor was asked to take over the inquiry. Even the accused did not refuse this, since he was more afraid of the bias of the people and of the Senate; he knew that Tiberius, by contrast, had enough strength of mind to despise scandal, and was also involved in his mother's complicity in the plot. A single judge would also be more able to distinguish the truth from perverse misrepresentation; where there were more they could be swayed by hatred and ill will.

Tiberius was not unaware of the formidable difficulty of the inquiry and of the rumours that were swirling. Having therefore summoned a few of his closest friends, he listened both to the threats of the prosecutors and to the pleadings of the accused. Finally he decided to refer the whole case to the Senate.

[11] The defendant began to seek legal help, asking Lucius Arruntius, Marcus Vinicius, Asinius Gallus, Aeserninus Marcellus and Sextus Pompeius. After they declined for different reasons, Marcus Lepidus, Lucius Piso, and Livineius Regulus became his counsel. Meanwhile whole country was full of speculation about how much fidelity would be shown by the friends of Germanicus, on what the accused rested his hopes, and how far Tiberius would repress and hide his true feelings. Never were the people more keenly interested; never did they indulge themselves more freely in secret whispers against the emperor or in the silence of suspicion.

[12] On the day the Senate met, Tiberius delivered a speech of studied moderation. "Piso," he said, "was an officer of my father and his friend. He was appointed by myself, on the advice of the Senate, to assist Germanicus in the administration of the East. Whether he had provoked Germanicus there through obstinate opposition and rivalry, and had rejoiced at his death or wickedly destroyed him, is for you to determine with unbiassed minds. Certainly if a subordinate oversteps the bounds of duty and of obedience to his commander, and has rejoiced in his death and in my affliction, I shall hate him and ban him from my house. But I shall avenge personal quarrels without resorting to my power as emperor. If, however, a crime is discovered that needs to be punished, it doesn't matter who the murdered man may be, it is for you to give just reparation both to the children of Germanicus and to us, his parents.

"Consider this, too, whether Piso dealt with the armies in a revolutionary and seditious spirit; whether he sought popularity with the soldiers through corruption; whether he attempted to retake his earlier province with arms, or whether these are falsehoods that his accusers have exaggerated. As for them, I am justly angry at their intemperate zeal. For what purpose was served in stripping the corpse and exposing it to the pollution of the vulgar gaze? or in circulating a story among foreigners that Germanicus was killed by poison, if all this is still in doubt and requires investigation? For my part, I mourn my son and shall always mourn him. Nevertheless, I shall not prevent the accused from producing all the evidence that can prove either that he is innocent or that Germanicus was unfair to him, if there is any. And I implore you, even though this case is intimately bound up with a personal sorrow of my own, do not to believe that any of the charges are true merely because of this. Those of you who are representing the defendant because of ties of blood or your own sense of loyalty must help him in his peril using all of your eloquence and dedication. I make the same appeal to the prosecutors. In this, and in this only, shall we place Germanicus above the laws, by conducting the inquiry into his death in this house instead of in the forum, and before the Senate instead of before a panel of judges. In all other ways, let this case be tried in the same way as others. Let no one heed the tears of Drusus or my own sorrow, or any stories invented to discredit us."

[13] The process would be as follows. Two days were allocating for the bringing forward of the charges; then would come a six 'days' adjournment followed by three days for the defense. Fulcinius Trio began with some old and irrelevant accusations about corruption and extortion during Piso's government of Spain many years before. These charges, even if proven, would not have been fatal to the defendant, provided that he manage to clear himself on the later accusations. But a refution of these charges would not

have secured his acquittal, if he were convicted of the greater crimes. Next, Servaeus, Veranius, and Vitellius spoke, all with equal earnestness. Vitellius' speech was striking for its eloquence. They all alleged that Piso, acting out of hatred of Germanicus and a desire for revolution, had corrupted the common soldiers through permissiveness and oppression of the allies. The extent of this corruption was shown by the fact that his nickname among the lowliest of them was "father of the legions". Meanwhile he had behaved outrageously towards all the best men, especially to the companions and friends of Germanicus. Lastly, they alleged that Piso had killed Germanicus himself by means of magic and poison, which explained the ceremonies and horrible sacrifices performed by himself and Plancina. He had also threatened the state with war, and had been defeated in battle, before he could be tried as a prisoner.

[14] Piso's defense failed on all points but one. Piso could not deny that he had tampered with the soldiers' loyalty, or that his province had been at the mercy of the worst of them, or that he had insulted a superior officer. The only charge that he was successful in refuting was that of poisoning. The prosecutors' case on this point was exceptionally weak: alleging that at a banquet given by Germanicus, his food had been poisoned by the hands of Piso because he happened to sit next to him. It seemed unthinkable that Piso would have dared such an attempt in front of someone else's servants, in the sight of so many bystanders, and under Germanicus' very own eyes. And, besides, Piso offered his own slaves to be cross-examined under torture, and insisted that the attendants serving on that occasion be examined in the same way. Different judges, however, were merciless for different reasons: the emperor, because Piso had made war on a province; the Senate because they could not be sufficiently convinced that Piso had not been involved about the death of Germanicus.

At the same time shouts were heard from the people gathered in front of the Senate House, threatening violence if Piso should escape the verdict of the Senators. They were actually in the process of dragging Piso's statues to the Gemonian stairs, and were breaking them into pieces, when the emperor ordered that they be rescued and replaced. Piso was then put in a litter and accompanied home by a tribune of one of the Praetorian cohorts, while people argued whether the tribune was meant to guard Piso's person or to be his executioner.

[15] Plancina was hated just as much but had stronger connections, so people were uncertain how far the emperor would be allowed to proceed against her. For as long as any hope remained for Piso, she swore that she would share his lot, whatever it might be, and even be his companion in death, if worst came to worst. But as soon as she had secured her pardon through the secret intervention of Augusta, she slowly began to withdraw from her husband and separated her defense from his. When Piso saw that this was fatal to him, he was unsure whether he should still persist, but at the urgent request of his sons steeled himself for the struggle and once more entered the Senate. There he patiently endured the repeated accusations, the furious voices of the Senators, and savage opposition from every quarter. What especially intimidated him, however, was to see Tiberius, pitiless and stonefaced, resolutely refusing to allow any scope for emotion. Piso was conveyed back to his house, where, under the pretext of preparing his defense for the next day, he wrote a few words, sealed the paper and handed it to a freedman. Then he undertook his ordinary end of day activities. A little while later, late at night, his wife left his chamber, and he ordered the doors to be closed. At daybreak he was found

with his throat cut and a sword lying on the ground.

[16] I remember having heard old men say that during this period a document was often seen in Piso's hands. He himself never revealed the contents of this document, but some of his friends repeatedly declared that it contained a letter from Tiberius with instructions referring to Germanicus. They also alleged that Piso had intended to produce it before the Senate as a reproach to the emperor, and would have, except that he was tricked by empty promises of Sejanus. Nor did he perish, they said, by his own hand, but by someone sent as executioner. I am unable to establish the truth of either of these statements; still it would not have been right for me to conceal what was related by those who lived up to the time of my youth.

The emperor, assuming an air of sadness, complained in the Senate that the purpose of such a death was to bring hatred on himself, and he asked repeatedly how Piso had spent his last day and night. Receiving answers which were mostly judicious, though somewhat incautious, he read out a note written by Piso, which said roughly the following: "I have been crushed by a conspiracy of my enemies and by the hatred deriving by a false accusation. Since there is no room for my truth and innocence in this world, I call the immortal gods to witness that I have lived loyally towards you Caesar, and have always shown dutiful respect towards your mother. I implore you to think of my children. One of them, Gnaeus is in no way implicated in my actions, whatever they may have been, seeing that all this time he has been at Rome. My other son, Marcus Piso, urged me not to return to Syria. How I wish that I had yielded to my young son rather than he to his aged father! Because of this I pray all the more fervently that the innocent may not pay the penalty of my wickedness. Consider my forty-five years of loyal service; consider my association with you in the consulate, and how I had earlier won the esteem of the Divine Augustus, your father. As someone who is your friend and will never again ask a favour, I implore you to save my unhappy son." About Plancina he wrote nothing.

[17] Tiberius then acquitted the young Piso of the charge of civil war, since a son could not have refused a father's orders. At the same time he expressed his sorrow for the downfall of a noble family and the terrible fate of Piso himself, however much he might have deserved it. His words about Plancina were spoken with shame and conscious disgrace; as an excuse Tiberius offered the intervention of his mother, about whom all good men were making increasingly stringent complaints. "Was it the duty of a grandmother," people asked, "to meet face-to-face with her grandson's murderer, to converse with her, and then rescue her from the Senate? Germanicus alone was denied the things that the laws are supposed to secure for every citizen. Vitellius and Veranius had used their voices to mourn a Caesar, while the emperor and Augusta had defended Plancina. She might as well now turn her poisons and other vicious skills against Agrippina and her children, and thus quench the thirst of this terrible grandmother and uncle with the blood of a most unhappy house."

Two days were frittered away over this mockery of a trial, with Tiberius urging Piso's children to defend their mother. While the accusers and their witnesses pressed the prosecution with competitive zeal, and there was no reply, pity rather than anger was on the increase. Aurelius Cotta, the consul, was first called on for his vote (for when the emperor put the question, even those in office went through the duty of voting). He held that Piso's name ought to be erased from the public register, half of his property confiscated, half given up to his son, Gnaeus Piso, who was instructed to change his first name; that Marcus Piso, stripped of his rank, with an allowance of five million sesterces, should be banished for ten years, Plancina's life being spared in consideration of Augusta's intervention.

[18] Much of the sentence was softened by the emperor. ...

Later, when Valerius Messalinus and Caecina Severus proposed respectively the erection of a golden statue in the temple of Mars the Avenger and of an altar to Vengeance, Tiberius interposed his veto, protesting that victories over the foreigner were commemorated with such monuments, but that domestic woes ought to be clothed in silent grief.

Adapted from A.J. Church and W.J. Brodribb, *Annals of Tacitus* (London: Macmillan and Co., 1876)

Chapter 10

Roman Religion

READING 10A. LIVY ON THE REFORMS OF NUMA

Roman religion took many forms and incorporated many different kinds of rituals, most of which originated in the earliest period of Roman history. Although the Romans themselves often did not know or fully understand the meaning of their most deeply held religious traditions, they nevertheless maintained them scrupulously. Roman state religion, cults that were administered by the state, was among the most important aspects of religious activity because it was closely tied to the notions of Roman citizenship and identity. Every good citizen was obligated to participate in these cults, and avoidance of them was viewed almost as a form of civil dissent and could be severely punished.

According to tradition, it was King Numa (ca. 715-673 B.C.), the successor to Romulus and the legendary first law-giver of Rome, who first set out many of the oldest cults of Roman state religion. In particular, the Romans believed that Numa organised the priestly colleges. While there is no evidence for the existence of a real Numa, nor any contemporary record of his activities, belief in his involvement in religion attests to the antiquity of many aspects of religious practice.

The following passage is taken from Livy, History 1.19-20, which is the most accessible account of this early material, although Livy himself wrote much later in the last first century B.C. Consider the following questions:

- What were Numa's concerns, according to Livy, and how did he try to address them in his organisation of religious institutions?
- What is the purported historical context of this passage, and how does it reflect the political and social developments of that time?

Livy, Histories 1. 19-20 Livy. History of Rome.

19. Having in this way obtained the kingship, Numa prepared to give to his city, which had so recently been founded by force of arms, a new foundation in laws, statutes, and customs. He saw that it was impossible to do this while a state of war existed, for war brutalised men. [2] Realizing that the ferocity of his subjects might be softened through a decreased use of arms, he built the temple of Janus at the foot of the Aventine. This temple would serve as an index of peace and war, signifying when it was open that the State was under arms, and when it was shut that all the surrounding nations were at peace. [3] Since the time of Numa's reign this temple has been shut only twice: once after the first Punic war in the consulship of T. Manlius; the second time, which the gods allowed our generation to witness, following the battle of Actium, when peace on land and sea was secured by the emperor Caesar Augustus. [4] After forming treaties of alliance with all his neighbours and closing the temple of Janus, Numa turned his attention to domestic matters. He feared that removing external danger would induce his subjects to fall into luxury and idleness, since they would be no longer restrained by the fear of an enemy or by military discipline. To prevent this, he strove to inculcate in their minds the fear of the gods, regarding this as the most powerful influence which could act upon an uncivilised and, in those ages, a barbarous people. [5] But, as this would fail to make a deep impression without some claim to supernatural wisdom, he pretended that he had nocturnal interviews with the nymph Egeria: that it was on her advice that he was instituting the ritual most acceptable to the gods and appointing for each deity his own special priests.

[6] His first reform was to divide the year into twelve months, corresponding to the moon's cycles. But since the moon does not complete thirty days in each month, and so there are fewer days in the lunar year than in that measured by the course of the sun, he inserted intercalary months and so arranged them that every twentieth year the days should coincide with the same position of the sun as when they started, the whole twenty years being thus complete. [7] He also established a distinction between the days on which legal business could be transacted and those on which it could not, because it would sometimes be advisable that there should be no business transacted with the people.

20. Next he turned his attention to the appointment of priests. He himself, however, conducted a great many religious services, especially those which belong to the Flamen of Jupiter. But Numa realized that in a warlike state there would be more kings like Romulus than like himself, and that these would often be leading military campaigns. To prevent, therefore, the interruption of the sacrificial rites that the king was supposed to perform, he appointed a Flamen as perpetual priest to Jupiter, and ordered that he should wear a distinctive dress and sit in the royal curule chair. He appointed two additional Flamens, one for Mars, the other for Quirinus, and also chose virgins as priestesses to Vesta. [3] This order of priestesses came into existence originally in Alba and was connected with the descendents of the founder. He assigned to them a public wage so that they might give their whole time to the temple, and made their persons sacred and inviolable by a vow of chastity and other religious sanctions.

…

[5] The next office to be filled was that of the Pontifex Maximus. He appointed the son of Marcus, one of the senators —Numa Marcius

—and all the regulations bearing on religion, written out and sealed, were intrusted to him. These defined what victims were to be offered on what days, and at what temples the various sacrifices were to be offered, and from what sources the expenses connected with them were to be defrayed. [6] He placed all other sacred functions, both public and private, under the supervision of the Pontifex, in order that there might be an authority for the people to consult, and so all trouble and confusion arising through foreign rites being adopted and their ancestral ones neglected might be avoided. [7] Nor were his functions confined to directing the worship of the celestial gods; he was to instruct the people how to conduct funerals and appease the spirits of the departed, and what prodigies sent by lightning or in any other way were to be attended to and expiated. To elicit these signs of the divine will, he dedicated an altar to Jupiter Elicius on the Aventine, and consulted the god through auguries, as to which prodigies were to receive attention.

21. The deliberations and arrangements which these matters involved diverted the people from all thoughts of war. Not only had they something to occupy their minds, but their constant preoccupation with the gods, now that it seemed to them that concern for human affairs was felt by the heavenly powers, had so tinged the hearts of all with piety, that the nation was governed by its regard for promises and oaths, rather than by the dread of laws and penalties. [2] And while Numa's subjects were spontaneously imitating the character of their king as their only example, the neighboring peoples also took note. Up to this point they had viewed Rome less as a city than as a miliary camp placed in their midst as a menace to the general peace. Now they came to feel such respect for their religious scruples that they thought it sacrilege to injure a nation so wholly dedicated to the worship of the gods. ... [5] There were many other sacrifices appointed by him and places dedicated for their performance which the pontiffs call the Argei. The greatest of all his works was the preservation of peace and the security of his realm throughout the whole of his reign.

[6] Thus the greatness of the State was advanced by two successive kings, each in a different way. One promoted the state through war; the other, through peace. Romulus reigned thirty-seven years, Numa forty-three. The State was strong and disciplined by the lessons of war and the arts of peace.

Adapted from Rev. Canon Roberts, *Livy. Books I and II With An English Translation*. (Cambridge, MA. Harvard University Press. London. William Heinemann Ltd. 1919.)

READING 10B. CICERO: ADDRESS TO THE PONTIFICES

Priests and Priestesses. Priests and priestesses played a different role in Roman religion than modern clergy do in contemporary religions. First, holding a state priesthood was not a full-time occupation, but an honour bestowed on senators who were expected to fill these functions as part of their on-going responsibilities. Second, there many different kinds of priests, some serving only specific deities. The most important preiests were organised into priestly colleges, each with its own set of responsibilities. The duties of different kinds of priests could differ signficantly. Some were responsible for specific religious festivals, which numbered in the hundreds on the Roman calendar. They arranged all aspects of the festivals, seeing to it that animals were properly prepared for sacrifice, and that prayers and rituals were carried out in the appropriate manner.

The colleges of priests were overseen by the chief priest of Rome, the pontifex maximus. Before the late Republic, most priests were co-opted into their colleges, by which we mean that the existing college of priests decided who would fill any vacancy. In 121 B.C., however, priests began to be elected to office, and thus the office became increasingly associated with political activity. In fact, serving in one of the priestly colleges was considered a mark of a senator's social standing. Moreover, state priests carried out their duties in public, thus providing the ambitious Roman politician with an excellent public context to demonstrate his qualities as a statesman and dutiful citizen. Unlike political office, however, priesthoods were held for life.

The following passage had been taken from a speech of Cicero's, who was appearing before the pontifical college. Cicero's house had been destroyed while he was in exile in 58 BC by one of his personal enemies, who then consecrated it to the gods, thus preventing Cicero from rebuilding it. Cicero appealed to the *pontifices* (which is the plural of pontifex) to rule that the dedication was invalid, thereby releasing Cicero from the obligation to adhere to it.

Cicero, On His House, 1.1

1. Gentlemen of the pontifical college, our ancestors invented and established many things under divine inspiration. No action of theirs, however, was wiser than their decision that the same men should supervise both what relates to the religious worship due to the immortal gods, and also what concerns the highest interests of the state. Because of this such men can preserve the Republic both as its most honourable and eminent of the citizens, by governing it well, and as its priests by wisely interpreting the requirements of religion. But if there has ever been a time when an important case has depended on the decision and power of the priests of the Roman people, this indeed is that case. Indeed, the dignity of the whole state, the safety of all the citizens, their lives, their liberties, their altars, their hearths, their household gods, their properties and condition as citizens, and their homes, all appear to be committed and entrusted to your wisdom, integrity, and power. [2] As members of the pontifical college, it is your responsibility to decide this day whether you prefer for the future to deprive frantic and profligate magistrates of the protection of wicked and unprincipled citizens, or even to arm them with the cloak of religion and of the respect due to the immortal gods. For what if my enemy—disgrace and disaster of the Republic that he is—succeeds in defending the mischievous and damaging actions of his tribunate by appealing to divine religion, when he cannot maintain it by any considerations of human fairness? Then it is clear that we must find other ceremonies, other ministers of the immortal gods, other interpreters of the requirements of religion. If, however, actions which were committed by the madness of wicked men in the Republic at a time when it was oppressed by one party, deserted by another, and betrayed by a third, are annulled by your authority and your wisdom, O priests, then we shall have full justification to praise the wisdom of our ancestors in selecting the most honourable men of the state for the priesthood.

Adapted from C. D. Yonge, *The Orations of Marcus Tullius Cicero* (London: George Bell & Sons, 1891).

Reading 10c. Plutarch on the Vestal Virgins

The worship of the goddess of the hearth, Vesta, was another of the oldest and most venerated of Roman cults. Her temple was a small circular structure located in a prominent place in the Roman forum. Within it was a hearth with the sacred fire, which symbolised the prosperity of Rome itself and which was tended by six maiden priestesses, the Vestal Virgins. These were young girls, ages 6-10, who took a vow of chastity and service to the goddess Vesta. Chosen by the pontifex maximus from elite Roman families to serve for a minimum of thirty years, after their retirement Vestal Virgins could and often did marry and have families. Living together in a special house beside the Temple of Vesta in the Roman forum, their tasks included sacrifice and prayer, but the most important duty was maintenance of the sacred fire, since it was a symbol of Rome's power. The extinction of the sacred flame was also interpreted as a sign of sexual transgression by a Vestal virgin; thus, their activity was closely scrutinised, because misbehaviour on their part could spell difficulty for Rome.

The following passage was written by Plutarch in his biography of the early Roman king Numa. It records the foundation of the cult of Vesta and the establishment of rules of conduct for the Vestal Virgins.

- How are the rules for the Vestal virgins consistent with the main characteristics of Roman religion?
- Compare the role of the Vestal virgins to the priestly colleges occupied by men. What are the particularly feminine elements, and how might they be explained?

Plutarch, Life of Numa 9-10

The leader of the Pontifical college, the Pontifex Maximus, had the duty of expounding and interpreting the divine will, or rather of directing sacred rites. He was not only in charge of public ceremonies, but also of supervising private sacrifices and preventing any departure from established custom, as well as teaching whatever was required for the worship or propitiation of the gods. [5] He was also overseer of the holy virgins called Vestals, who were responsible for the worship and care of the perpetual fire. The consecration of the Vestal virgins is ascribed to Numa, which he did possibly because he thought the nature of fire pure and uncorrupted, and therefore entrusted it to chaste and undefiled persons. It is also possible that it is because he thought of it as unfruitful and barren, and therefore associated it with virginity. For comparison, wherever in Greece a perpetual fire is kept, as at Delphi and Athens, it is committed to the charge, not of virgins, but of widows past the age of marriage. [6] And if by any chance it goes out, ... as during the Mithridatic and the Roman civil wars the altar was demolished and the fire extinguished, then they say it must nor be kindled again from other fire, but made fresh and new, by lighting a pure and unpolluted flame from the rays of the sun. ... [8] Some, moreover, are of the opinion that nothing but this perpetual fire is guarded by the sacred virgins; while some say that certain sacred objects, which none others may behold, are kept in secret by them. ...

10. In the beginning, then, they say that Gegania and Verenia were consecrated to this office by Numa, who subsequently added to them Canuleia and Tarpeia; it is also reported that two others were added by Servius at a later time, making the number which has continued to the present time. The king ordained that the sacred virgins should vow themselves to chastity for thirty years; during the first decade they are to learn their duties, during the second to perform the duties they have learned, and during the third to teach others these duties. [2] Once the thirty years had passed, a Vestal who wishes is free to marry and adopt a different mode of life, after laying down her sacred office. We are told, however, that few have welcomed the indulgence, and that those who did so were not happy, but were plagued by regret and depression for the rest of their lives, thereby inspiring the rest with superstitious fears. The result is that that until most stay steadfast in their virginity until old age and death.

[3] Numa bestowed great privileges upon the Vestals, such as the right to make a will during the lifetime of their fathers, and to transact and manage their other affairs without a guardian, like women who had given birth to three children. When Vestals appear in public, the fasces are carried before them, and if they accidentally meet a criminal on his way to execution, his life is spared; but the Vestal must make oath that the meeting was involuntary and fortuitous, and not intentional. [4] If anyone passes under the litter on which a Vestal is being carried, he is put to death. For their minor offences the virgins are punished with whippings, the Pontifex Maximus sometimes scourging the culprit on her bare flesh, in a dark place, with a curtain interposed. If a Vestal breaks her vow of chastity, however, she is buried alive near the Colline gate. At this place a small ridge of earth extends for some distance along the inside of the city-wall; the Latin word for it is 'agger.' [5] Under it a small chamber is constructed, with steps leading down from above. In this are placed a couch with its coverings, a lighted lamp, and very small portions of the necessaries of life, such as bread, a bowl of water, milk, and oil, as though they would thereby absolve themselves from the charge of destroying by hunger a life which had been consecrated to the highest services of religion. [6] A guilty vestal is placed on a litter, over which coverings are thrown and fastened down with cords so that not even a cry can be heard from within, and carried through the forum. All the people allow the litter to pass in silence, and they follow it without uttering a sound, escorting the litter in dreadful sorrow. No other spectacle is more appalling, nor does any other day bring more gloom to the city than this. [7] When the litter reaches its destination, the attendants unfasten the cords of the coverings. Then the high-priest, after stretching his hands toward heaven and uttering certain mysterious prayers before the fatal act, brings forth the culprit, who is closely veiled, and places her on the steps leading down into the chamber. After this he turns away his face, as do the rest of the priests, and when she has gone down, the steps are taken up, and great quantities of earth are thrown into the entrance to the chamber, hiding it away, and making the place level with the rest of the mound. Such is the punishment of those who break their vow of virginity.

Adapted from Bernadotte Perrin, *Plutarch. Plutarch's Lives with an English Translation* (London: William Heinemann, 1914).

Reading 10d. Pliny on Early Christians

The persecution of the Christians stands in direct contrast to the otherwise open and tolerant nature of Roman religion. Whereas other religions and cults were accepted, even welcomed, by the Romans, Christianity was met with distrust, fear, and eventually persecution. For example, the historian Tacitus records that in A.D. 64 the Emperor Nero sought to shift the blame for the great fire of Rome from himself to the despised and distrusted Christians:

> But neither human effort, nor imperial liberality, nor sacrifices to the gods, was able to counter lingering suspicions that the fire had been started by Nero. As an attempt to undermine this rumour, Nero found scapegoats — the notoriously depraved Christians, as they were known — and punished them with every torture. The founder of this religion, Christ, had been executed by Tiberius' governor of Judaea, Pontius Pilatus. In spite of this, however, the pernicious superstition had broken out anew, not only in Judaea (where the thing had started), but now, too, Rome. (Every degraded and shameful practice finds its way to the capital and and flourish there.) As a first step, admitted Christians were arrested. Then, on their information, large numbers of others were tried — not so much for arson as for their anti-social tendencies. (Tacitus, Annals, 15.44)

One reason for the antipathy was Christianity's exclusiveness. Whereas most other ancient religions were open to the worship of other gods and goddesses, Christians were forbidden from worshipping any other deity. A devotee of Isis, for example could also venerate the traditional Roman state gods (which included the deified Roman emperors) and participate in their religious festivals. A Christian, on the other hand, was required to worship only one god and to reject all others. This exclusiveness in effect involved rejecting much of Greek and Roman society and culture and because of this to threaten the moral, political and social order. In addition, because they did not participate in the religion of their neighbours, Christians remained aloof from the rest of society and their own meetings were attended only by themselves. These actions only deepened the misunderstanding and suspicions of treason and subversion.

Pliny the Younger (c. A.D. 61-c. 112) was a prominent Roman lawyer and senator whom the Emperor Trajan (ruled 97-117) sent as governor of the province of Bithynia-Pontus in northern Asia Minor. Pliny is known to us because of his published correspondence, which was shared with many important people on a great variety of topics. One section of this correspondence contains Pliny's letters to Trajan (and Trajan's replies) concerning problems which he encountered as the emperor's representative in Bithynia-Pontus. The following letter was written to Trajan in about A.D. 112 asking for the specific instructions regarding the Christians. Trajan's response follows. It established the official Imperial policy for the punishment of this group. Before this time, attacks on the Christians had been sporadic and motivated by local prejudices.

Some questions to consider as you read:

- Is it Pliny or others who instigate the attacks on Christians?
- What is Pliny's opinion of the Christians? Does he hate them?
- In the eyes of Romans what are the Christians guilty of?
- How are the accused Christians to prove their innocence?
- What is the Imperial policy established by Trajan's response?

Pliny's Letter to the Emperor Trajan (10. 96)

It is my practice, Sir, to ask you about all issues that I have doubts about. For who can give me better guidance when I'm in doubt or inform me when I am ignorant?

I have never previously been present at examinations of Christians. I therefore do not know what offenses are supposed to be punished or investigated, and to what extent. Also, I have been quite unsure on a number of questions. Should there be any distinction on account of age? For example, should the very young be treated differently than adults? Should a pardon be granted for repentance? or should it do a man no good to cease being a Christian once he's become one? Is it the name itself, even without offenses, that is to be punished, or only the offenses associated with the name?

For the moment this is the procedure that I've followed in the cases of those who were accused in my court of being Christians. First, I have asked them in person whether they were Christians. If they admitted it, I asked a second and a third time, threatening them with punishment. Finally, those who persisted I ordered to be executed. (Whatever the actual nature of this religion, their stubbornness and inflexible obstinacy surely deserves to be punished.) There have been others engaged in the same foolishness; but because they were Roman citizens, I ordered them to be transferred to Rome for trial.

Once these proceedings started, accusations began to grow in number (as so often happens), and several incidents occurred. An anonymous document began to circulate containing the names of a number of alleged Christians. Some of the people named denied that they were or ever had been Christians. In cases like this, I thought a discharge was the right thing to do, on several conditions. I insisted that they invoke the gods according to a formula that I prescribe and then pray to your image while offering a sacrifice of incense and wine. (I had brought along for this purpose, together with statues of the gods.) I also insisted that they curse Christ because it is said that true Christians absolutely refuse to do this. Others named by the informer admitted to having previously been Christians, but claiming that they had ceased to be adherents for various periods: some three years, others many years, a few even as much as twenty-five years. All these individuals worshipped your image and the statues of the gods, and cursed Christ.

They also admitted that they were guilty of foolishly engaging in the following practices. They were accustomed to meet on a fixed day before dawn and chant a responsal hymn to Christ as to a god. At that meeting they would swear a binding oath not for some criminal purpose, but instead that they would not commit fraud, theft, or adultery, would commit no breach of trust, and would not refuse to return a deposit when called upon to do so. When this ceremony was finished, it was their custom to depart and to assemble later to share a meal of ordinary and innocent food. They had ceased to do even these things, they said, after my edict had been published (in accordance with your instructions) forbidding political associations. Accordingly, I decided it was necessary to learn the truth by examining under torture two female slaves who were deaconesses in this cult. But I discovered nothing else but a depraved superstition taken to excessive lengths.

I therefore postponed my inquiry in order to consult you. Such consultation seemed warranted in this case, especially because of the numbers of people involved. For it seems that every age, every rank, and both sexes have been affected by this and will continue to do so. For this superstition and its contagion have infected not only the cities but also the villages and countryside. It also seems possible, however, to stop its spread and provide a cure. This is suggested by the fact that the temples, which had been practically deserted, again seem to be have greater attendance. It is also the case that established religious rites, which had long been neglected, are being resumed, and that sacrificial animals (which there seemed to be no market for) are now everywhere. The implication seems to be that a great multitude of people will be reformed if they are given an opportunity to repent.

Trajan responds to Pliny (10. 97)

In handling the cases of those who had been accused before you of being Christians, you have followed the proper procedure, my dear Pliny. In this matter, it is impossible to establish any general rule to serve as a fixed procedure. These people are not to be hunted out; but if they are accused before you and proven guilty, they are to be punished. Those who deny being Christian, however, and who prove it by worshipping our gods, shall be pardoned because of repentance, regardless of how guilty their conduct had been in the past. But anonymously submitted accusations ought to have no place in any prosecution. For this is both a dangerous precedent and not at all in keeping with the spirit of our age.

Translation by C. Eilers.

Reading 10E. Apuleius on the Cult of Isis

Roman religion is notable for its flexibility and capacity to accept foreign religious cults. This, combined with the cosmopolitan nature of the city of Rome, meant that by the Imperial period traditional Roman religion was practiced side by side with new foreign cults. The popularity of foreign religions, however, increased in the Imperial period because these religions were both exotic and often more personal than traditional Roman religion. The religions of Isis, Mithras, Jehovah, and Christ all spread throughout the Roman Empire, increasingly gaining more converts.

Lucius Apuleius was a wealthy Roman of the second century A.D. He was born into a wealthy family and, after pursuing higher education in Carthage and then Athens, eventually became a travelling orator. While a youth he lived a dissolute lifestyle, dabbling in magic and squandering his money on wine and women. His life, however, was transformed when he became an initiate into the cult of Isis, in which he discovered new purpose and moral guidance.

In *The Golden Ass*, Lucius Apuleius provides us with a semi-autobiographical tale of a man's conversion to a life of enlightenment and religion. In this work (also known as the *Metamorphosis*), the character Lucius is transformed into a donkey through his association with magic. As a donkey, an animal which symbolized lust, wickedness and ill-luck, he experiences many adventures. Eventually he is saved and transformed back into the shape of a man through the agency of the goddess Isis. In his address at the beginning of the work, Apuleius expresses his hope that the reader will not only learn something about the goddess Isis but will also enjoy the story:

> If you are not put off by the Egyptian story-telling convention which allows humans to be changed into animals and, after various adventures, restored to their proper shapes, you should be amused by this queer novel, a string of anecdotes in the popular racy style, but intended only for your private ear, which I will call my Metamorphosis.

The goddess Isis, an Egyptian deity, became increasingly popular during the Hellenistic period when she was gradually absorbed into the Greek pantheon and equated with other deities. By the time of the Roman Empire, she was revered throughout the Mediterranean world. In her roles as life-giver, healer, and protector, she was worshipped as a 'mother' goddess. Her followers were primarily women and slaves, to whom she offered protection, hope and freedom from fate. The cult of Isis was what we describe as a mystery cult: initiation into the cult was a secret affair and devotees were not permitted to speak to outsiders about their religious practices. Because of this secrecy, we know little about its rituals. In *The Golden Ass*, for example, Lucius speaks of his own conversion in language that is intentionally vague. This tale is an allegory of the journey from the sensual, physical world of everyday experience to the world of the spiritual. The tale was apparently written to express Apuleius' own gratitude to Isis for saving him.

Some questions:
- In what ways does the cult of Isis appear different from traditional Roman religion (as represented in the previous sources)?
- Do you see any similarities between the Isis cult and Christianity?
- Why do you think the details of such religions were secret?

Apuleius, The Golden Ass, 11. 4-23

[3] When I had completed my prayer and poured forth to the goddess all my wretched requests, I fell asleep again upon that same bed. After a short time (for mine eyes had only just closed), a divine face appeared to me as from the midst of the sea, a face so holy that it was worshipped even of the gods themselves. Then, little by little, the whole figure of her body appeared to me, bright and arising out of the sea and standing before me....

[4] The air was filled with the smell of the pleasant spices of fertile Arabia, and the goddess deigned to speak these words to me with her holy voice: "Behold, Lucius, I have come. Your tearful prayer has moved me to help you. I am the natural mother of all things, mistress and governess of all the elements, the original maker of worlds, first of the powers divine, queen of all who are in the underworld, the leader of those who live in heaven, the sole manifestation of all gods and goddesses. All the planets of the sky, the wholesome winds of the seas, and the lamentable silences of the underworld depend on my will. My name and my divinity is worshipped through the entire world, in different ways, in various customs, and by many names. For the ancient Phrygians call me 'the Mother of the gods at Pessinus'; the Athenians, who are sprung from their own soil, 'Cecropian Minerva'; the Cyprians, who live by the sea, 'Paphian Venus'; the arrow-carrying Cretans, 'Dictynnian Diana'; the trilingual Sicilians, 'infernal Proserpina'; the Eleusians, 'their ancient goddess Ceres'. Some call me Juno; others, Bellona; still others, Hecate or Rhamnusia. But both races of the Ethiopians who dwell in the East and are the first to see the morning rays of the sun, and the Egyptians, who excel in every kind of ancient doctrine and are accustomed to worship me with proper ceremonies, address me by my true name, Queen Isis.

"I have come to take pity on your ill-fortune and tribulations! I am here to help you and to take pity on you. Put an end to your weeping and lamentation, Lucius! Put an end to all your sorrow! The day of your deliverance has come, ordained by my providence. Therefore prepare yourself and listen to my instructions. Tomorrow is a day dedicated to my worship by an eternal religion. My priests and ministers are will be offering me as a first-fruit of the new sailing season the dedication of a new ship. The ceremony marks the end of the winter storms of the sea and the calming of its waves. You must wait for this ceremony with a mind that is solemn and a heart that is calm. [6] In this procession the great priest shall carry in his right hand, at my instruction, a garland of roses tied to his rattle. Without hesitation, and trusting in me, join that procession as it passes through the crowds; approach the priest and act as if you are about to kiss his hand. Then gently take the garland of roses in your mouth. By doing this you will finally shed the skin and shape of an ass, which is an animal that I have always hated and despised. More than anything else, however, have faith. Do not fear that any of my instructions are hard to obey. For in this same hour that I have come to you, I have also appeared to the priest in a vision and told him what he must do. Tomorrow, all the people shall be compelled by my will to make way for you and say nothing. ... But know this, too, with certainty: that the remainder of your life until the hour of your death shall be dedicated to my service. In no way should it be burdensome to serve me as long as you live, since it is by my favour that you will again become a man. Under my guidance and protection you will live a happy life in this world and will become famous. Even after your allotted years have passed and you descend into the underworld, there again you will see me as you see me now, shining in the darkness of Acheron, and reigning in the deep halls of Styx. In that place you worship me for having saved you. And if I see that you are obedient to my ordinances and observe my religion faithfully through continued chastity, know that I will extend your days beyond the time that the fates have appointed and ordained."

[7] When the invincible goddess had spoken these words and ended her holy oracle, she vanished. The next morning, I awoke with my body covered in sweat, and I got up filled with both fear and joy, since I was still in awe of the recent presence of her divinity. After I had splashed myself with sea water, I carefully recalled her instructions, memorizing her every order. Soon after the golden sun arose and chased away the last shadows, I turned and saw the streets filled with people, moving together as if in a religious triumph. The whole world seemed to be full of joy. The animals, the houses, even the day itself seemed to rejoice. For the previous night's chill had been followed by the warmth of the sun. Song birds, assured that spring had arrived, began chirping and singing melodiously, welcoming with their sweet songs the mother of the seasons, the parent of time, and mistress of the whole world....

[8] Now the front ranks of the procession came closer and closer, with every one dressed in their finest clothes according to their choice. One man wore a large belt around his waste like a soldier; another carried a spear and wore a hitched up cloak and a hunter's boots; still another was dressed as a woman, with a silk robe, gilded sandals, fine jewelry, and a wig; then there was a man wearing heavy boots, a shield, a helmet and a spear as if he were a gladiator. ...

[9] These strangely dressed participants were running in and out of crowd while the goddess' parade was steadily marching onwards. At the head of the parade were women dressed in white with garlands of flowers on their heads. They had aprons full of flowers which they scattered along the road where the devout procession was about to pass. Their every gesture proved their joy. Behind them came women with mirrors strapped to the back of their heads. This was so that the goddess' image would be reflected back towards those marching behind. ... Then came a great number of men and women carrying lamps, candles, torches, and other lights of every sort, which was meant to signify that the goddess was born of the celestial stars.

Next in sequence came pipers and flute-players playing in the most pleasant harmony. They were followed by a delightful choir made up of youth wearing white festive vestments. They were singing a beautiful hymn that some learned poet had composed with the help of the Muses; the words of this hymn explained the origins of this great procession. Meanwhile the pipers of the mighty god Sarapis had arrived. They were playing an anthem proper to the temple and the god on pipes held sideways, which curved back behind their right ears. Next came many to shout that room be made for the goddess to pass.

[10] Then came great crowds of the goddess' initiates: men and women from every station of life and every age group, whose garments of the whitest linen glistened in the streets. The women had their hair anointed and covered their heads with light linen. The men had their heads completely shaven and shining bright, representing the shining stars of the goddess, and held in their hands rattles of brass, silver, and even gold, which were producing forth a continuous tinkling.

The leading priests, in charge of the sacred rites, were also there, wearing white tunics around their torsos that hung down to the ground.

They carried the relics of all the most powerful gods. ...

[12] At last came the destined moment of my good fortune, according to the promise of the most powerful goddess. Coming into view was the priest who was bringing my fate and my very safety by the commandment of the goddess. As he came ever closer, carrying in his right hand both the rattle and the garland of roses that had been foretold to me. To me it was much more than a garland, but the means by which, with the help of the greatest goddess, I would overcome the misfortune that had beset me with so much calamity and pain and with so many perils.

Although I was overcome by sudden joy, I resisted the temptation to gallop forward, not wanting to disturb the quiet procession with the sudden movement of an animal. Instead, I eased forward like a man wriggling through a crowd of people, which was influenced by divine order and made way for me on every side. Now I approached the priest.

[13] Then the priest, who had clearly been warned of this the night before, looked on in amazement as what had been prophesied was now actually happening. And so he stopped suddenly and held out his hands offering the garland of roses to me while I took it in my mouth. My body was trembling and my heart pounding, and I devoured it with a great relish. As soon as I had eaten it, I knew that the promise made to me was fulfilled. For my bestial face began to change; the coarse hair on my body began to shed; my thick skin melted and became soft again; my fat belly tightened; the hoofs on my feet turned into toes; my fore-hooves ceased being feet and instead were restored for human work; my neck grew shorter; my head and mouth became round; my long ears shortened; my great buck-teeth returned to normal size; and my tail, which had up to now grieved me most, vanished completely.

Onlookers were shocked. The priests praised the goddess for this miracle, which had been foreshadowed by the visions seen in the night, this sudden restoration of my shape. They lifted their hands to heaven and with one voice praised the great favour that I had received from the goddess. ...

[21] From this time, I devoted myself more diligently to the service of the goddess in hope of greater benefits, regarding what I had already received as tokens to hope for more marks of her favour. My desire to take holy orders at the temple increased every day and I frequently discussed this with the priest, begging him to make me an initiate in the mysteries of the holy night. He was a man of serious religiosity, well known for his precise observance, and he gently and kindly put off my request every day with consolations, as often parents rebuff the unreasonable requests of their childen. He explained that no one would be admitted into their order except on a day appointed by the goddess, that the priest to administer the sacrifice is chosen by her; and that the costs of the ceremonies would be assigned on her instructions. He encouraged me to endure this disappointment with attentive patience, explaining that I should avoid being too eager or too obstinate. I should not be unresponsive if called, or hasty if not. He also said that no brother in his order had been so wrong-minded or so rash as to think of receiving the mysteries without the invitation of the goddess; to do so would be to commit a deadly sin. He added that both the gates of the underworld and the power of salvation were in the goddess' power, and that the rites of initiation were like a voluntary death, from which hope of resurrection could be precarious. Because of this those deemed capable of receiving the deep mysteries of the goddess are

usually those near the point of death and at the end of their lives, but not so senile as to give away its secrets. By her divine power they might be reborn and restored to the path of health. Finally he added that I must therefore await the goddess' call, although it was clear that the goddess had already decided to call and appoint me to service in her ministry. Because of this he said that I must refrain from forbidden food, just as current priests do, so that so that I might enter the secret mysteries of the religion more quickly when my vocation came.

[22] I accepted his words and continued to serve the goddess patiently. I attended the temple daily to prove my meekness and quietness. In the end the goddess did nothing to deceive me and did not torment me with a long delay. One dark night she appeared to me in a vision, declaring clearly that the day had finally come that I had longed patiently for. She told me what provision I should make for the ritual, and that she had ordered her high priest Mithras to administer the ritual for me, since his destiny was joined to mine (as she said) by the planets.

When I had heard these and the other divine instructions of the great goddess, I was exceedingly happy, and arose before daybreak to speak with the high priest, whom I happened to see coming out of his chamber. I greeted him, and was about to ask more forcefully that he allow me to be initiated as something that I had been granted. As soon as he noticed me, however, he began to speak: "Dear Lucius, now I can see clearly that you are both lucky and blessed because the divine goddess has decided to honour you in this way. Why are you standing here idle? Why do you delay? The day that you have been praying for has come! The goddess of many names has ordered me to initiate you into her most holy mysteries."

Then the old man took me by the hand, and led me to the gate of the great temple, which he opened in a solemn way and performed the morning sacrifice. Next, he went into the secret place of the temple and brought out some books written in strange characters: some of them were animal hieroglyphs; some ordinary letters whose tops and tails were looped in the fashion of a wheel with their tops joined together like vines in order that they would be illegible to outsiders. He explained to me what things I would need to acquire for the initiation. [23] This done, I diligently set about acquiring what I needed. Some things I got friends to purchase for me; others I bought myself. When the time had come, the priest took me to the nearest baths, along with a group of priests. First, I underwent an ordinary bath. Then the priest prayed for the gods' forgiveness and then purified my body by sprinkling water. Then, in the middle of the afternoon, he brought me back again to the temple where he presented me before the feet of the goddess. At this point he gave me certain orders that were whispered to me secretly, and then instructing me before everyone to fast for the next ten days, without eating of any meat or drinking of any wine. I obeyed these instructions in complete reverence.

The appointed day finally came for my sacrifice of dedication. When the sun declined and evening came, a great multitude of priests gathered around me bring me many presents and gifts, as was the ancient custom. Then the high priest ordered all the uninitiated to depart; when they had left, he put a new linen robe over my shoulders, took my hand, and led me into the most secret and sacred part of the temple.

I have no doubt, curious reader, that you want to know what was said and done there. I would happily tell all if I were allowed to speak of this and if you were allowed to hear it. As it is, however, your ears would be punished for hearing and my tongue for telling. I have no desire, however, to leave you in a state of suspense, especially if you are inclined towards religious devotion. Listen therefore to my words and believe them to be true. *I came near to the very gates of death and stepped on the threshold of Proserpina, and then after that I was carried through all the elements and returned to my proper place. At midnight I saw the sun shining brightly. I approached the gods above and the gods below, and worshipped them in their presence.*

I have now told you. But although you have heard it, it is something that you cannot understand.

Adapted from Stephen Gaselee, *The Golden Ass, being the Metamorphoses of Lucius Apuleius* (London: William Heinemann, 1915).